Gestalt Therapy on the

The Gestalt Therapy Page is the ....
comprehensive web resource for information, resources, and
publications relating to the theory and practice of Gestalt therapy.

Visitors can subscribe to News and Notes, a free email calendar of
conferences, training programs, and other events of interest to the
worldwide Gestalt therapy community.

The Gestalt Therapy Page includes an on-line store that offers the
most comprehensive collection of books and recordings available
– many available nowhere else!

Visit today: www.gestalt.org

The Gestalt Journal Press was founded in 1975 and is currently the leading
publisher and distributor of books, journals, and educational recordings
relating to the theory and practice of Gestalt therapy. Our list of titles includes
new editions of all the classic works by Frederick Perls, Laura Perls, Paul
Goodman, Ralph Hefferline, and Jan Christiaan Smuts. Our catalog also
includes a wide variety of books by contemporary theoreticians and clinicians
including Richard Hycner, Lynne Jacobs, Violet Oaklander, Peter Phillipson,
Erving & Miriam Polster, Edward W. L. Smith, and Gary Yontef.

In 1976, we began publication of The Gestalt Journal (now the International
Gestalt Journal), the first professional periodical devoted exclusively to the
theory and practice of Gestalt therapy.

Our collection of video and audio recordings features the works of Frederick
(Fritz) and Laura Perls, Violet Oaklander, Erving & Miriam Polster, Janie Rhyne,
and James Simkin.

The Gestalt Journal Press, in conjunction with the University of California,
Santa Barbara, maintains the world's largest archive of Gestalt therapy related
materials including original manuscripts and correspondence, published and
unpublished, by Gestalt therapy pioneers Frederick & Laura Perls and Paul
Goodman. The archives also include more than six thousand hours of audio
and video recordings of presentations, panels and interviews dating to early
1961.

Gianni Francesetti (Ed.)

Panic Attacks
and Postmodernity
Gestalt Therapy Between
Clinical and Social Perspectives

FrancoAngeli | PSYCHOTHERAPIES

Distributed in the United States and Canada by:

The Gestalt Journal Press

Cover: Detail from Vincent Van Gogh, *Starry Night*

To Luisa

Contents

Preface to the English Edition

by Dan Bloom

The United States is at least a nation of immigrants, their children and grandchildren. This was true for the ethnically mixed neighborhood of New York City where I grew up. It was a common occurrence on special days for unfamiliar cars to drive up in front of one of my friend's houses and for people to gather, embrace, and greet one another with the sounds of what were to me foreign languages. More often than not, I, a stranger, would be caught up in the whirlwind of family love, embraced and kissed while Italian endearments were murmured in my ear.

These memories came to mind as I read this volume. Page after page, I found myself reading familiar material, family material as it were, written by my European relatives. This analogy is apt. Gestalt therapy was originated by European émigrés, who brought it with them to the United States, codeveloped with the American Paul Goodman, and, after some time budding further in America's cultural soil, was returned to Europe through, among others, the teachings of Laura Perls, Isadore From, and Richard Kitzler, three of my own principal teachers. The authors of the essays in this book, then, are in my gestalt therapy family, brothers, sisters, and cousins. They are taking the model of gestalt therapy of The New York Institute for Gestalt Therapy, founded in 1952 by the Perls's and others, and are applying and developing it, within their own cultural context, and by so doing, shining a clarifying light on it. As I read the essays, I see what elsewhere I have called "the foundational model" (Bloom, 2004) in all its glory, but I also see the richness of their European perspective, their direct application of phenomenology, hermeneutics, and postmodernism. The stream of gestalt therapy inevitably acquires the character of the land through which it flows.

But more than merely being a fine book of basic gestalt therapy, this volume is itself an important original contribution to our literature. It is a phenomenological and clinical discussion of a specific disorder we find in our psychotherapy practices. Gestalt therapy traditionally excels as an experiential practice; but the literature in gestalt therapy has been deficient in serious scientific research and clinical case material. This book from the Italian branch our gestalt therapy family is a continuation of the foundational model and, moreover, fills a deficiency in gestalt therapy literature.

Despite the claim of some that gestalt therapy is a system built upon intuitive understanding rather than theory, gestalt therapy is in fact a psychotherapeutic modality with a unity of theory and praxis, an approach to clinical work that attends to the passage of experience itself as a function of the phenomenal field of the therapist and patient. In foundational gestalt therapy, there is no separate theory from practice, and no separate practice from theory. We hold, paraphrasing Immanuel Kant, that practice without theory is empty, and theory without practice is blind. Gestalt therapy is built upon the foundation of the arts and sciences, that is, all the achievements of our culture. Our work as gestalt therapists is that of our *intuitions informed by our knowledge*, integrated and integrating one with the other in a whole process as we continue to develop our art, our science (Bloom, 2004). Our art and science will develop further as we engage with one another in meaningful dialogues about our work, utilizing the concepts of our theory together with the experience of our clinical practices. This book is such a meaningful dialogue in this development.

Yet, to have a meaningful dialogue, we must use a common vocabulary. The original texts of gestalt therapy began to create the language for our method. First, in *Ego, Hunger, and Aggression* (F. Perls, 1942/1947), Frederick Perls (with Laura Perls) first outlined his radical departure from classical psychoanalysis which would later be called "gestalt therapy," and presented such notions as dental aggression, creative indifference, and mental metabolism. It was with the 1951 publication of *Gestalt Therapy: Excitement and Growth in the Human Personality* written by Frederick Perls, Ralph Hefferline, and Paul Goodman, that gestalt therapy was presented as a new modality with complex terms sufficient to describe human experience. The model of gestalt therapy presented in Perls et al. is the foundation upon which the authors of this book practice their art.

The authors develop *contact, contact-boundary*, the *sequence of contact*, the critical role of *support for contact making*, the *interruptions to contact*, *self functions and structures, creative-adjustment*, and the *relationship of therapist to patient*, and show these concepts deployed in the successful treatment of panic disorders. These are the central ideas of Frederick and Laura Perls (L. Perls, 1992), Paul Goodman, and Isadore From, which were transplanted to Italian soil. The terms found in the glossary to this book itself are words first defined in Perls et al., and are continuing to be refined and developed in the worldwide practice of gestalt therapy. Look closely at this glossary: The definitions are not mere repetitions from Perls et al. or any subsequent source, but a careful synthesis of those sources with this book's authors own research. In this unity of theory and practice, the contributors bring new understanding to basic themes of gestalt therapy.

One of the threads connecting the various essays is how the nature of our concerns as psychotherapists changes over time. What were significant clinical concerns at the time of gestalt therapy's emergence in the 1950s were no longer crucial in the 1970s, and similarly, the concerns of society in the 1990s could no longer be central in this new century. Consequently, how therapists respond to these concerns must likewise change. This is the hermeneutics of gestalt therapy, our understanding that meaning is inevitably changing and always co-created by therapist and patient as partners in the ongoing creative-adjusting in our clinical work. The authors ask us, then, to consider panic disorder to be the disorder of our time.

The temporal and cultural contingency of meaning is at the heart of gestalt therapy. The narratives and metanarratives which inform our work have long been our concern. The authors of this publication take this from gestalt therapy and link it explicitly to postmodern ideas. Drawing on sociology, psychology, and philosophy, the authors show the relevance of gestalt therapy to other contemporary approaches that consider panic disorders from a broad cultural perspective. By doing so, they firmly establish gestalt therapy as a continuingly developing psychotherapy, not as an artifact of any time or fashion. Moreover, they do this while using the concepts of the foundational model itself, clearly and succinctly applied to the clinical situations of their research. It is gratifying to read how clearly the phenomenon of panic can be understood when viewed through the lens of gestalt therapy.

Importantly, this volume is not restricted to the clinician's perspective. In keeping with gestalt therapy's attention to experience as emergent of the social field, and that psychotherapy itself as a phenomenon of the contact-boundary *par excellence*, this work includes a chapter written from the perspective of an actual patient. This is both a dramatic entry into the world of someone suffering from panic disorder and a direct example of the phenomenological research method of the authors.

It has been a privilege for me to write an introduction to this book. I expect it will produce in you the same desire for the translation into English of more writings from this community of Italian foundational gestalt therapists as it does in me, a member of their English-speaking family.

References

Bloom, D. (2004). The emergence of foundational gestalt therapy within a Teaching/Learning Community. *International Gestalt Journal, 27*(1), 97–109.

Perls, F. S., Hefferline, R. F., & Goodman, P. (1951). *Gestalt therapy: Excitement and growth in the human personality*. New York: Julian Press.

Perls, F. S. (1947). *Ego, hunger, and aggression: A revision of Freud's theory and method*. London: Allen & Unwin. (Original work published 1942)

Perls, L. (1992). *Living at the boundary: Collected works of Laura Perls* (J. Wysong, Ed.). Highland, NY: Gestalt Journal Press.

Preface to the Italian Edition

by Eugenio Borgna

With the large number of books being published on the topic of anxiety from many different perspectives, this volume, superbly edited by Gianni Francesetti, stands out for its methodological and epistemological approaches that distinguish it in its originality and authoritativeness.

In particular, focusing on aspects of rigor and critical awareness, I would like to stress the distinct clarity that characterizes the discussion of anxiety and anxiety so heightened as to become panic. This discussion is presented here in all its historical, psychopathological, and psychotherapeutic dimensions within the context of such a great school of thought as Gestalt psychotherapy. (We should note that panic attacks, although only now concisely defined in clinical terms as such, are nonetheless manifestations of a psychopathological and human condition already known by the great clinical psychiatrists of the nineteenth and twentieth centuries.) This thematic and expressive clarity, free of ideological bias, is evident in each of the contributions to the volume: starting with the emblematic title that draws us into a network of inexorable correlations between individual psychic experience, such as anxiety, and models of social life, characterized as they are by a tendency towards fragmentation.

The expressive clarity is all the more to be admired considering that the discussion of anxiety and panic attacks addresses not only psychopathological and clinical aspects but also existential and philosophical issues. These are approached with an acute awareness of the intrinsic problematics that characterize philosophical and metapsychological theories. At the same time this clarity characterizes the discourse structures that lie at the very foundation of Gestalt psychotherapy—structures indicated and made explicit through their epistemological background and in their various dialectical and semantic connotations. (The very useful glossary provided enables the essential thematic elements of Gestalt psychotherapy to be learned and relearned in all their endless correlations between the I and the Other, that is, between the I and the World. This occurs in the wake, of course, of an epistemological revolution of a radical phenomenological matrix that, in the schematic though emblematic Heideggerian affirmation, identifies being-in-the-world—*In-der-Welt-Sein*—as the fundamental basis of the human condition.) In this approach to therapy and critical reflection, which unfolds through rigor and discursive cogency, the extensive bibliography is never an external ancillary. The references are critically drawn upon and brought to converge into the overall unifying horizons of each and every contribution to therapeutic strategies marked out in the book.

A second important aspect of this volume is the wealth of cases illustrated in their psycho(patho)logical and human dimensions, which strike a chord through their emotional immediacy and direct emotional expression, through the lived experiences represented. The cases offer not just reflections on the outcomes of therapy, but also the very words and emotions of patients, of men and women who tell of their anguish and their unease, and the changes they go through over the course of therapy. In this way, we are confronted with the throbbing reality of anxiety, which rises and falls at distressing rates, and which is crystallized into what we call panic attacks.

Putting aside symptomatological reductionism, the experience of anxiety as lived by men and women is described with all its radically phenomenological and anthropological connotations. That is, in its simple human dimension and in the hermeneutical foundations which these states of being conceal within themselves, and in their interpersonal and environmental echoes. After all, it is only in this way that we can gather the sense of psychopathological phenomena (and of anxiety and panic in particular) and interpret such phenomena from a theoretical but above all therapeutic perspective—a psychotherapeutic perspective.

Through the Gestalt interpretation of panic attacks, which is another emblematic aspect of the discussion unfolding through the contributions to the volume, beyond the intrinsic and distinctive models specific to Gestalt psychotherapy, meaning structures can be identified. The psychological and human dimensions of these meaning structures, when inserted into a clinical context (note that my own training is clinical), can be expanded and radically explored. This would seem to me to be one of the most exciting insights that emerge from this book. Bringing at least some fragments of

Gestalt psychotherapy into everyday psychopathological and clinical discourse, together, of course, with Jungian and Freudian elements, means truly extending the epistemic and therapeutic value of rigorous theoretical approaches, with the involvement of all those interested in reintroducing into psychiatry and psychology the *meaning* that lies hidden within behavior and exteriority, in the sense introduced by Emmanuel Lévinas.

I believe this is important, as it would seem to me that the theoretical boundaries of Gestalt psychotherapy, as with phenomenology per se, are much more open than other schools of thought to the perception and appreciation of the categories of the sayable and the unsayable, as understood by Edmund Husserl.

At any rate, moving beyond clinical and nosological categorizations, which are themselves elusive if not perhaps quite useless, the heart of panic attacks lies in the lacerating and distressing wound torn open by anxiety, a dizzyingly Kierkegaardian expression of freedom. And it is precisely this existential and phenomenological dimension that cannot but lead us to reflect upon the profound eidetic core of all illnesses and break free of the unsustainable dichotomy of illness and nonillness. This dimension allows us to appreciate, rather, the transitions and shifts which lie at the heart of the models and meaning horizons of Gestalt psychotherapy, as so rigorously illustrated in this volume and outlined with great originality, not only in its reality, but also in its theoretical and practical perspectives.

Anxiety is understood as the expression of a radical crisis of the world and society in which each and every one of us is necessarily immersed. Anxiety is understood as the reflection of the shattering—or at least the fragmentation—of society and interpersonal relationships, which are increasingly splintered and devoured by feverish individualism.

Even these quintessentially phenomenological aspects are present, albeit necessarily expressed in the language of Gestalt theory of forms—a language not unlike the language of phenomenology itself.

There is one last aspect I wish to underline. This regards the mutual relationship posited between psychotherapy and pharmaceutical treatments. I cannot but agree with the argument so clearly expressed in the book that there can be no effective pharmacological solution without psychotherapy. Pharmacological agency is always in some way influenced by the relational and, thus, psychotherapeutic context (be this understood either in a strict or in a general sense) existing between patient and therapist. Pharmaceutical therapy can treat intense symptoms (and thus is often essential), but it does not modify the psychological landscape within which anxiety has flared up and spread. Notwithstanding this, even the temporary relief of symptoms immediately improves the chances for psychotherapeutic success.

In short, this is an immensely interesting book, not only from the point of view of doctrine (whereby the radical epistemic and methodological importance of Gestalt psychotherapy and of Gestalt theory is brought to light), but also from a clinical and therapeutic perspective. From the various contributions to the book emerge concrete models for the understanding of panic attacks and psychotherapeutic strategy, unfailingly anchored in the social context that necessarily affects therapy.

This book is of great interest and use for those interested in discovering, or exploring in further depth, what Gestalt psychotherapy is and what panic attacks are, both symptomatologically and phenomenologically (or eidetically) speaking. It further teaches us about the necessity to subjectively confront the boundless growth of anxiety, and to intuitively perceive the unsayable that lies concealed within all human experience torn apart by suffering and solitude. A book for all practitioners of psychotherapy and of psychiatry—which itself cannot survive without psychotherapy.

Acknowledgments for the Italian Edition

First of all, I would like to thank the directors of the Istituto di Gestalt H.C.C., Italy, Dr. Margherita Spagnuolo Lobb and Dr. Giovanni Salonia. Their teachings lie at the root of the key ideas behind this project. The clarity of their teachings and their skilled command of theory, together with their wealth of clinical experience, have guided and enriched this text. This publication would not have been possible without their generous contributions and support at every stage of its development.

Thanks are also due to all the members of the Istituto di Gestalt H.C.C., which provided the broader framework of contacts, exchange, and reflections from which the text developed. Particular thanks go to Dr. Maria Mione, Dr. Elisabetta Conte (directors of the Venice branch of the Istituto H.C.C.), and to Dr. Michela Gecele for stimulating exchange and continuous support. I also wish to thank Paola Argentino for her generous assistance.

My heartfelt thanks go to Professor Eugenio Borgna, author of the preface at the beginning of this book. His wise and invaluable words bear witness to the depth and epistemological rigor needed to venture into the complex territory of psychological illness.

I am grateful to Susan Gregory, Dan Bloom, and Rachel Brier of the New York Institute of Gestalt Therapy, for some valuable input on certain theoretical concepts. Celeste Borgnino, Luisa Brachet, Ida Cravero, Jessica Ghioni, and Paola Grandis kindly edited parts of the text.

My heartfelt thanks go to the various patients suffering from panic attacks with whom I have worked. Although only some of their stories are told in this volume, my firsthand encounters with all of them were the principal source of inspiration behind this book.

Finally, I would like to thank my wife Luisa for her incessant encouragement and for never losing her temper, even though her infinite well of patience was put to the test on several occasions during the preparation of this volume. Thanks also go to my children, Chiara and Emanuele, for their resources of *im*patience that proved similarly bottomless.

Acknowledgments for the English Edition

A lot of people have contributed to the creation of this book. Without their encouragement and enduring faith I would never have been able to complete this project.

First of all, I wish to thank the directors of the Istituto di Gestalt H.C.C., Italy, Giovanni Salonia and Margherita Spagnuolo Lobb, for appreciating and promoting this volume. If the Italian edition had not been so successful, I would probably never have chosen to produce this English version.

My heartfelt thanks go to the book's various authors, who believed that the text was worth translating and who have supported me at every stage of the translation process.

I wish to say a special "thank you" to Margherita Spagnuolo Lobb, without whose editorial experience this volume would never have been completed.

I would like to thank the editor, Ilaria Angeli, who believed that this text might attract the interest of an international public.

My warmest thanks go to Alice Spencer, the translator of this volume, and to Nele Brauner, our copyeditor. Their patience and skill provided us with the most accurate edition possible.

I particularly wish to thank Nancy Amendt-Lyon for making herself available to read drafts and for freely offering valuable editorial comments.

Finally, I wish to thank Dan Bloom, not only for offering useful comments and writing the preface to the English edition, but also and above all for the warmth and enthusiasm he has always shown in encouraging my work. He has always been a great source of support for me.

These are just some of the ties of belonging that have created the fabric of support, sustaining me in the course of my work.

I hope that my acknowledgment and gratitude will flow back to them along the multiple ties that bind together these networks, reaching even those sources of nourishment I myself have been unable to perceive.

Introduction

by Gianni Francesetti

This book has its origins in a research project that sought to reach a better understanding of panic attacks, using the theoretical and clinical instruments of Gestalt[1] therapy within the social field in which such symptoms emerge.

It originates, more generally speaking, in the need to "read" the phenomena of our time on the basis of psychotherapeutic experience and to simultaneously understand personal distress not only in an idiographic context, but also in the social and cultural settings from which it emerges. "A symptom is a word looking for a sentence," as Giovanni Salonia declares. We therefore find ourselves right in the middle of a hermeneutic circle where individual experience (even and, indeed, especially if such experience is psychopathological) acquires meaning only if it is understood against its relational and social background. Vice versa, we can only attain a satisfactory understanding of social phenomena if we take personal experience as our starting point. The play of figures and backgrounds gives rise to questions and opens up new pathways that enable us to understand each problem in the full complexity of its fragmented social context.

From another point of view, as Margherita Spagnuolo Lobb so effectively highlights, panic poses a genuine challenge to clinical psychotherapy today. We are required to find appropriate therapeutic responses to a symptom that is unsayable, apparently incomprehensible, and that often arises all at once, like a sudden bolt of lightning against a clear sky.

---

[1] Notwithstanding Dan Bloom's encouragement that we should write the term *Gestalt* with a lower case "g" (as is normally the practice with other therapeutic approaches: psychoanalysis, cognitive therapy, etc.), we decided to use a capital letter. Gestalt is a German noun and in German nouns always begin with a capital letter. Despite the differing positions adopted by our authors on the matter, we believe that this choice represents the most faithful rendering of the term's semantic field.

This text stems from a long period of research and reflection on the part of the directors of the Istituto di Gestalt H.C.C., Italy. It will treat panic attacks not only as an individual clinical symptom, but also in relation to the context in which they occur—that is, in relation to postmodernity. This perspective has stimulated, oriented, and nourished the research on which this book is based.

The present volume is the fruit of a group effort. It originates from an ongoing dialogue between its various authors. Such an approach is vital in sustaining the necessary plurality of perspectives required by the topic. Even though the study can still not claim to be exhaustive, at least we hope we will be able to give an idea of the complexity of the phenomena in question.

Every effort has been made to avoid oversimplification and reductionism. We have sought to follow a method that explores panic attacks from various points of view, casting light on the issue from diverse angles and enabling our readers to investigate all its various psychological, phenomenological, psychotherapeutic, social, and cultural dimensions.

Moving on to consider the book's structure, the first two chapters outline the background for our Gestalt-based approach to panic attacks, from both a clinical and a social point of view.

In the first chapter, Margherita Spagnuolo Lobb presents a new interpretation of panic, following some of the most recent and innovative new directions in psychotherapeutic research. Panic comes to represent a place where the unsayable, as a constituent part of human experience, acquires sense and dignity. This prospect lights up a whole new horizon to be explored, in which the limitations of language find the way for new therapeutic possibilities that are implicit yet essential, taken as read yet unknown. It thus becomes possible to outline the ineffable "founding grounds" of the relational landscape, which sustain the dance of relationships, life, and health.

The second chapter, written by Giovanni Salonia, takes an in-depth look at the relationship between psychic distress and social context and thus, more specifically, between panic and postmodernity. This is a fundamental issue in current psychotherapeutic debate, which, in the various manifestations here discussed, represents the basis and the common theme of all the essays in this volume. The issue is approached without having recourse to a causal form of logic, which would presuppose some kind of scission. It is rather viewed from the perspective of figure/ground dynamics, which prevents us from straying from the relevant hermeneutic field. Panic, from this outlook, becomes an individual figure, which emerges from a collective ground, requiring a social reading, with implications that are not only clinical but also more broadly cultural and pedagogical.

The third chapter offers a phenomenological and clinical reading of panic attacks, using conceptual tools from Gestalt psychotherapy. These include figure/ground dynamics, contact intentionality and interruptions, the functions of the self, the play of opposites (with particular reference to the autonomy–belonging polarities), the cycle of experience, and some key aspects of specific support. In this light, panic comes to represent a setback to the individual's acquired creative adjustment. At the same time, however, it also generates new opportunities in the individual's life, revealing new directions that can lead the individual to new and more up-to-date creative solutions. Psychotherapy often plays a defining role in supplying the support needed to enable the individual to handle such new opportunities and in facilitating the functional and positive reorganization of the individual's relationships and life in general.

The fourth chapter is written by an individual who has suffered from panic attacks. The various trials undergone in seeking out an effective course of treatment provide a clear illustration of the difficulties and needs of patients suffering from this particularly intense and debilitating problem.

The fifth chapter deals with the theme of belonging, drawing on a number of key concepts of Gestalt therapy to provide an overview of social and generational changes. Observing and seeking to understand the changes taking place in this era of fragmentation enables the practitioner not only to adapt therapy accordingly, but also to interpret changes to networks of belonging from one generation to the next.

The authors of the sixth and final chapter explore the complex relationship between panic attacks and the contemporary social context. The individual symptom, inasmuch as it is a figure through which the troubles of the contemporary ground can be perceived, inevitably places the psychotherapist (considered both personally and professionally) in a "political" context, of which he or she must necessarily be aware.

Finally, a short glossary of some specialized Gestalt terminology with brief definitions and a bibliography has been included at the end of the volume.

This text will be of use, not only to therapists who are already practicing the Gestalt approach, but also to those from other backgrounds who, faced with cases of panic attacks, are looking for new solutions to clarify and relieve the problem.

I sincerely hope that such therapists will find this material stimulating and beneficial, not just for their everyday clinical practice, but also more generally for their deeper considerations of the relationship between society and psychological disturbance.

For those who are suffering from panic attacks, I hope that this text will prove useful in clarifying certain aspects of the problem and its clinical treatment, outlining the direction and the significance of psychotherapeutic treatment. Moreover, considering panic as a field phenomenon can provide patients with a broader perspective that may help them to make sense of this distressing condition.

That which will inevitably be lacking in this volume is, on the one hand, the freshness of every new therapeutic encounter, with its unrepeatable poetical uniqueness and, on the other, a real sense of the suffering that mars the lives of those who are afflicted by panic attacks. Even though it is not always made explicit, every page of this book is steeped in the struggles and the pain of the patients. Fortunately, however, this is not the whole story. These pages also tell the story of the patients' new lease on life, our reciprocal understanding, and the challenging, sometimes playful nature of our encounters.

1. Why Do We Need a Psychotherapeutic Approach to Panic Attacks?

by Margherita Spagnuolo Lobb

1.1 A Story Similar to Many Others

A patient sits down in the armchair in my psychotherapy office. It is his first appointment. He seems self-contained. He is a distinguished person, who wishes to project a dignified self-image. He establishes eye contact while he addresses me. However, he often averts his gaze so as not to betray the sense of fear, consternation, and panic by which he is overcome. In this way, he is able to maintain his dignity as he explains why he has come.

> I am a medical doctor, a well-known specialist. I have always carried out my professional duties—I am a pediatrician—with dedication, and my patients have rewarded me with their gratitude and esteem. The children's mothers always tell me that I am good at calming their anxieties. This is because I am a good listener and I keep them fully informed about what is happening to their children at any given moment. This calms them down and helps them go back to being the kind of mother they aspire to be. I also love exchanging ideas and cooperating with my colleagues. I have coordinated various professional associations and organized significant national and international conferences. My life in general is thoroughly satisfactory. I have a wonderful family: Two children and a wife with whom I continue to get along very well. I do a lot of sport: I always do what I want. I go canoeing and I attained my pilot's license ten years ago. My dream of flying consequently came true, and I bought a microlight.

All of this comes out very fast, as if it is a necessary preface without which it will be impossible for me to fully appreciate the drama of his situation. He then continues:

It all started two years ago. I was in the car with my wife, on the expressway from Florence to Rome. There was a traffic jam and we were queuing. I was chatting calmly with my wife. Then, all of a sudden, my hands started sweating. I felt nauseous and my heart was beating very fast. I had never experienced such symptoms, and I thought it must be a stroke, or some kind of circulatory problem. I am a doctor, so I am familiar with bodily sensations, and not just those of my patients. A good doctor can only understand his patients' symptoms if he is able to imagine experiencing them with his own body. Yet, in that moment I did not feel lucid enough to discern that what was happening to my body was not a physically pathological process—that I was rather the victim of a purely mental, psychological condition. I tried to resist the impulse, asking myself if I should go straight to the emergency room or wait to understand my symptoms better ... Then I could reason no longer and I asked my wife to take me straight to hospital. There they diagnosed me as having suffered an anxiety attack. Nothing physical. I thought it was because I was going through a stressful period at the time. I was very tired from overwork, but it would have been a lie—would still be a lie—to say that at that particular moment I was under any more professional or emotional stress than usual. I had been through far worse. Nonetheless, I did not worry too much about the episode, and got on with my everyday life.

Then, about three months later, I went out in my microlight. It was a beautiful day. There was not a cloud in the sky and a light breeze was blowing. I was alone, enjoying the wonderful sensation of flying and admiring the beautiful landscape. All of a sudden, the following thought crossed my mind: If someone were sitting there with me, I might not be able to land the plane safely. The anxiety suddenly hit me out of nowhere. The catastrophic process I was undergoing was absolutely beyond my control. It was as if I had suddenly entered into a tunnel, from which there was no way out. I broke out in a cold sweat and my heart was beating very fast. I felt an overwhelming urge to land the plane and to get out of the situation, which, illogically, I had begun to conceive of as fraught with peril. I have no idea how I managed to land the plane safe and sound. However, as soon as I was back on the ground, my physical symptoms were immediately alleviated. Those around me will not have noticed that I had experienced anything out of the ordinary.
It was now clear to me that the symptoms were nothing more than the product of my imagination. I did not go to hospital on that occasion.

However, from that day on I have felt unable to fly my plane. Indeed, I do not believe I could even be a passenger on a plane flown by someone else, as I know that I would be afraid of not being able to help in a case of need.

From that moment on—every now and then but with increasing frequency—I started experiencing thoughts that would suddenly overwhelm me, sending me plummeting into a dark abyss of extreme anxiety. I visited a neurologist friend, but he told me that my problems were not neurological in origin. My psychiatrist friend, instead, told me that I was going through a stressful period and prescribed some psychotropic drugs. I took them for a couple of months and felt much better. It felt as if everything was going to be all right. I decided of my own accord to reduce the dosage of pills, believing that I had tamed the beast. However, just a few weeks later, the symptoms began to creep back.

His eyes fill with tears and he struggles to suppress a sob. "Sorry ... I just can't keep back the tears ... I cannot cope any more." "This is a good place for crying," I tell him, and he bursts into tears. I pass him a tissue, letting him cry, while I breathe calmly. I know that this is the only environment in which he is able to vent the terrible suffering of his incomprehensible state of mind. When he has calmed down, he looks at me, and begins to speak again. He says "sorry" again, but seems calmer.

I started taking the pills again, and continue to take them now. However, I'm always worried that I won't have them when I need them, or that I won't have enough of them, or that my sickness will be too strong for them to work. I came here because I have heard others speak well of you ... I do not know how you can help me, but my scientific knowledge does not offer me any explanations about what is happening to me. This is something completely illogical. What am I lacking? I feel as if I've been involuntarily thrust into a spiral of aging and depression. I feel that my situation is pretty hopeless. How about you? I've always been very positive and active in my life. I have made all of my important choices with a great deal of energy and faith in life, and with a great deal of faith in other people too—in my patients and my family. Now I am no longer able to help anyone, not even myself. I feel like I have turned into a loser in both my family and my professional life. How can my life possibly have turned into this?

For many of those seeking to provide help, be they doctors, psycho-therapists, counselors, coaches, or even friends and partners, such stories have become commonplace.

1.2 The Psychotherapist and Panic Attacks

Panic attacks have become almost an emblem of the elusive affliction of our times: A malaise that appears to lack any logical cause and that can also afflict those who seem to have everything, including those who have lived not just an ordinary, but even a particularly successful, positive, courageous life.

Considering an *excursus* of psychotherapeutic researches in the last decades, we can say that we now have the theoretical and methodological tools to appropriately treat the narcissistic personality disorders that typified the 1980s.[1] Then, since a few decades, serious psychic disorders—which begin with a severe mental agitation, and are often accompanied by a state of delirium—have been studied extensively and have been linked to the development of relational skills.[2] These are accompanied by the need for support, which arises at transitional moments in life, and by a repeated failure to creatively adjust to a difficult field (Spagnuolo Lobb, 2003b). Psychotherapy continues to find more and more theoretical and methodological tools to effectively cure even this serious form of disorder.

As far as panic attacks are concerned, we are currently witnessing a period of considerable evolution in both theory and practice.

If we may assume that every historical moment breeds its own form of psychic malaise, closely linked to the cultural trends of society at any given time (Salonia, 2001)—and if, therefore, we consider psychotherapy and society to be inextricably connected (Spagnuolo Lobb et al., 1996)—then panic attacks would appear to be the sickness of our time. This is a suffering without rhyme or reason, a suffering almost "needed,"[3] a suffering in which we, too, find ourselves in a state of panic.

---

[1] Characterized by anxiety as to whether choices should be made in one's own interests or in the interests of others and whether life should be lived for ones own good or for the good of others (Müller Ebert, Josewski, Dreitzel, & Müller, 1989; Iaculo, 1996; Miller, 1996).

[2] Cf. Mahler, Pine, & Bergman, 1975; Winnicott, 1957; Salonia, 1989.

[3] The following passage from Friedrich Nietzsche (1882/1909–13) springs to mind: "sickness: Is it not almost tempting to ask if we could do without it? Great pain is the only extreme liberator of the spirit, inasmuch as it is the master of *great suspicion*" (Translated from the Italian by A. Spencer).

The therapist's reaction to the kind of story described above is, in fact, often a sense of impotence and emptiness—sometimes even of panic. Initially, s/he will try to deploy the methods that s/he has always been taught. S/he may seek to gain access to life experiences that have prevented the construction of a solid ground for the patient's personality. Alternatively, s/he may try to develop the patient's assertive skills, so that s/he will begin to define him-/herself—through more positive mental constructions. Again, s/he may seek to acquire a sense of the individual's actual phenomenological situation. There are many possible paths to take. However, individuals subjected to such methods (and genuinely wishing to be cured as soon as possible) often feel as if they are wasting their time, or argue that they have already made concerted efforts to think positively and calm themselves down, but that it has proved useless.

The therapist may eventually begin to suffer from a suffocating, debilitating fear not dissimilar to that of the patient, finding that the tools of his rational world, including those that have enabled him to become a psychotherapist (e.g., certain diagnostic and therapeutic systems), have suddenly become useless. S/he can feel s/he is of little help for the patient to get out of the dark tunnel of panic in which s/he finds him-/herself. The psychotherapist, too, feels as if s/he has lost control of the therapeutic relationship, just as the patient feels as if s/he has lost control of part of his social life. The therapist will sometimes feel that s/he lacks the necessary tools to cure the *unsayable*, elusive anxiety afflicting his patient.

Both psychotherapist and patient consequently begin to ask themselves whether psychotherapy can really be useful in curing panic attacks. If they continue to believe that the answer is "yes," then they will go on to ask themselves what lines psychotherapy should move along if it is to fully respond to the social needs connected to this kind of disorder, considering the apparent ineffectiveness of their methods so far.

This is an important question, as panic attacks constitute the main challenge being faced by psychotherapists today, similar to psychosis 10 years and narcissistic disorders 20 years ago. Too many patients continue to consider attempts to cure their panic attacks through psychotherapy to be a failure. As one patient says:

> The most common approach is to look for causes in the past ... as if seeking out guilty parties or scapegoats. I felt as if my therapist was constantly trying to put my life into rewind, watching it again and again in a vain hope to change the ending.

If, as Eugenio Borgna (1999) maintains, psychotherapists are morally bound to help those who ask for help in making sense of their suffering and—as we would have it, in finding that meaning at the contact-boundary between patient and therapist (Spagnuolo Lobb, 2004b)—then, what new ethical and methodological principles should inform their methods?

1.3 The Unsayable and the Sayable in Psychotherapy

Patients suffering from panic attacks tend to describe their condition as something unsayable. "If you have never experienced it, you cannot possibly understand it," is the typical statement with which they disarm their listeners. This unsayability would seem to lie at the very heart of the panic attack experience. It represents its very essence. In every other sense, the patient retains his/her logic. S/he knows that s/he is not going to die, although s/he continues to be afraid of dying. He knows that his accelerated heartbeat does not mean s/he is at risk of having a stroke, yet s/he continues to fear that his/her heart will explode from one moment to the next. S/he knows that his sense of suffocation is triggered by a psychological mechanism, yet s/he is still anxious that this may not be the case. The sense of the arcane, which characterizes this kind of experience, does not, then, stem from a failure of language in the patient. Rather, it has its origins in the nature of the experience itself. In other words, the psychotherapist needs to ask him-/herself: "*Is it possible to cure an experience that is constitutionally unsayable?*" Can therapy make the unsayable *sayable*, or do we need to find new ways of expressing the therapeutic process in the context of the unsayable?

Sigmund Freud was born (and thus was psychoanalysis) into a cultural climate in which "curing" psychological disorders involved rationalizing all the aspects of the patient's pathology. Freud's innovation did not, therefore, consist so much in rationalizing the irrational as in recognizing the existence of the unconscious—of an irrational domain that effectively determines human behavior. Freud's axiom that "Where id was, there ego shall be" was based on a faith in reason that had its origins in the Enlightenment and that was quite normal at the time. His notion of "interpretation-as-cure" was the natural methodological application of such a vision. In the century that has passed since then, despite the many cultural transformations that the field has undergone, this notion of making conscious that which belongs to the unconscious remains at the heart of all the various schools of psychotherapy, varying only slightly according to their differing notions of the self, of normality, and of pathology. Some approaches refer to the conscious and the unconscious, others to the rational and the irrational, others again to conscious as opposed to notconscious. However, at the end of the day, the final aim of psychotherapy is still seen as making the unsayable sayable. Gestalt psychotherapy, which is well-known for basing on the process, focuses above all on the relational patterns through which the individual makes contact with the environment, from bodily functions to the relational meaning of dreams recounted to the therapist. This approach seeks to renew the individual's spontaneity in a holistic sense (bodily, affective, intellective, and spiritual). It has the virtue of having overcome the dichotomy between what is healthy and what is sick, between the individual and society, between the body and the mind, favoring instead a holistic perspective on the organism–environment relationship and on the successful integration of all personal experiences. Nonetheless, even Gestalt psychotherapy has yet to develop a satisfactory method based on the unsayable. Gestalt practitioners continue to use techniques based on making the implicit explicit, as if a cure should only consist in an explicit consciousness of relational processes.

How can the sayable be effectively defined? It is an experience that can be told to someone. Making the unsayable sayable would therefore involve socializing an experience. The notion of sayability or narration as a cure presupposes the fact that the source of the disorder lies in what is not said, in what remains closed inside the heart. Articulating an experience, making it sayable through words, restores it to the relationship from which it arose. However, should the therapeutic relationship only have to deal with this aspect of the unsayable? Or is there a whole other series of experiences and kinds of communication that keep us in contact with each other and that are also unsayable? The accelerated heartbeat during a panic attack might be one such case. One part of this experience is sayable. However, the individual who describes the experience always feels as if something has been left unsaid, however well he chooses his words. The therapeutic relationship provides us with another such example. Therapist and patient can be said to "sniff each other out" as they try to decide whether they are suited for one another. Something is always unsayable and, in the case of panic attacks, this "something" is the defining feature.

That being so, we have to ask ourselves whether the possibility of psychological cures always depends on the sayability of the disturbing experience. Does the sense of liberation experienced by patients who have been able to describe their experiences to a psychotherapist represent a cure *par excel-*

lence, or do we need to find *a therapeutic dimension that lies beyond the sayable*? Daniel Stern, who has always worked at the crossroads between research and psychotherapy, as well as between the observation of children and clinical activities with adults, has reached the following conclusions:

> Implicit knowledge that has never been verbalized ... plays a huge role in the context and in how people change in psychotherapy ... Explicit knowledge is verbal, symbolic, and declarative. It's also what narration is made of: All interpretations are by definition explicit. Implicit knowledge is nonverbal. It is not symbolic, and it is not conscious, but not repressed: It has simply never come into consciousness ... We ... used to think that implicit knowledge ... progressively becomes explicit, because it becomes symbolized and talked about. According to this perspective, the development supposedly implies that implicit knowledge turns into explicit knowledge. (Stern & the Boston Change Process Study Group, 2003, pp. 21ff.)

Development theorists would support us on this point, specifying that some experiences are preverbal and cannot be sayable, because they belong to a language without words. During the individual's relational life, this nonverbal consciousness develops and matures entirely independently of the verbal or verbalized forms of consciousness.

The most significant changes to therapy being made today are in response to this implicit type of relation. The theme of the sayable and unsayable is being discussed a great deal by the psychotherapy community nowadays. This is both because certain researchers, such as Stern (2004), are reviewing the concept of the conscious and the unconscious in the psychoanalytic method and because certain new disorders, such as panic attacks, do not respond to psychotherapeutic methods based on making the unsayable sayable. It seems that neither words nor therapeutic methods seeking to make the unsayable sayable can generate positive change. Solutions are instead to be found in the sphere of the unsayable (Stern, 1998a; 1998b), of perceptions at the contact-boundary (Spagnuolo Lobb, 2003a). The changes that psychotherapy is undergoing at the moment will have particularly strong repercussions in determining cures for panic attacks.

From the 1960s onwards, scientific interest in the experiences and behavior of patients with serious psychic disorders has increased exponentially. Thanks to the studies that followed, the concept of psychotherapeutic care has been freed from the naïve notion of a purely dyadic relationship and been firmly situated in a broader context, in which therapy (be it in an individual, group, or family setting) influences and is influenced by relational and field factors. The formulations of object relational theoreticians (Greenberg & Mitchell, 1986) have clarified the qualitative differences between the experiences of patients with severe psychic disorders and the experiences of neurotics. The experience that accompanies severe psychic disorders is therefore now seen to be qualitatively different from the experience that accompanies neuroses, the first consisting in anxiety linked to existential security and the second focused on aspects of the individual's social role. Nevertheless, both are the product of relationships and are accordingly curable in a relational context (Spagnuolo Lobb, 2001).

Panic attacks occupy a middle territory between these two poles. Although the individual would appear to have all the "existential security" he needs, he sometimes feels that it is lacking.

Any psychotherapeutic approach needs to start by identifying how the experience of the patients in question is qualitatively different. Starting out from a given anthropological perspective, which includes a notion of healthy (evolutionary) and unhealthy (psychopathic) development, psychotherapy needs to "grow" together with society if it is to be able to respond to new pathologies. It is for this reason that panic attacks (as were severe psychic disorders ten years ago) presently represent the main challenge faced by all the various schools of psychotherapy. I sincerely hope that the attention currently being paid to this increasingly common condition will stimulate an evolution in the language of psychotherapy. This will by no means preclude the prevalence of a multiplicity of approaches.

1.4 Gestalt Psychotherapy and the Cure of the Unsayable

Gestalt psychotherapy[1] is a process-based approach, which was devel-

---

[1] Gestalt therapy is a post-Freudian school of psychotherapy. It was developed in the U.S.A. in the 1950s by humanistic psychotherapists (for a summary of the birth and evolution of Gestalt psychotherapy up to the present day, see Spagnuolo Lobb, 1997 & 2006; Salonia, 1991; Bowman, 2005). *Gestalt* is a German word that can be roughly translated as "meaningful whole." A Jewish German couple, Friedrich S. Perls and Laura Perls, Perls, née Posner, who emigrated to the U.S.A. in the late 1940s, became aware of an aspect of human relations which had been obscured by psychoanalysis. They suggested that the capacity to bite and chew, which individuals acquire as their teeth develop, foregrounds the aggression (which they view in a positive light) of a survival instinct. This capacity allows the individual to assimilate the novel through a process of deconstruction, thereby growing in a creative and active, as opposed to a negative and introjective manner. This new perspective offered a means to overcome the dualism between individual impulse and social order present

oped in order to overcome the dualism between individual and society found in Freud's psychoanalytic thought. It was the brainchild of a group of psychoanalysts who had developed a revolutionary new conception of human nature. This was characterized by a *polar and holistic vision* (suggesting that "sick" and "healthy" are two sides of the same coin), a *positive anthropology* (i.e., the notion that human beings are animals-for-contact, who function by creatively adjusting to the situations in which they find themselves) and by a love of *phenomenology*, whereby the basic concept of intentionality inherent in every experience is defined as intentionality to make contact. Every kind of human behavior thereby comes to be understood in terms of contact-related tension in the context of a spontaneous contact-making between organism and environment. Psychic distress thereby comes to represent the consequence of an intentionality of contact which has not been brought to fruition (Salonia, 2001). Which intentionality of con-

in Freud's metapsychology. This implies that, from the very moment in which the individual begins to deconstruct and reconstruct, s/he is living a fulfilling life in this world.

"The elaboration of these intuitions together with a group of American intellectuals, who had a deep knowledge of psychoanalysis, led to the development of a set of terms with which to express this organismic perspective (Perls, *Ego, Hunger, and Aggression*, 1942) and, ultimately, to the foundation of a new psychotherapeutic system based on the theory of experience of contact (Perls et al., 1951). The basic premise of this group is that every experience necessarily takes place at the contact-boundary of a human organism (to use the organismic terms employed by the founders of Gestalt psychotherapy) and his or her environment. Therapeutic interventions are therefore to be based on what we are able to observe of the goings on at this boundary. The contact-boundary is the space where the self, i.e., the capacity of the individual to find his or her bearings in the world and to enter into and withdraw from contact with his or her surrounding environment, unfolds. The concept of *function* thus replaced the psychoanalytic notion of instance, thus doing justice to the individual's capacity to orient him- or herself in the world and to act on it creatively for his or her self-preservation. At the same time, the technique of concentration (derived from Elsa Gindler's bodywork and Zen Buddhistic philosophy, and particularly compatible with a phenomenological approach) replaced that of free association (which was based on the mechanistic notion that we must boycott our defence mechanisms in order to attain access to the deepest structures of our psyches). At the contact-boundary it is thus possible to combine *creativity* (which expresses the individual's uniqueness) with *adjustment* (which expresses the reciprocity necessary for social life). An individual's psychic functioning thus comes to be described in terms of how he or she makes or does not make contact with his or her environment. Psychic functioning is no longer understood in terms of a univocal standard of health (From, 1985), but is rather modulated through parameters of creativity and adjustment. The criteria for reading it are no longer evaluative in terms of standard norms, but are rather process-based and aesthetic (Bloom, 2003). Individual and community needs can be integrated without any a priori sacrifices" (Spagnuolo Lobb, Salonia, & Sichera, 1996. Translated from the Italian by A. Spencer).

tact cannot be satisfactorily realized in a person's life? The strictly humanistic concept of self-regulation casts a positive light on intentionality in human behavior, seeing such distress as a creative-adjustment to a difficult field. The initial question hence becomes: *Which kind of creative-adjustment is the individual undergoing when panic attacks happen?* And, secondly, *Which kind of organismic and relational spontaneity is being sacrificed in the process?*

Our approach conceives of awareness in a manner that revolutionizes the Socratic edict "know thyself." The intellective power of consciousness and self-control is replaced by (a) the human capacity to "stay awake" and be aware of their own senses as a normal condition; (b) the direction of the experience, stemming from the intentional nature of contact (the way the self is at the contact-boundary with the environment and contributes to its creation); and (c) the strength and courage implied by such a holistic vision (at once bodily, affective, mental, and spiritual) of the energies involved in this being at the boundary, which are no longer conceived of in prevalently intellective terms.

Neurosis consists in maintaining isolation (in the organism–environment field) through the overexercise of consciousness. Awareness serves the opposite function, and represents the evolution of the opposite function, that is, spontaneous being at the contact-boundary. The first theoretical formulations and examples of awareness by practitioners of Gestalt psychotherapy mark a transition from the psychoanalytic culture of Freud's edict to "Where id was, there ego shall be" to a culture in which *experience* reigns supreme. According to the existentialist perspective of Gestalt therapy, which blossomed from the 1950s to the 1970s, experience (*Erlebnis*) is opposed to consciousness, and the organism's creative faculty (creative-adjustment) is opposed to its capacity to sublimation as the only way in which individuals can respond to the demands of the community. Besides, the organism self-regulation and holism is opposed to the necessity from the ego to control the id.

Today the humanistic movement belongs to our roots. We are currently experiencing a new cultural movement centered on relationships or, rather, on the experience of relationships. Thereby, Gestalt psychotherapy has been involved in developing the aspect of awareness that concerns itself with the nature of "being-with"—of being at the contact-boundary. This perspective has enabled us to pass beyond intrapsychic notions of awareness as a process linked to the satisfaction of needs to a fully postmodern, phenomenological outlook on relations. We need to begin conceiving of awareness in terms of *situation* or *field* (Robine, 2003) rather than of *relation*. This is because, as

Gestalt therapists, we see every experience as a part of (i.e., as relative to and stemming from) a situation, with all the limitations and richness of meaning that this implies. In sum, awareness is a contact quality, which may be more or less open to the senses and to the risks involved in intentionality in the course of every significant experience. It is the self's waking presence at the contact-boundary (Spagnuolo Lobb, 2004b).

These anthropological presuppositions of Gestalt therapy shed a new light on panic attacks, foregrounding the proactive tension experienced by sufferers: The excitement towards the realization of an intentionality of contact. *And this presents us with the possibility of a cure.* Only by believing in the individual's innate capacity to spontaneously reach out for contact with the environment—through which s/he will attain fulfillment—only through faith in each individual's capacity to do the right thing at any given moment can Gestalt therapists be in the therapeutic relationship without depending on external diagnostic schema. S/he can rather be guided by awareness, the being fully present at the contact-boundary, and this will enable him/her to find a new therapeutic solution for each therapeutic situation, as it is co-created by patient and therapist.

Besides, by paying more attention to the process than to the content, the therapist will be able to focus on the "mathematical" elements of the relationship. A patient who breathes in quickly, holding his/her breath, and only breathing out imperceptibly, is revealing something about his/her relationship with us. The therapist's capacity to observe these procedural aspects and to explore how the person seeks to develop his/her relational patterns, to help him/her in what s/he as an organism would like to do but does not manage, enabling him/her to breathe and to feel free to live, allows the patient to modulate the "music" s/he would like to play with the therapist.

Gestalt therapy defines treatment as the support that allows the individual to regain his/her capacity to live spontaneously and to spontaneously make contact with others. Herein lies the key to individual integrity and harmony—in other words to health itself. The therapist establishes a context in which the patient can develop his/her own integrity. This context is established by means of a kind of "dance" between therapist and patient. Therapy is not, therefore, just a technique that an expert implements upon a patient who has asked for help. It is rather the co-creation of a contact-boundary within which values, personalities, and personal attitudes towards life, play a fundamental role. Two people work together to find a new way of realizing interrupted intentionalities (Spagnuolo Lobb, 2003a). This is the elaborate dance that the therapist, with all his/her skills and humanity, and the patient, with all his/her suffering and desire to get better, create. They are able to reconstruct the ground on which the patient's relational life, his/her sense of security in the world and in others, and consequently his/her ability to abandon him-/herself to intimacy are based.

To sum up, the cure of panic attacks in Gestalt therapy consists in the co-construction of the ground of relational experience. It does not consist in creating a new figure. It rather creates a new narrative in which the implicit, the unsayable, the ground, and that which is usually taken for granted plays a key role. This notion of therapy is based on a positive anthropological perspective on humanity's inherent capacity to adjust creatively to situations, using both deconstructive skills and its ability to co-create.

Returning briefly to research carried out on the experience of patients with severe psychic disorders, Gestalt therapy theory maintains that these individuals are lacking the *ground provided by acquired contacts* (Spagnuolo Lobb, 2001). As a child gradually gains more and more experience of the world, s/he comes to take certain forms of contact for granted. For example, when a child is ready to start walking, s/he has already fully acquired a whole series of proprioceptive notions and sensory-motor skills which enable him/her to stand safely on his feet. The child acquires a number of relational and affective securities in much the same way. As s/he gradually learns to react to the primal and often catastrophic fears of early infancy (Winnicott, 1957), learning to feel supported and protected by his/her surrounding environment (through the realization, for example, that the caregiver will not abandon him/her), the child learns to draw on a series of contacts that permit him/her to realize a fully integrated self, distinct from that which is outside him-/herself, and consequently to face the world.

Psychiatric patients are lacking in these very "ground contacts," which are usually taken for granted. They are still struggling with primal fears and they are unable to clearly define themselves in relation to the world. As a result of this incapacity to differentiate between that which is within and that which is outside the self, chronic patients are defenseless in the face of environmental stimuli, which neurotics would find normal or even banal. In the former, the self is not differentiated in relationships. It is therefore intensely "permeable" to all that which happens ("If my friend is angry, what have *I* done to make him angry?"; or "How will his anger penetrate inside me and probably destroy me?"). Everyday social activities thereby become highly stressful and, above all, are not of primary importance to chronic patients.

What can, then, be said of *the experiences of those who suffer from panic*

39

attacks? The normality of their everyday existence is suddenly interrupted, as if they had suffered a severe trauma. It is no coincidence that panic disorder (PD) is often associated with post-traumatic stress disorder (PTSD). Nevertheless, whereas in the case of PTSD there are clear physiological and psychological reasons for the distress suffered, when panic attacks occur, there do not seem to be any words or any explanations that might relieve the sufferer's pain. There does not seem to be any phenomenological source for the patient's anxiety, yet the effects resemble those of a trauma. That there has been a trauma is clearly evident. However, its precise nature is unsayable. It may date back to the death of the father or mother years ago. Perhaps the patient's son had a motorcycle accident some time ago, during a period in which there was no time to reflect on how life could have changed had it proved fatal. Again, the episode might originate from other events that have taken place but have been somehow bypassed by the mind, because it was preoccupied with other matters or because the environment did not allow the individual to dwell on what had happened at that time. Our culture does not allow us to linger on the subject of death or on the profound pain of loss.

The trauma is therefore real, but it has been kept into the realm of the unsayable, taking the sufferer unawares with sudden attacks of primal fear which seem to creep up on them in silence, pushing them to their breaking point, and triggering crises and emergent properties. Upon discovery, the sufferer should like to be treated with the swiftness with which one would respond to the discovery of a tumor. The afflicted individual suddenly experiences the sense of panic and emergency that s/he should have felt at the moment of the trauma. It is this very unsayability that leaves the individual who suffers the panic attack defenseless in the face of a loss of control over what s/he is experiencing.

Which development of therapeutic approach should we search for in dealing with panic attacks? *Which aspects of the therapeutic relationship should we bring out* in order to support the patient in the sudden "plummet into the abyss" that characterizes the experience of the panic attack?

We have, by now, ascertained the ineffectiveness of approaches seeking to induce the patient back into "normality." Such methods tend to be rather forced, resulting in an involutional process. We need, instead, to deal with the consequences of a trauma that has not been fully experienced. We cannot restore the "naïve" sense of security in which the PD patient previously lived. Our task, instead, is to construct a new ground of security, which will have its origins in a full awareness of the fragility of existence and in a decision to live life to the full, seeking to contrast the fear of losing what one has with the positively aggressive determination to actively give and take what one wishes. This therapeutic turn can only be brought about through the unsayable, through providing a support that is co-created by patient and therapist and rests upon implicit knowledge. This conception of therapy for PD cases could serve to explain the swiftness with which some patients claim to have been cured in contexts that are not always therapeutic—for example through the intervention of a coach who simply offered to wait on the opposite pavement for a patient afraid of crossing the street. This is not to say that this style of coaching has discovered the cure for panic attacks. Rather, the coach in question has perhaps discovered the right course of action and the right moment, an implicit support, which is simple but difficult to formulate with the tools of the sayable.

1.5 Coming Back to Our Patient

So how does our patient's story finish? Naturally, I cannot describe all the details of the case. However, I can reproduce a short text that describes a turning point in the patient's ability to spontaneously participate in both therapy and life in general.

Alfonso (as we will call him) is the second of two sons. The older brother always fully occupied the role of firstborn, supporting and caring for the rest of the family. Alfonso, on the other hand, had always been the younger brother. He had traveled widely, enjoyed a number of unusual new sports, and allowed himself to get into a number of scrapes, which his brother had always been generous and effective in getting him out of. The two brothers were very fond of each other and complemented each other perfectly. They always did a lot of things together. When their mother became seriously ill and died, however, it was Alfonso, the younger brother and the doctor in the family, who felt responsible for overseeing her treatment. Although he did so willingly, the stress involved was considerable. Nevertheless, the close support of his brother proved invaluable. Next, however, the two brothers had to deal with a financial problem. Just as they were trying to make the best of the situation, the older brother suffered a stroke and died a few days later. Alfonso did not allow himself to fully experience the pain that resulted from this loss, and over the years he found it increasingly difficult to process it. Alfonso's feeling of self-assurance was gradually eroded. There was something in the realm of the unsayable that made the existence of this skilled doctor resemble a three-legged table.
One day, recalling the times past in which he was able to fly, to go ca-

noeing, to drive, and to travel to distant lands without any problems, Alfonso told me: "I want to be bigger, to behave like a grown-up. I do not want to seem like a baby who is scared of everything and needs someone to hold his hand if he wants to do anything." The way he said "I want to be bigger" reminded me of a child who, feeling ashamed of his diminutive stature, admits how much better s/he would feel if s/he were just a little bit taller. This leads me to recall the situation in which Alfonso grew up as the youngest in the house, always comforted and reassured by the presence of his older brother. An image of a small child, naked and alone before the big world springs to mind. This was the implicit situation that this man experienced as the ground of his social life. With a sudden moment of insight and with the aim of providing a support for this implicit situation, I say to him: "But you ARE big now. In fact, now you're the oldest brother in the family." This sentence, which redefines the ground for his experience of responsibility on the basis of a very palpable variable, to which he had never adjusted, has a noticeable effect on his body, on his breathing, and on his posture. He breathes more deeply and he opens up his shoulders. His whole body somehow becomes bigger. Neither he nor I say anything immediately. In the next session, Alfonso seems very happy when he arrives. He tells me he feels much better and that the words "Now you're the big brother in the family" have echoed in his mind all week, bringing on a strong sense of loss and mourning, for the death of his brother, but also of calm, of freedom to breathe. His shoulders felt more relaxed, broader, and higher. He felt, in his own words, "more able to live in the world." He examined his young patients with his usual enthusiasm, enjoying their company. He went for walks around the town and even visited the airfield. He met his fellow pilots and admired his microlight "without feeling anything of what I felt before, without my heart beating faster, or my head spinning."

From that moment onwards, I work to "accompany" my patient back to a normal life. We never discuss that sentence of mine again. It is nonetheless the ground of our relationship, on which our understanding of things is based. We are dealing in words, but these have a powerful implicit resonance. Alfonso has been able to change the ground that was creating his anxiety, whereby the younger brother was left without the older.

Only on one occasion did Alfonso ask: "But why am I feeling better now?" I explained to the best of my ability, outlining the complexity of the situation. I did so partly because his interest in the process was, to some extent, professional. However, he did not seem particularly taken by what I said. It seemed that my words were unconnected to his personal experience of recovery.

1.6 Concluding Notes on Aesthetic Values in Therapy

I have discussed panic attacks and the role of psychotherapy, suggesting that this kind of disorder is particular to our time. I have defined the unsayable as the essence of this complaint, underlining the importance of a process-based aesthetic approach. I have proposed a therapeutic perspective, focusing on enabling the patient to spontaneously "dance" out his relationships, rebuilding lost confidence through the language of the implicit.

It seems to me that, in this case, we must yet again conclude that our society needs to be reeducated in beauty. By beauty, I do not mean that which is promoted by mass media. I am rather referring to that sense of beauty that springs from being fully present in contact-making with the world.

If aesthetics formed the basis of the ethics of human relations in our society, traumas (including those unrelated to actual events) could be undergone in the measure of time and with the kind of rhythms that the organism requires to live through them adequately. A father whose son had escaped unharmed from a motorcycle accident would be free to wholly experience the anxiety caused by the incident, instead of being impelled by the surrounding environment to move on as before, to be happy with things as they are—perhaps even happier than before. Such a father should, instead, be encouraged to entirely acknowledge the experience that he will tend to deny, as it takes a long time to thoroughly process such traumas.

Like all disorders affecting our relational life, the panic attacks that afflict our society should lead us to reflect on the vacuum that characterizes the day-to-day habits and values on which society is based—to posit alternative values that might support us today.

In accordance with my arguments in this essay, I would uphold the following epistemological values that our society could support in helping relationships: (a) individual–environment unity, (b) contact intentionality as a key to understanding relationships, (c) education in beauty and creativity (Spagnuolo Lobb, 2004a).

These principles will help us to recognize a sort of "universal code" that enables us to appreciate the music and the "rhythms" of relationships and to "digest" our experiences, allowing ourselves to pause when necessary.

References

Bloom, D. J. (2003). "Tiger! Tiger! Burning bright"—Aesthetic values as clinical values in Gestalt therapy. In M. Spagnuolo Lobb & N. Amendt-Lyon (Eds.),

Creative license: The art of Gestalt therapy (pp. 63–78). Vienna & New York: Springer.

Borgna, E. (1999). "Le pietre del silenzio." Il contributo della letteratura alle conoscenze della psicologia ["The stones of silence": The contribution of literature to psychological knowledge]. *Le sfide della modernità, 4*, Liceo Scientifico Statale "Alessandro Antonelli," Novara, recording of the conference 1999, March 16 (with handouts for the students).

Bowman, C. E. (2005). The history and development of Gestalt therapy. In A. Woldt & S. Toman (Eds.), *Gestalt therapy: History, theory, and practice* (pp. 3–20). Thousand Oaks, CA: Sage Publications.

From, I. (1985). Requiem for "Gestalt." *Quaderni di Gestalt, 1*, 22–32.

Greenberg, J. R., & Mitchell, S. A. (1983). *Object relations in psychoanalytic theory*. Cambridge, MA: Harvard University Press.

Iaculo, G. (1996). Tempo e relazione nel processo terapeutico con la struttura esperienziale "narcisistica" [Time and relationships in the therapeutic process when dealing with "narcissistic" experience]. *Quaderni di Gestalt, 22/23*, 149–170.

Mahler, M., Pine, F., & Bergman, A. (1975). *The psychological birth of the human infant: Symbiosis and individuation*. New York: Basic Books.

Miller, A. (1996). *The drama of the gifted child: The search for the true self*. New York: Basic Books.

Müller Ebert, J., Josewski, M., Dreitzel, P., & Müller, B. (1989). Il narcisismo nella terapia della Gestalt [Narcissism in Gestalt therapy]. *Quaderni di Gestalt, 8/9*, 7–44.

Nietzsche, F. (1909–1913). The gay science and idylls on Messina. In O. Levy (Ed. & Trans.), *The complete works of Friedrich Nietzsche: The first complete and authorised English translation*. Edinburgh & London: N. Foulis. (Original work published 1882)

Perls, F. (1942). *Ego, hunger, and aggression: A revision of Freud's theory and method*. Durban, South Africa: Knox.

Perls, F., Hefferline, R., & Goodman, P. (1951). *Gestalt therapy: Excitement and growth in the human personality*. New York: Julian Press.

Robine, J.M. (2003). Intentionality in flesh and blood: Toward a psychopathology of fore-contacting. *International Gestalt Journal, XXVI*(2), 85–110.

Salonia, G. (1989). Dal noi all'io-tu: contributo per una teoria evolutiva del contatto. *Quaderni di Gestalt, 8/9*, 45–53. (Successively published 1993 as From We to I-Thou: A contribution to an evolutive theory of contact. *Studies in Gestalt Therapy, 1*, 31–41)

Salonia, G. (2001). Disagio psichico e risorse relazionali [Psychic disorders and relational resources]. *Quaderni di Gestalt, 32/33*, 13–23.

Spagnuolo Lobb, M. (1997). Gestalt. In J. M. Prelezzo (Ed.), *Dizionario di Scienze dell'Educazione* (pp. 465–468). Leumann, Turin, & Rome: LDC, LAS, & SEI.

Spagnuolo Lobb, M. (2001). La psicoterapia della Gestalt nelle strutture psichiatriche [Gestalt psychotherapy in psychiatric institutions]. *Quaderni di Gestalt, 32/33*, 34–48.

Spagnuolo Lobb, M. (2003a). Therapeutic meeting as improvisational co-creation. In M. Spagnuolo Lobb & N. Amendt-Lyon (Eds.), *Creative license: The art of Gestalt therapy* (pp. 37–50). Vienna & New York: Springer.

Spagnuolo Lobb, M. (2003b). Creative adjustment in madness: A Gestalt therapy model for seriously disturbed patients. In M. Spagnuolo Lobb & N. Amendt-Lyon (Eds.), *Creative license: The art of Gestalt therapy* (pp. 261–278). Vienna & New York: Springer.

Spagnuolo Lobb, M. (2004a). Diventare genitori nella società post-moderna [Becoming parents in postmodern society]. In R. G. Romano (Ed.), *Ciclo di vita e dinamiche educative nella società postmoderna* (pp. 211–228). Milan: Angeli.

Spagnuolo Lobb, M. (2004b). L'awareness dans la pratique post-moderne de la Gestalt-thérapie [Awareness in the postmodern practice of Gestalt therapy]. *Gestalt*, Société Française de Gestalt (Ed.), *XV*(27), 41–58.

Spagnuolo Lobb, M. (2007). Psicoterapia della Gestalt [Gestalt Psychotherapy]. In F. Barale, V. Gallese, S. Mistura, & A. Zamperini (Eds.), *Dizionario storico della scienza della psiche* (pp. 900–904). Turin: Einaudi.

Spagnuolo Lobb, M., Salonia, G., & Sichera, A. (1996). From the "discomfort of civilization" to creative adjustment: The relationship between individual and community in psychotherapy in the third millennium. *International Journal of Psychotherapy, 1*, 45–53. (Successively published 1997 as Dal "disagio della civiltà" all'adattamento creativo. Il rapporto individuo/comunità nella psicoterapia del terzo millennio. *Quaderni di Gestalt, 24/25*, 96–106)

Stern, D. (2004). *The present moment in psychotherapy and everyday life.* New York: Norton.

Stern, D., Bruschweiler-Stern, N., Harrison, A., Lyons-Ruth, K., Morgan, A., Nahum, J., et al. (1998a). The process of therapeutic change involving implicit knowledge: Some implications of developmental observations for adult psychotherapy. *Infant Mental Health Journal, 3*, 300–308.

Stern, D., Bruschweiler-Stern, N., Harrison, A., Lyons-Ruth, K., Morgan, A., Nahum, J., et al. (1998b). Non-interpretive mechanisms in psychoanalytic therapy: The "something more" than interpretation. *International Journal of Psycho-Analysis, 79*, 903–921.

Stern, D., & the Boston Change Process Study Group. (2003). On the other side of the moon: The import of implicit knowledge for Gestalt therapy. In M. Spagnuolo Lobb & N. Amendt-Lyon (Eds.), *Creative license: The art of Gestalt therapy* (pp. 21–36). Vienna & New York: Springer.

Winnicott, D. W. (1957). *Mother and child: A primer of first relationship.* New York: Basic Books.

2. Social Changes and Psychological Disorders. Panic Attacks in Postmodernity

by Giovanni Salonia

> If, as we now believe, individual identity stems not automatically from a combination of genes, but rather from a process of development—that is through the individual's interaction with the environment in which he or she is born—we must acknowledge that individual psychopathology will change according to the sociocultural environment in which the individual identity is formed (cf. Rangell, 1975). In fact, the incidence and distribution of mental illness tends to vary both quantitatively and qualitatively from one society to another and in individual societies as they change with time. (Gaddini, 2002)

These are the opening words of one of Eugenio Gaddini's most famous papers, significantly entitled *Se e come sono cambiati i nostri pazienti fino ai nostri giorni* (On Whether and How Our Patients Have Changed).

Taking the same question as a starting point (as we know, while the fundamental questions are always the same, their answers tend to differ!), I will here posit a series of reflections from the perspective, not of psychoanalysis, but rather of Gestalt psychotherapy.

At this juncture we should clarify that when we speak of changes in psychopathology, or rather of "new" kinds of patient, we are not only referring to symptoms that are new on a behavioral level (such as, for example, internet addiction). Instead, we will also take into consideration the increased occurrence of specific disorders, which pose new questions for therapists (e.g., borderline disorders). It is in this sense that we ask ourselves the question: Why is it that the epidemiology of psychic disorders varies quantitatively and qualitatively on both the diachronic (i.e., in the same society) and the synchronic (i.e., in different social contexts) levels?

Before we can answer this question, we must deal with another, which is perhaps embarrassing but which certainly proves to be illuminating: Why do approaches to therapy change? In over 100 years of psychotherapy, we have witnessed the birth of many different schools of thought (often differing significantly from each other) and we have also witnessed some significant changes of practice within the individual schools. What does all this mean? Both the naïve response to this question, which attributes these changes to the genius or personal characteristics of the movement's founder,[1] and the more ideological approach, which attributes such changes to the "acting out" of therapists rebelling against their predecessors, do not seem to tell the whole story.

We are faced, then, with two questions:

Why (and how) do patients (and psychopathologies) change in different social contexts?

Why (and how) do psychotherapeutic approaches change (via both the "birth" of new schools and changes within existing models)?

2.1 Basic Relational Model

Gestalt psychotherapy[2] reads psychic disorders as originating in a disorder of the individual's relational competences. Psychic disorders spring up within relationships, manifesting themselves in and recurring to an incapacity to conduct valid relationships in the here-and-now. They can be cured through and within the context of a "reparative" relationship. From this point of view, the various symptoms are understood as different manifestations of the patient's inability to have a healthy relationship with others.[3] The symptom interpreted as "calling for a relationship" (Sichera, 2001) thus becomes the expression of a short circuit between the irrepressible intentionality to enter into contact with the other and an insurmountable inability to do so.

Relational competence, in turn, requires an ability to integrate two constitutive and elementary (i.e., universally recognized) needs of the human heart: The need to realize oneself (i.e., to be oneself) and the need of be-

---

[1] On this point, see Carotenuto, 1982.

[2] For readers who are new to Gestalt psychotherapy: The classic texts on the subject are Perls, Hefferline, & Goodman, 1951; Polster & Polster, 1973; Zinker, 1978. For new developments, see Spagnuolo Lobb, 2001; Spagnuolo Lobb & Amendt-Lyon, 2003.

[3] On the psychopathology of Gestalt psychotherapy, see Salonia, 2001 and Spagnuolo Lobb, 2003.

longing (i.e., "living-with").[1] Many differences between human beings (with regard to the manner in which relations are conducted and decisions made) derive from the very way in which these two needs (which are never entirely convergent or divergent) are combined and recombined. In their various manifestations, psychic disorders result from a failure in the individual's capacity to balance these two impulses in a positive way (i.e., one or another tends to be cancelled out). Three main factors influence the individual in developing this competence and in elaborating the style in which relations will be conducted—the manner in which the individual will choose to relate these two needs (i.e., Which will be prevalent? How? At which moments?). These are the individual's own relational experiences, the imprint received from his or her initial relations (i.e., his or her family of origin and the environment in which he or she was first socialized), and the kinds of relationality prevalent in his or her own sociocultural context. Social context is the most influential of these three, inasmuch as it provides the basis of and the key for understanding the other two. This is because, for reasons we will explore later, every group (or community) chooses its own relational model—its own way to integrate these centripetal (i.e., reaching for belonging) and centrifugal (i.e., reaching inwards, towards the fulfillment of the self) forces.[2] Considering relations from this perspective, we can adopt the basic relational model of cultural anthropology[3] for our own purposes. This model, whereby the group integrates its centrifugal and centripetal impulses, depends upon the factors that determine the group's survival.

When a society immediately and simultaneously recognizes an imminent threat to its survival (e.g., war or famine), it spontaneously organizes its relational model so as to prioritize "living-with" or belonging to the group at the expense of individual self-fulfillment (thereby following the old saying: "*primum vivere deinde filosofari,*" or "first live, then fulfill yourself"). In such situations, the need to feel oneself protected leads naturally to a sacrifice (or repression) of personal freedom and of any expression of individual subjectivity. Indeed, any attempt at self-differentiation or autonomy at such a moment is likely to provoke a sense of guilt. Furthermore, in these contexts the value of unity in the face of a common danger

---

[1] For a more detailed study on this point, see Salonia, 2004, pp. 101–112.

[2] See Salonia, 2004.

[3] See Kardiner's classic analysis (1939) of *basic personality*. According to our perspective, and in contrast to that of this scholar, it is the structure of society (in this case the *basic relational model*) which determines the frame of reference for the networks of relationships which are experienced in the family life and are learned at the first stages of socialization.

tends to be at the foremost, with a consequent emphasis upon obedience to one's superiors (who are seen to be the most capable of overcoming the current peril). Belonging is accordingly viewed positively and with feelings of pride. The fact that those without decision-making power are denied creativity is not viewed in a negative light. An army is needed, and that army will consist in many who will sacrifice their individuality for the survival of the group. For an individual to emerge, he or she must either become a hero, making a radical sacrifice for the common good (the *mystique* of the hero is always associated with danger), or, more negatively, a scoundrel or even a traitor, putting the community at risk. The thoughts of the group (their very conceptions of maturity and immaturity) revolve around themes of belonging (e.g., guilt, the superego, or repression). Psychic disorders are manifestations of a fear of emerging from the crowd as a responsible, unique individual (nervous hysteria, phobias, obsessive–compulsive disorders, hypochondria, etc.). The growth of individuals within such a social context will depend on their developing faith in themselves, the courage to rise above the protective blanket of society and overcome the fear and guilt of being themselves. When society is strong, the individual is weak. Sigmund Freud's analysis in *Civilization and its Discontents* (1930/1994) hence remains valid. Freud argued that, as it was impossible to avoid conflict between the individual and society, it is necessary to have recourse to a superego, even if it is domesticated, and a censor, even if it is easily dupable. He reached this conclusion because he believed it was impossible for an individual who is not a "hero" to fully express him- or herself against society.

The relational models that emerge in societies in which the group does not perceive its survival to be at risk (or under threat of war or famine) are significantly different (Salonia, 2004, pp. 129–142). Without the uniting force of a perceived common danger, centrifugal impulses are decidedly more prevalent. Self-interest and the desire for self-fulfillment bring about conflict, followed by disaffection where the individual is faced with the demands of belonging. As Constantinos Kavafis has written, in the absence of external threats it becomes difficult to stimulate any interest in belonging ("What are we to do now that there are no more enemies?").[1] In such contexts, the individual gradually, first with feelings of anger and then with euphoria, regains the liberty that had been sacrificed to security. Without the impulse to unite in the face of danger, the connective tissue of society is

---

[1] "What would we do without the barbarians? At the end of the day, they were a solution" (Kafavis, 1992, p. 36).

lacerated. Society becomes fragmented (or "liquidized" as Zygmunt Bauman would put it[1]) into multiple subjectivities that do not consider living together to be a number one priority and who have lost their uniting valences, their metanarratives, and their ideologies.[2]

Since every subjectivity legitimizes its own values, nobody feels the need to refer to others in order to authenticate the truthfulness of their positions. Self-sufficiency is the only logic (i.e., learning is conceived of in terms of "do it yourself") and self-realization (over and above affective ties) is the only aim. Once the initial sense of guilt (because one has ceased to belong) has been overcome, the individual experiences a sense of (narcissistic) euphoria in the discovery and the appreciation of his or her own subjectivity. Subsequently, in the postnarcissistic period, difficulties emerge both as to how to construct an identity (it is difficult to recognize oneself in a narcissistic world made up of isolated individuals) and as to how to fulfill oneself in the face of an infinite number of possibilities and attractions and a scarcity of tools and genuine pathways. The very meaning of existence, which is clearly defined in periods of danger (i.e., as working together for the survival of the group), becomes obscure and difficult to identify. As we only live once (and, as Milan Kundera would put it, "*Once is never,*" 1984), inventing (or discovering) a meaning for our unique and unrepeatable lives proves a dramatic challenge.

In periods in which society emphasizes subjectivity over and above belonging (i.e., in narcissistic societies), disorders manifest both narcissism (the subjectivity that feels unable to entrust itself to society) and the loss of identity (the subjectivity that feels unable to define itself in the face of multiple possibilities and opportunities).[3] Borderline disorders are also common in fragmented societies, where clear boundaries are lacking and where an overwhelming sense of confusion and entanglement prevails. Individuals who have been socialized in an environment in which they have received contradictory messages are particularly vulnerable to confusion with regard to their own identities.

Fear of individuation and fear of belonging are the key poles of psychic disorders, as Otto Rank observed.[4] The former is typical of societies joined by a common threat, the latter of societies where the absence of a threat has

[1] Amongst the many texts written by the prolific analyst Bauman on postmodern society, see especially 1998, 2000, & 2001.

[2] On this point, see Salonia, 1999.

[3] Frankl's psychoanalytic exploration of the quest for the meaning of life as a primary need belongs to this period (see 1946/2004).

[4] See Becker (1973/1997) for a fascinating presentation of these ideas of Rank's.

pushed the individual subjectivity to the forefront. In both cases, the psychic disorder is always triggered by a search for personal identity and self-realization. In some contexts, the individual is afraid to say the word "I," because it would mean abandoning the security of belonging. In others, the individual can say "I" freely, but is incapable of reciprocity ("I-Thou"), or of having a clear personal and relational identity.

2.2 Evolutive Theories and Social Changes

It is interesting to note how changes to the basic relational model do not only generate different kinds of disorders but also different conceptions of maturity. The notion of maturity is central to any developmental theory and to all of the various schools of psychotherapy (Salonia, 1997).

We need only examine the dominant theory of child development in the last century to observe how developmental models have changed. Both the stages of the child's growth and the various key moments of development and evolution are described in very different terms. For Freud, child development culminates in the genital stage—that is, the moment at which the individual becomes able to love and to work, which is reached as he or she becomes aware ("Where id was, there ego shall be"[1]) of his or her own instincts (or drives) and of the various forms of repression being carried out in fear of the superego. Freud thus defines maturity as a compromise between the requirements of the social (and the superego) and those of the individual. The highest levels of maturity are expressed by the hero and the saint (Freud, 1905/1962; 1930/1994). In the 1950s, Gestalt theory redefined maturity in terms of *creative-adjustment*, the capacity to "bite" into experience so as to learn how to join adaptation (belonging) and creativity (subjectivity). In accordance with Rank's seminal ideas, the ideal model of maturity is the artist. Margaret Mahler developed a model of infantile development in a narcissistic society which laid a great deal of emphasis on personal autonomy, attaching just value to the significance of the child's learning to walk (which she viewed, not as a means to walk towards the mother but as the capacity to walk away from her) and defining maturity as "constancy of object" (Mahler, Pine, & Bergman, 1975). Such a paradigm conjures up the image of someone strong who is challenging the whole world, like the lead cowboy in a Western or, in a more adolescent manifestation, Jonathan Livingstone Seagull who breaks away from the group because he

---

[1] Freud, 1933/1961, p. 80.

feels special (Bach, 1970/1994). In the subsequent postnarcissistic period, it became imperative to find a compromise with others (for how could a society of "Narcissi" possibly live together?). Daniel Stern posited a developmental theory connected to the theory of the self (1985). He thereby unknowingly revived the key concepts of Gestalt therapy, suggesting that there is no such thing as individual maturity, as maturity can only be conceived of in relational terms. The self is, in fact, always relational. It is narrative, inasmuch as it represents a capacity to tell stories and to account for itself, to relate to others in a triadic manner. Gestalt developmental theory defines a child's maturity in terms of his or her contact skills (Salonia, 1989). In summary, it is interesting to note how, during a period of war, a child is obliged to "join in," obeying and accepting the rules necessary for common survival. In a narcissistic period, by contrast, maturity consists in being autonomous and expressing one's own potentials. Finally, in a postnarcissistic period, a mature being is defined as one able to express him- or herself in the context of a relationship.

2.3 Psychotherapeutic Models and Social Changes

Having established these initial premises, we can now ask ourselves a somewhat more complex question—namely, can a single clinical model serve in all historical periods and contexts? Or rather: "Can clinical procedures established decades ago in entirely different historical and cultural contexts continue to satisfy the needs of a world that has now completely changed?" (Spagnuolo Lobb, 2001b, p. 9).

There is a broad spectrum of possible answers to this question. Some would argue that their own school is atemporal and aspatial both in theory and in practice and that all other approaches (be they earlier or later) are partial or superficial. For others, objectivity can only be achieved through a descriptive approach to psychopathology (e.g., *Diagnostic and Statistical Manual of Mental Disorders–IV*). However, such attempts at creating integrated psychotherapeutic models (i.e., by juxtaposing shreds of theory with bits and pieces of practice) is but another way of denying the need for the constant updating of existing psychotherapeutic models.

It is this very lack of a connection between psychotherapy and social context that makes it so difficult to develop an entirely satisfactory psychotherapeutic approach. Let us take, for example, the case of psychoanalysis, which is commonly considered to be the mother of all other branches of psychotherapy. Freud sought to anchor his ingenious and seminal intuitions on social life in legends of the origins of humanity (*Totem and Taboo*, 1913/1960), in Greek mythology, and in literature, drawing on these bases to formulate future predictions (1930/1994). Paradoxically, Freud's assumption that he had thus discovered *the* immutable principles behind life in society became the weakest link in psychoanalytic theory. Indeed, it was one of Freud's own disciples who first pointed out (with understandable hesitance) that we have now passed from the "guilty man" phase to that of the "tragic man" (Kohut, 1971). While Freud's patients were suffering from guilt because they were unable to separate themselves from their surrounding communities, patients nowadays (i.e., from the last two decades of the twentieth century onwards) are afflicted by a tragic incapacity to formulate a relational identity, participation in the community having become at once "necessary and impossible" (Esposito, 1998).

Gestalt psychotherapy holds that any psychotherapeutic theory must necessarily and constantly respond to sociocultural changes. To this end, in a manner coherent with the epistemology of its experiential–relational principles, Gestalt psychotherapy has recourse to hermeneutics (Sichera, 2001). Such hermeneutic tools facilitate a process of understanding which takes into account—as part of an inevitably and revealingly circular process—text, author, and reader. That is, on the one hand, therapist, patient and therapeutic model and, on the other, the model itself, the context in which it was originally formulated, and the context in which it is being applied. Sociocultural contextualization therefore proves to be an absolutely indispensable element for any program of therapy. The history of Gestalt psychotherapy provides us with a fine illustration of this hermeneutic choice. Frederick Perls, one of the movement's founders, summarized his theory in the so-called "Gestalt prayer":

> I do my thing and you do yours. I am not in this world to live up to your expectations, and you are not in this world to live up to mine. You are you and I am I, and if by chance we find each other, then it is beautiful. If not, it can't be helped. (Perls, 1969)

Perls wrote this in America in the 1960s, that is, in a setting in which people felt unable to separate themselves from dysfunctional forms of belonging. In such a context, Perls' affirmations had a genuine therapeutic value. Transferred to a different setting (e.g., the "narcissistic" society of the 1970s), such a statement would instead be nonsensical. "Don't tie yourself down" and "follow your own path" are instructions that narcissists have no problems following in their day-to-day life. Such individuals need, instead, to learn to overcome their phobia of forming attachments in order to be able to experience belonging and trust in others.

A further consequence of this contextualization of psychic disorders—that is, of their being understood in the context of the basic relational model—is that their significance can change dramatically. An individual whose personality tends towards excessive levels of dependence will view his or her disorder differently, depending on whether the primary impulse of his or her social context is towards belonging ("How can I possibly overcome this sense of guilt?") or towards self-fulfillment ("Why am I different from everyone else?"). The basic relational model is, therefore, the principal key for understanding every psychic disorder and directing therapy.

All of the above provides us with a key for interpreting the emergence of the various schools of psychotherapy over the last 60 years (Salonia, 1997). In societies that are strongly united in the face of a common danger, the psychoanalytical school, with its rigid therapist–patient hierarchy (that is to say, the analyst alone makes sense of the senseless outpourings of the patient: free associations, lapsus linguae, dreams), will tend to prevail. The psychotherapeutic process is regulated by and accountable to the superego. The ego is seen as the fruit of the superego–id conflict. The patient's task consists in "introjecting" the interpretation (or illumination) that the analyst provides. When, instead, subjectivity comes to assume primacy in the sociocultural context, therapeutic value is attributed to the patient's capacity for opposition (e.g., in Rank's *Gegenwille* or *counterwill*, 1932). Perls' first important intuition (which first catalyzed his detachment from the psychoanalytic schools and laid the foundations for the Gestalt approach) was that children learn by deconstructing (hence the value of teething), not by swallowing (Perls, 1942/1969). Subjectivity thus comes to the forefront, not only in society, but also in psychotherapy. This is the profound meaning behind the Rogerian nondirective approach to therapy (Rogers, 1951), and behind the importance attached to experience by Gestalt psychotherapy (both schools have often been overhastily accused of superficiality! See Cavalieri, 2003). These therapists effectively adopt and adapt, albeit in very different ways, the brilliant but isolated theories of Karl Jaspers on the importance of patient experiences and on the value of *Einfühlung* over explanation. "Feeling expression" has become the new principle of therapy, inasmuch as it manifests the patient's renewed ability to express his or her subjectivity.[1] For example, in periods of danger, it makes little sense to free

---

[1] Such was the slogan of the humanistic therapies of the 1960s. Compare Buhler & Allen, 1972.

up space for the expression of personal experiences. In situations in which we need to fight for our survival, it is unwise to pay attention to expressions of fear or to take fear too seriously, unless it can be defined as positively "psychiatric." From the 1960s on, a risk has arisen from subjectivities that have entirely freed themselves from all sense of belonging, which is conceived of as a dependence. It proves necessary to reinstate relations and a nondependent sense of belonging. Therapy, as a reflection of its social and philosophical context, has come to focus on the family and on relationships. This is an era of "therapies of the self," which lay emphasis on the inevitable social and relational dimension of the subject.[1] Gestalt psychotherapy further refines the existing theoretical and clinical corpus on the self and develops the theory of contact as the hermeneutic key to all future clinical and theoretical procedure. Gestalt therapy in particular made explicit a key fundamental notion, revolutionary even compared to the developments of the 1950s: that the organism's self-regulation had to be understood in terms of a broader context—that of the self-regulation of the relationship (Salonia, Spagnuolo Lobb, & Sichera, 1997). The notion that the relationship self-regulates radically transformed our understanding of what it means to experience relationships, including those between therapist and patient. It is interesting to note that, in the same period, psychoanalysis was undergoing a parallel transformation, both within its own confines and through the creation of new postpsychoanalytic paradigms. The most famous of these developments is the notion of object relations, which has developed over these last years largely due to the research of Stephen Mitchell and Daniel Stern (Mitchell, 2000; Stern, 1985). The effectiveness of the therapeutic relationship at any given stage of the therapy assumes a central importance according to this "relational model."

2.4 Panic Attacks and the Basic Relational Model

Panic attacks, which are increasingly frequent in postmodern society, are a case in point. All at once, the subject feels overwhelmed by a sense of hopeless loneliness, even if he or she is actually surrounded by many others. He or she is suddenly overcome by a profound anxiety and terror, ca-

---

[1] This interest for the Other, in philosophy, was advocated by philosophies of otherness and reciprocity (we need only think of Buber, Lévinas, Rosenzweig, etc.). In therapy it created the context of sensibility, which gave rise to family therapy and the attention paid to relationships (Salonia, 1992; Lévinas, 1961/1969 & 1949/1998; Buber, 1958/2004).

tastrophe seems imminent, and the individual is left desperately reaching out for figures that might provide some sense of security. The physiological reactions that follow (trembling, sweating, and faintness) intensify the sense of being near the end. A crevice, which seems like an abyss, has suddenly cleaved open the ground upon which all the subject's existential certainties rest. The presence of others—who are not figures of particular significance—is insufficient to assuage anxiety and provide support. After the first attack has passed, the sufferer, in addition to being stunned by the violent trauma experienced, is also completely fazed by his or her inability to explain what has just happened—how he or she has suddenly passed to a state so far removed from the serenity and self-confidence which have characterized his or her life so far. This inexplicability intensifies his or her feelings of insecurity and further limits movement. Upon entering this vortex, individuals feel unable to move in unfamiliar spaces without the support of a trusted companion (having medication with them is not always enough to placate anxiety).

Panic attacks are essentially a kind of fear—an absolute and overwhelming fear, which gives the sufferer the impression that everything is dangerous and running out of control. Fear is not, in itself, an illness. It is, in fact, a vital element of human nature. All living people experience fear—a fear above all related to pain and death (i.e., all other fears stem from these primal terrors). According to Arthur Janov (1970), fear is the real root problem of existence. With what instruments can human beings face up to fear? Or rather, in clinical terms, when does fear become pathological? Fear is physiological if it makes the individual aware of a danger and enables him or her to protect him- or herself in the best possible way (through fighting back, flight or immobility). Fear is pathological if it does not correspond to reality—if it is greater or lesser than a given danger requires (we are obviously here not taking into account the fear that is triggered by an unthreatening object, somehow recalling a previous trauma). During childhood, we learn how to accurately perceive and deal with fears through our relationships with our parental figures. In the early stages of infancy it seems, according to Donald Winnicott (1984), that fears consist in internal experiences and dramatic relationships whilst, later on, children begin to fear external objects, which often become spaces where relational fears can be fixated and where sense perceptions can be amplified. When a child receives support and containment which are "good enough" (to borrow from Winnicott's famous notion of the "good enough mother") he or she develops the innate and positive aggression that enables every human organism to face danger. Such support should consist, on the one hand, in allowing the child to express his or her fears and, on the other, in offering reassurances that help him or her to learn how to perceive and face danger. A good experience of belonging enables the child to develop a healthy sense of his or her own integrity and strength.

As we have seen, in periods when the group is in danger, a strong sense of belonging emerges. Fear of the danger in question is faced as an experience to be shared and responded to by the group as a whole, with the stronger members of the community supporting and reassuring the young and weak. Panic attacks (i.e., fear without external stimuli) will not occur in such contexts, because the community is in the grip of an externally stimulated fear (of something already experienced or impending), which is being directly, dramatically experienced. A danger being faced by the one becomes, in a certain sense, a danger to be faced by all. In situations where there is a strong sense of belonging, individuals may experience fear, but not panic. Panic is by definition a fear devoid of relation and support. Panic attacks cleave a deep crevice in the world of appearance, allowing the sufferer to glimpse, albeit painfully, the world beyond, the deeper world of relationships, involvement, and reliance on others. It is interesting to note how individuals who suffer from panic attacks are particularly good at distinguishing significant relationships (i.e., which have a calming and tranquilizing effect) from apparent relationships (i.e., which may be myriad but do nothing to contain anxiety). It is as if they experience firsthand and are consequently acutely sensitive to the difference between encounters leading to genuine contact with the other (i.e., Martin Heidegger's *Mit-Da-Sein*), and encounters whereby one is simply side-by-side with another (Salonia, 2001).

In the course of a panic attack, the patient has the vivid and agonizing sensation of being thrown out into the world without any protection (the experience Heidegger referred to as *Geworfenheit*). As we have seen, such an experience is highly dramatic, normally belonging to the primal terrors of childhood. Only with parental support can the child build up the necessary existential ground of security (i.e., a healthy faith in him- or herself and in life in general; Perls, Hefferline, & Goodman, 1951) to be able to face the difficulties of existence. We might, therefore, hypothesize that individuals suffering from panic attacks are lacking in (i.e., have not received) a "good enough" degree of (parental) containment to be able to bear a total opening of the self. Indeed, children who have grown up in social (and family) contexts that can be defined as narcissistic (i.e., in which self-fulfillment appears to take priority over belonging) are profoundly affected by the dilemma that is lacerating their parents, who are torn between ties to the family and opportunities for personal growth in the *polis*. The sense of belonging that such parents afford to their children is, in a certain sense, incomplete and labored (it by no means comes across as something automatically granted). The children of such families are thus obliged to become their own parents—to self-parent. Psychotherapy defines these individuals as "affective orphans"—children who have never experienced sufficient levels of support and containment (Spagnuolo Lobb & Salonia, 1993). They learn to conduct relations in an entirely self-sufficient manner, expecting nothing from their surrounding environment, in which they have very little faith. Such security as these individuals can offer to others (and to themselves, for that matter) rests on a fragile ground, which is built on the denial of and the failure to respond sufficiently to their own weaknesses and vulnerability. When faced with new and stressful situations (e.g., any key events in the personal or family life cycle), they will need a greater level of support that they will be unable to find within their basic ground of security. A rift (of a clearly relational nature) will therefore open up in those areas of the ground where the support of others was lacking. Feelings of weakness and need, which had long been suppressed in the subject's inner life, rise up so suddenly and inexorably that the individual cannot help asking for support, and often from individuals whom it had always seemed he or she could do without. This is the situation that Erik Erikson defined as the "moratorium stage" (1950/1995)—the moment at which the individual is obliged (and, for that matter, desires) to be restored to specific relational experiences that he or she has been denied, and also to acquire necessary relational skills. Panic attacks can be defined as a dramatic way of reaching out for a relationship, helping to reconstruct the belonging, which is a constituent part of any integrated and full identity (on this point, see chapter 3).

The first objective of the program of therapy must thus be to attach a meaning to an apparently meaningless and alien symptom—to identify the panic attack as a relational appeal. The patient will then gradually learn to have faith in even his or her weakest facets and to trust in and rely on the therapist (and the outside world). Such a restored faith will enable the patient to attain a new confidence in him- or herself.

2.5 Psychotherapy and Life

In conclusion, returning to the question of "if and how our patients have changed," I would posit a rather different answer to that proposed by Gaddini (as I wrote before, while questions unite us, answers divide us!). It does not seem to me that the increased appearance and possibility of treating patients suffering from complaints, which would once have been incomprehensible, is due to the fact that therapists are more methodologically and emotionally refined today than they were in the past. Every social context breeds a specific kind of patient, and therapists are required to abandon the securities of tradition in order to invent new strategies and methods in collaboration with their patients, or, we should rather say, "standing at the feet of their growth and development" (Luzi, 1998). They need to respond to new demands arising from new disorders, new manifestations of the inability to reconcile the two impulses (towards belonging, on the one hand, and fulfillment, on the other) that have provided our hermeneutic key in this chapter (Salonia, 2004, pp. 129–139). The first instance of socialization, which provides the imprint on which each individual will base his or her "being-with" relations, is a variable. It always depends on the vast potential horizon afforded by the basic relational model, upon which every reflection on the human condition and its disorders and each new therapy should be founded.

This reflection brings us back to one of the basic and fundamental principles of psychotherapy: Its intimate connection with life. Individuals need to grow and mature through the full experience of existence, in all its complexity—through sorrow and joy, meetings and partings, birth and death. Only in this way can human beings find true fulfillment. To paraphrase Alessandro Manzoni, life "both wearies and comforts." In existential and psychotherapeutic terms, this means that each human being has a capacity for growth which is innate but only germinal (i.e., it needs a favorable environment in which to develop)—an innate and germinal ability to self-regulate and self-fulfill in even the most difficult situations. Psychotherapists are called upon to help when this vital skill has not been sufficiently nurtured, with the effect that the individual is unable to positively face up to the events of his or her life. The psychotherapist's job is to renovate (or even recreate) the skills that will enable the individual to mature and repair him- or herself. The psychotherapist's role is one of support, recalling the role occupied by the individual's parents and social network, in situations such as those described in Arnold van Gennep's *Rites of Passage* (1908/1977). This close connection between psychotherapy and life means that, if the therapeutic program is to be carried forward in collaboration with the patient, the therapist must closely interrogate both society and life itself.

The relationship between psychotherapy and life is essentially circular.

Life challenges psychotherapy to give expression to all its possible therapeutic valences, while the psychotherapist draws on life for the direction
and meaning of therapy.

References

American Psychiatric Association. (1994). *Diagnostic and statistical manual of
mental disorders* (4th ed.). Washington, DC: American Psychiatric Associa-
tion.
Bach, R. (1994). *Jonathan Livingston Seagull: A story*. London: HarperCollins.
(Original work published 1970)
Bauman, Z. (1998). *Globalization: The human consequences*. Cambridge: Polity
Press.
Bauman, Z. (2000). *Liquid modernity*. Cambridge: Polity Press.
Bauman, Z. (2001). *The individualized society*. Cambridge: Polity Press.
Becker, E. (1997). *The denial of death*. New York: Free Press. (Original work pub-
lished 1973)
Buber, M. (2004). *I and Thou* (R. G. Smith, Trans.) (2nd ed.). London: Continuum.
(Original work published 1958)
Buhler, C., & Allen, M. (1972). *Introduction to humanistic psychology*. Monterey,
CA: Brooks/Cole Publishing Co.
Carotenuto, A. (1982). *Discorso sulla metapsicologia* [Discorse on metapsycho-
logy]. Turin: Bollati Boringhieri.
Cavaleri, P. (2003). *La profondità della superficie* [The depth of surfaces]. Milan:
Angeli.
Chessick, R. D. (1993), Psychology of the self and the treatment of narcissism.
Northvale, NJ: Aronson.
Erikson, E. H. (1995). *Childhood and society*. London: Vintage. (Original work
published 1950)
Esposito, R. (1998). *Communitas. Origine e destino della unità* [Communitas: Ori-
gin and destiny of unity]. Turin: Einaudi.
Frankl, V. E. (2004). *Man's search for meaning* (I. Lasch, Trans). London: Rider.
(Original work published 1946)
Freud, S. (1960). *Totem and taboo* (J. Strachey, Trans.). London: Routledge.
(Original work published 1913)
Freud, S. (1961). New Introductory Lectures on Psycho-Analysis. In J. Strachey
(Ed. & Trans.), *The standard edition of the complete psychological works of
Sigmund Freud* (Vol. 22). London: Hogarth Press. (Original work published
1933)
Freud, S. (1962). *Three essays on the theory of sexuality* (J. Strachey, Ed. &
Trans.). London: Hogarth Press. (Original work published 1905)
Freud, S. (1994). *Civilization and its discontents* (J. Riviere, Trans.). New York:

Dover Publications & London: Constable. (Original work published 1930)

Gabbard, G. O. (1990). *Psychodynamic psychiatry in clinical practice.* Washington, DC: American Psychiatric Press.

Gaddini, E. (1984). Se e come sono cambiati i nostri pazienti fino ai nostri giorni [If and how our patients have changed]. In E. Gaddini (2002), *Scritti 1953–1985* (pp. 644–662). Milan: Cortina.

Greenberg, J. R., & Mitchell, S. A. (1983). *Object relations in psychoanalytic theory.* Cambridge, MA: Harvard University Press.

Heidegger, M. (1996). *Being and time: A translation of Sein und Zeit* (J. Stambaugh, Trans.).

Albany, NY: State University of New York Press. (Original work published 1927)

Janov, A. (1970). *The primal scream. Primal therapy: The cure for neurosis.* New York: Putnam.

Jaspers, K. (1997). *General psychopathology* (J. Hoenig & M. Hamilton, Trans). Baltimore: Johns

Hopkins University Press. (Original work 1913)

Kardiner, A. (1939). *The individual and his society.* New York: Columbia University Press.

Kavafis, C. (1992). Aspettando i barbari [Waiting for the barbarians]. In C. Kavafis, *Settantacinque poesie* (pp. 36–40). Turin: Einaudi.

Kohut, H. (1971). *The Analysis of the self: A systematic approach to the psychoanalytic treatment of narcissistic personality disorders.* New York: International Universities Press.

Kundera, M. (1984). *The unbearable lightness of being* (M. H. Heim, Trans.). London: Faber.

Lévinas, E. (1969). *Totality and infinity* (A. Lingis, Trans). Pittsburgh, PA: Duquesne University Press & The Hague: Martinus Nijhoff. (Original work published 1961)

Lévinas, E. (1998). *Discovering existence with Husserl and Heidegger* (R. Cohen & M. Smith, Trans.). Evanston, IL: Northwestern University Press. (Original work published 1949)

Luzi, M. (1998). *Poesie* [Poetry]. Milan: Mondadori.

Mahler, M., Pine, F., & Bergman, A. (1975). *The psychological birth of the human infant: Symbiosis and individuation.* London: Hutchinson.

Mitchell, S. A. (2000). *Relationality: From attachment to intersubjectivity.* Hillsdale, NJ: Analytic Press.

Perls, F. (1969). *Ego, hunger, and aggression: The beginning of Gestalt therapy.* New York: Random House. (Original work published 1942)

Perls, F. (1969). *Gestalt therapy verbatim.* Lafayette, CA: Real People Press.

Perls, F., Hefferline, R., & Goodman, P. (1951). *Gestalt therapy: Excitement and growth in the human personality.* New York: Julian Press.

Polster, E., & Polster, M. (1973). *Gestalt therapy integrated: Contours of theory and practice.* New York: Brunner/Mazel.

Rangell, L. (1975). Psychoanalysis and the process of change: An essay on the past, present, and future. *International Journal of Psycho-Analysis, 56*, 87–98.

Rank, O. (1932). *Art and artist: Creative urge and personality development* (C. F. Atkinson, Trans.). New York: Knopf.

Rank, O. (1950). *Will therapy and truth and reality* (J. Taft, Trans.). New York: Knopf. (Original work published 1930)

Rogers, C. (1951). *Client-centred therapy.* London: Constable.

Salonia, G. (1989). Dal noi all'io-tu: contributo per una teoria evolutiva del contatto. *Quaderni di Gestalt, 8/9*, 45–54. (Successively published 1993 as From We to I-Thou: A contribution to an evolutive theory of contact. *Studies in Gestalt Therapy, 1*, 31–41)

Salonia, G. (1992). Tempo e relazione. L'intenzionalità relazionale come orizzonte ermeneutico della Gestalt Terapia. *Quaderni di Gestalt, 14*, 7–21. (Successively published 1993 as Time and relation: Relational deliberateness as hermeneutic horizon in Gestalt therapy. *Studies in Gestalt Therapy, 1*, 7–19)

Salonia, G. (1997). Maturità [Maturity]. In J. M. Prelezzo (Ed.), *Dizionario di Scienze dell'Educazione* (pp. 663–665). Leumann, Turin, & Rome: LDC, LAS, & SEI.

Salonia, G. (1999). Dialogare nel tempo della frammentazione [Dialogue in the time of fragmentation]. In F. Armetta & M. Naro (Eds.), *Impense adlaboravit. Scritti in onore del Card. Salvatore Pappalardo* (pp. 571–585). Palermo: Pontificia Facoltà Teologica di Sicilia S. Giovanni Evangelista.

Salonia, G. (2001). Disagio psichico e risorse relazionali [Psychic disorders and relational resources]. *Quaderni di Gestalt, 32/33*, 13–22.

Salonia, G. (2004). *Sulla felicità e dintorni* [On happiness and thereabouts]. Ragusa: Argo Edizioni.

Salonia, G., Spagnuolo Lobb, M., & Sichera, A. (1997). Postfazione [Afterword]. In F. Perls, R.

Hefferline, & P. Goodman, *Teoria e pratica della Terapia della Gestalt* (pp. 497–500). Rome: Astrolabio-Ubaldini.

Sichera, A. (2001). Un confronto con Gadamer: per una epistemologia ermeneutica della Gestalt [A confrontation with Gadamer: Towards a hermeneutic epistemology of Gestalt]. In M. Spagnuolo Lobb (Ed.), *Psicoterapia della Gestalt. Ermeneutica e Clinica* (pp. 17–41). Milan: Angeli.

Spagnuolo Lobb, M. (Ed.). (2001a). *Psicoterapia della Gestalt. Ermeneutica e Clinica* [Gestalt psychotherapy: Hermeneutics and clinical practice]. Milan: Angeli.

Spagnuolo Lobb, M. (2001b). Presentazione [Preface]. In M. Spaguolo Lobb (Ed.), *Psicoterapia della Gestalt. Ermeneutica e Clinica* (pp. 9–12). Milan: Angeli.

Spagnuolo Lobb, M. (2003). Creative adjustment in madness: A Gestalt therapy model for seriously disturbed patients. In M. Spagnuolo Lobb & N. Amendt-Lyon N. (Eds.), *Creative license: The art of Gestalt therapy* (pp. 261–277). Vienna & New York: Springer.

Spagnuolo Lobb, M., & Amendt-Lyon, N. (Eds.). (2003). *Creative license: The art of Gestalt therapy*. Vienna & New York: Springer.

Spaguolo Lobb, M., & Salonia, G. (1993). Verso un'ecologia della competenza genitoriali. Il contributo della psicoterapia della Gestalt [The contribution of Gestalt psychotherapy to an ecology of parenting skills]. In S. Lupoi, D. di Cara, A. Ferruccio, R. Mazzaglia, & C. Panebianco (Eds.), *Genitori e figli—La salute mentale nelle relazioni familiari* (pp. 437–445). Atti del 1° Convegno Studi S.I.P.P.R. Taormina: Grafo editor.

Stern, D. N. (1985). *The interpersonal world of the infant: A view from psychoanalysis and developmental psychology*. New York: Basic Books.

Stern, D. N. (1999). *Diario di un bambino* [A child's diary]. Milan: Mondadori.

Van Gennep, A. (1977). *The rites of passage* (M. Vizedom & G. Caffee, Trans.). London: Routledge. (Original work published 1908)

Winnicott, D. W. (1984). *Deprivation and delinquency*. London: Tavistock.

Zinker, J. (1978). *Creative process in Gestalt therapy*. New York: First Vintage Books Edition.

3. The Phenomenology and Clinical Treatment of Panic Attacks

by Gianni Francesetti

> *Anxiety, as a basic state-of-mind, belongs to Dasein's*
> *essential state of Being-in-the-world.*
> (Heidegger, 1927/1962)

> *Once,*
> *the great misery of living seemed to him to consist*
> *in the passage of time.*
> *Now, the bewilderment lay*
> *in time's having stopped,*
> *suspended,*
> *fractured.*
> *What if the breeze stopped blowing?*
> *What if the seasons ceased to alternate?*
> *What if the setting sun tumbled down from its peak?*
> *He asked himself all this with terror.*
> (Said Bahaudin Majrouh, 1995)[1]

In this chapter, we will present a reading of panic disorder based on the theoretical and clinical perspective of Gestalt therapy (Perls, Hefferline, & Goodman, 1951/1994). Our research method will be based on the principles of phenomenology (Borgna, 1989; Galimberti, 1991; Ballerini & Callieri, 1996; Moustakas, 1994)—one of the main epistemological roots of this approach.

Our research, then, will not be founded on a statistical kind of investigation. These inquiries will, instead, seek to gather together and narrate from a Gestalt perspective the experiences of those who have lived through the episodes we refer to as "panic attacks." We cannot assume, and indeed have no intention of assuming, the role of the detached observer in developing this research. Instead, one of the most fundamental elements throughout has been our own firsthand experience in carrying out research. The road we have followed has required a continuous presence, a continuous "being-

---

[1] Translated from the Italian by A. Spencer.

with" the other. Attention has always been paid to "We" as the dimension in which experience is born and on which intentionality focuses. However, at the same time, we have never ceased to distinguish between our own experiences and those of the "Other." From the perspective afforded by this state of "being-ourselves-with" others, figures of meaning have gradually arisen, together with a strategy for reading and narrating the experiences of those who know more about panic attacks than anybody else—that is to say, those who suffer from them.

In this kind of research, the responsibility of choosing one figure from many possibilities is clearly evident and should not to be obscured by numbers. That which we have experienced, and that which will be narrated here, is to be seen as *our* reality, not *the* reality.

Two of the founding methodological principles of this study is our awareness of the inevitable partiality of our narrative and the care with which we seek to develop a discourse that is co-constructed and not self-referential.

Intersubjective experience (i.e., the weakness that is a constitutive part of "being-ourselves-with") thus becomes a precious gift, to be cherished and passed on, and an invaluable point of reference in taking care of those who ask us for help, hope, and strength in staying together in the face of all the irreducible complexity of the world.

3.1 A Descriptive Framework

> *Anxiety is replete with disturbance and disorientation, vertigo and insecurity, unknowability and spatial–temporal metamorphoses, which submerge the psychic lives of patients like high seas.*
>
> (Borgna, 1997)[1]

The term "panic" derives from the name of the Greek god Pan, a creature half man and half goat, able to instill a sudden and inexplicable fear in the human soul. Greek mythology tells us that Pan appeared at the side of the Athenians at the Battle of Marathon, forcing the Persians to flee in terror. He would also sometimes appear besides passersby, giving rise to an extreme and irrational fear. In modern times, Rabelais appears to have been

---

[1] Translated from the Italian by A. Spencer.

the first to use the term *peur panique* in 1534, and from that time on the use of the term has gradually spread across Europe (Schmidt & Warner, 2002, p. 5).

In the clinical field, the origins of the term are much more recent. Whilst today panic attacks are a well-defined symptom, which can arise in various situations of anxiety, the early classics on the subject referred instead to "acute anxiety crises." They thus referred to particularly intense episodes of anxiety usually without paying specific attention to the phenomenology of the experience or describing symptoms in any detail. There was, indeed, a certain degree of controversy as to whether panic anxiety should or should not be considered as a clinical condition in its own right in relation to other forms of anxiety-related disturbance (Borgna, 1997, p. 53).

Nowadays, psychiatric nosography uses grids of reference to recognize and classify psychopathological conditions, which have the advantage of providing a codified language with which to describe the symptoms of the disorder.

It is important to underline the fact that these "diagnostic trees" neither pretend to provide etiological diagnoses (and they must not be used for such purposes), nor do they claim to comprehend the phenomenological meaning of the psychopathological experience. They do not, therefore, provide us with an exhaustive description of subjective experience.

Unfortunately, in clinical practice, these innate limitations are often forgotten, and we risk, perhaps unconsciously, confusing such a code with "reality" (for some criticisms of such an approach, see chapter 6). When this happens, the symptomatological grid to which the therapist restricts his or her patient comes to represent a distortion and a negation of personal experience. From a methodological point of view, presuppositions lose their clarity, as the therapist forgets that descriptive classification is neither a neutral nor an objective language, but is rather a statistically (yet arbitrarily) founded point system, which is shared (but impoverished in that it can be shared). It is thus essential to bear in mind Rousseau's monumental edict that "there is no such thing as sickness. There are only the sick" (Rousseau, paraphrased in Wulff, Pedersen, & Rosenberg, 1986).

With due caution, we will now examine the symptoms of panic attacks making reference to the criteria defined in the *Diagnostic and Statistical Manual of Mental Disorders* (DSM–IV), which has become the most broadly accepted reference grid in psychiatric nosography over the last decades.[1]

---

[1] The DSM–IV proposes a "categorical classification of mental disorders, upon the basis

According to such a classification, the panic attack cannot be codified as a disorder in its own right, as it can arise in various clinical (i.e., as part of various forms of anxiety disorder or in the course of organic illnesses, such as Graves' disease) and nonclinical situations (i.e., when triggered by experimental factors, e.g., hypercapnia).

DSM–IV does not therefore diagnose the panic attack as a disorder in its own right. Instead, it classifies a number of different anxiety disorders within which panic attacks can occur (e.g., panic disorders, social phobias, etc.) The present volume is concerned above all with individuals who have suffered from panic disorder. The distinguishing feature of this kind of disorder is that the individual in question has suffered, at least for a certain period of time, from unexpected panic attacks, which have no cause in particular or predictable situations.

What are the distinguishing features of a panic attack? The essential characteristic of a panic attack, according to this classification, is a precise period of intense fear or discomfort, accompanied by at least 4 out of 13 somatic or cognitive symptoms. The attack begins suddenly, reaches its peak rapidly, and is often accompanied by a sense of impending doom or catastrophe and a sense of urgent need to leave the site of the panic attack (DSM–IV).

Panic attacks can occur as part of several forms of anxiety disturbance: panic disturbance, social phobia, specific phobia, post-traumatic stress disorder, and acute stress disorder.

Panic attacks can be divided up into three categories, on the basis of when symptoms begin to manifest themselves and of their causes:

1. Unexpected panic attacks, with no environmental cause. These occur "out of the blue" and cannot be predicted by the person involved.

2. Panic attacks caused by the situation in which they occur, in which symptoms are triggered by the appearance, or the anticipation of, an environmental stimulus or a specific context.

3. Panic attacks that are sensitive to the situation in which symptoms are frequently, but not always, triggered by exposure to a specific stimulus or circumstances (e.g., a subject might have a panic attack when he or

---

of descriptive criteria." The use of descriptive classification in this field originated in the need for a common and comparative language with which to describe patients and their symptoms, carrying out statistical analysis of the various forms of psychic disturbance. The DSM does not presume that any single definition can absolutely distinguish one disturbance from another.

The DSM, then, provides us with a descriptive system in which a series of signs (arising from clinical practice) and symptoms (from the patient) correspond, resulting in a diagnosis based on descriptive statistics.

she is just about to use public transport, yet might not have an attack once the journey is actually underway).

As we have said, panic disorder is only diagnosed when at least one unexpected panic attack takes place at some stage of the disturbance.

Panic attacks caused by situations are most typical of social phobias (where the attack is triggered when the subject is exposed to a social situation, such as having to speak in public) and specific phobias (where the attack is triggered by something very specific, such as a snake). In any case, subjects affected by panic disorder commonly—and above all at the advanced stages of the condition—tend to suffer from panic attacks caused by specific circumstances.

Subjects affected by unexpected panic attacks usually describe "the fear as intense and claim to have felt that they were near death, that they were losing control, that they were about to have a myocardial stroke or to 'go crazy.' They also describe an urgent desire to flee from the place in which the attack is taking place" (DSM–IV).

According to the DSM–IV, the diagnostic criteria for recognizing a panic attack are as follows:

[A panic attack is] a discrete period of intense fear or discomfort, in which four (or more) of the following symptoms developed abruptly and reached a peak within 10 minutes:
- (1)   palpitations, pounding heart, or accelerated heart rate
- (2)   sweating
- (3)   trembling or shaking
- (4)   sensations of shortness of breath or smothering
- (5)   feeling of choking
- (6)   chest pain or discomfort
- (7)   nausea or abdominal distress
- (8)   feeling dizzy, unsteady, lightheaded, or faint
- (9)   derealization (feelings of unreality) or depersonalization (being detached from oneself)
- (10) fear of losing control or going crazy
- (11) fear of dying
- (12) paresthesias (numbness or tingling sensations)
- (13) chills or hot flushes

This list of symptoms and signs provides us with the tools to recognize and carry out a *descriptive diagnosis* of panic attacks. The diagnosis of the disorder within which the panic attack is situated is, instead, made by considering, on the one hand, any possible organic causes (for example, a panic attack could be viewed as a symptom of an overactive thyroid) and, on the other, the disorders codified in the DSM. Panic attacks would be part of a panic disorder with or without agoraphobia, a specific or social phobia, or a post-traumatic or acute stress disorder.

Agoraphobia, which is present in about half of those who suffer from panic attacks, is not only a fear of open spaces but is also a fear of places from which it would be difficult to escape and situations in which it would be difficult to find help. From an epidemiological point of view, the number of people suffering from panic attacks and seeking help has increased exponentially in recent years. This phenomenon does not seem to stem exclusively from the increased availability of information on panic (and thus on the ability of clinical practitioners to recognize it). It appears, rather, that there has also been a considerable rise in the occurrence of such attacks (Gerdes, Yates, & Clancy, 1995).

The incidence of panic disorder (i.e., the number of people suffering from the disorder for the first time each year) is between 1.5 and 3.5%, depending on the source from which the statistics are drawn. It affects almost twice as many women as men. It is more common in cities than in the countryside and in more complex societies than in more traditional ones (Rovetto, 2003, p. 32).

3.2 The Collapse of the Ground During the Formation of the Figure

> *What distinguishes panic anxiety most of all is this unpredictable sliding from a condition of emotional compensation to a condition of emotional laceration. Apparently devoid of any interior motives and environmental causes, the subject is immersed in a Stimmung (i.e., a state of the soul) of imminent death.*
>
> (Borgna, 1997)[1]

In the founding text of the Gestalt therapy movement, Frederick Perls, Ralph Hefferline, and Paul Goodman's *Gestalt Therapy: Excitement and*

---

[1] Translated from the Italian by A. Spencer.

Growth in the Human Personality (1951/1994), panic is considered as a healthy and normal creative-adjustment of the organism to specific conditions. Panic, like every experience, is a field phenomenon, the expression of a particular manifestation of the organism–environment relationship at a particular moment. To quote the text, amongst the various possible situations where contact can be made, there are:

> The situation of danger: if the boundary becomes intolerably overworked because of environmental forces that must be rejected by extraordinary selectivity and avoidance; and ... the situation of frustration, starvation, and illness: if the boundary becomes intolerably tense because of proprioceptive demands that cannot be equilibrated from the environment. In both these cases, of excess of danger and of frustration, there are temporary functions that healthily meet the emergency with the function of protecting the sensitive surface. These reactions may be observed throughout the animal kingdom, and are of two kinds, subnormal and supernormal. On the one hand, panic, mindless flight, shock, anesthesis, fainting, playing dead, blotting out a part, amnesia: these protect the boundary by temporarily desensitizing it or motorically paralyzing it, waiting for the emergency to pass. On the other hand, there are devices to cushion the tension by exhausting some of the energy of tension in the agitation of the boundary itself, e.g., hallucination and dream, lively imagination, obsessive thought, brooding and, with these, motor restlessness. (Perls et al., 1951/1994, p. 37)

Panic, then, is a boundary phenomenon that serves to protect the individual in situations of extreme environmental danger. It occurs when the subject undergoes a sudden, immediate, and grave threat and can neither flee from nor effectively oppose the danger. It is a response to extreme stress: danger of death, torture, cataclysm, or the receipt of terrible news. It is interesting to note that such experiences do not generally lead to panic disorder, but tend to result in post-traumatic stress disorder, whereby the trauma suffered is suddenly and intensely relived.

A panic attack, instead, is an experience of panic in a situation in which no extreme, immediate, concrete threat is posed by the environment, and in which no traumatic experience is remembered, yet in which this acute and intense protective function is nonetheless activated at the contact-boundary.

Let us, then, seek to understand what exactly happens at the contact-boundary when a panic attack takes place. A panic attack is an episode of acute anxiety for which there is no support. The organism feels alone in the face of a danger perceived as extreme and with which the subject feels unable to deal. The excitement is so intense, uncontainable, and unsupported that the subject fears to be on the brink of death. Unlike normal panic episodes, panic attacks are not triggered by an environmental threat. Rather, they originate in a sudden rift that opens up between excitement and support. The organism feels his or her level of excitement grow and is unable to manage it, since neither the environment nor the individual's own resources offer a sufficient level of support.

Anxiety can emerge at any point along the contact sequence, when the organism–environment field comes to lack the support needed to deal with creative excitement. Likewise, panic can emerge at any stage of the contact sequence. Like anxiety, panic is not, therefore, born at a particular moment or at a particular point on the curve.[1]

We now need to discover which particular conditions lead to a panic attack as opposed to a simple episode of anxiety. At first sight, it is easy to note a clear, quantitative difference between anxiety and panic. Nonetheless, there are also a number of qualitative differences that are relevant not only for our understanding of the disorder, but also for its cure.

To highlight these differences, we will employ concepts related to the contact-boundary and the figure/ground dynamic, seeking to locate panic attacks in relation to experiences of neurotic anxiety and of psychotic anguish.

"The contact boundary, where the experience occurs, does not separate the organism and its environment; rather it limits the organism, contains and protects it, and at the same time it touches the environment" (Perls et al., 1951/1994, p. 5).

These two functions of the contact-boundary are the necessary bases upon which it is possible for experience to develop.[2] First of all, it is the boundary that makes contact possible (it is the point of contact) and contact interruptions constitute impediments to this boundary function. Contact is accompanied by a growing excitement, which, if it lacks support, becomes anxiety. In fact, when "the excitement is interrupted ... this is anxiety" (Perls et al., 1951/1994, p. 188).

[1] This conclusion is, in my opinion, implicitly suggested in Perls, Hefferline, & Goodman: "At whatever stage of contacting the interruption, fright and anxiety occur, the effect is to become cautious about the original appetite itself" (1951/1994, 189).

[2] I wish to thank Professor Antonio Sichera for his illuminating comments on this passage from Perls, Hefferline, & Goodman. For a detailed study of the concept of the contact-boundary in Gestalt psychotherapy, see Pietro Cavaleri's wonderful study entitled *La Profondità della superficie*, 2003.

Anxiety can emerge at any of the various moments of the contact sequence, when support proves insufficient. The contact process is then interrupted in order to avoid the anxiety. Contact interruption serves this purpose: It avoids anxiety where there is not enough support to proceed through the contact sequence. Anxiety reemerges in subsequent moments of contact where it is impossible to interrupt contact in the habitual manner (e.g., where it is impossible to retroflect) and the subject perceives him- or herself to be lacking in support. Therapy is a peculiar example of this type of situation, since it is the "place" where adequate support enables the patient to deal with the anxiety caused by not carrying out the habitual form of contact interruption. At this moment, therapy can permit the patient to experience contact with the freshness and vividness of immediate experience. It thus frees up the path for a new creative-adjustment. Where there was once evasiveness and contact anxiety, there is now a new creative synthesis. Avoidance of anxiety through contact interruption reduces the newness of experiences, making them seem mundane and clichéd. This is the so-called "neurotic" mode of experience, and it is linked, above all, to disorders of this first boundary function—the function of bringing organism and environment into contact.

With respect to the process of forming the figure/ground, when this function is disturbed, it becomes difficult to form a new figure, since the potential for contact has diminished and, with it, the possibility of encountering the new.

In conclusion, in neurotic anxiety, the difficulty, which is faced at the boundary, consists in permitting the formation of a new figure within which the freshness of experience can be gathered, inasmuch as the ground has grown rigid through noncontactable repressions.

The second function of the boundary is that of delimiting, containing, and protecting the organism.

A disturbance to this faculty, that is to say an underdevelopment of the protective qualities of the boundary, results in an experience distinct from the anxiety described above.

In this case, anxiety arises when the organism feels exposed to the environment in a manner that he or she feels could seriously damage his or her integrity and conservation. The less the support offered by the boundary to the organism, the lower his or her anxiety threshold grows. In extreme cases, anxiety could be aroused by any stimulus (as in the cases of hypersensitivity to stimuli which typify certain experiences of psychosis).

This is what happens in situations of extreme danger or psychotic experience. In this latter case, exceptional danger is perceived as present and real because the boundary organization is not up to protecting the organism's integrity. In both cases, this type of anxiety occurs because the protective capacities of the boundary are unequal to the environmental threat, with the consequence that it is impossible for the organism to feel protected. Anxiety arises when the boundary is incapable of protecting the organism from a perceived environmental threat.

In cases of psychotic anxiety the organism loses his or her protective "skin." Every stimulus becomes a potential figure (but never attains full figure status). There is no perceptive selection. The individual is, rather, hypersensitive to stimuli. The figure/ground dynamic is exceedingly unstable and the organism is therefore sensitive to every perceptive stimulus. In such situations, the environment does not provide a sufficient level of support to allow for the formation of a boundary able to protect the organism. The resulting experience is one of psychotic anxiety (or of a psychotic episode). The most extreme example of the ground being problematized is that of the delusional mood (*Wahnstimmung*) that precedes the development of delirium (Klaus Conrad considers Wahnstimmung to represent the gateway to schizophrenia). The structure of the world begins to vacillate, every connection and relationship becoming uncertain. The familiar world seems to be on the point of shattering, of physical and hermeneutic collapse. The organism is left breathless, stupefied, with a feeling of vertigo, anxiety, and impending doom, with an impression that the end of the world is nigh. Every predefined sense of belonging is in the balance and seems on the point of being eclipsed: "the patient is like a frightened child, walking alone in a forest" (Ballerini & Callieri, 1996, p. 99. Translated from the Italian by A. Spencer).

In such cases, anxiety cannot be avoided through intentional contact interruption, since there is no ground to support intentionality and its interruption. All sense of any consistency, continuity, and meaning in the world and in individual existence is terrifyingly dissolved.

Delirium comes to the patient's aid in such cases, through providing meaning and structure (albeit not shared) to the experience undergone, reestablishing some sense of "myself" and "the world" and of the relationship (albeit not shared) between the two. A therapeutic relationship, reconstructing the world through a dialogical relationship whereby the meaning and the structure of experience is reconstructed through sharing, is an alternative solution. Whilst delirium gives a pervasive structure, which immediately explains everything without any kind of dialogue (and in so doing reduces anxiety), the therapeutic relationship rebuilds the world by taking a few (often very few) points of communality as its starting point.

Where, then, should we situate panic attacks between neurotic anxiety and psychotic experience?

Panic attacks strike suddenly. The individual's habitual psychophysical and emotional state is devastatingly and unexpectedly reversed. The panic attack is perceived as a discontinuity in the continuum of experience. It can be precisely delimited in time.

As far as the figure/ground dynamic is concerned, during a panic attack the ground, against which a figure is being created, suddenly appears highly problematic and precarious, about to shatter and collapse. This is probably the defining characteristic that identifies an experience as panic anxiety, as opposed to just anxiety.

To clarify this point, it is worth recalling the distinction between intentional contact, contact that is taken for granted, and acquired contact (Spagnuolo Lobb, 2001b, p. 94).

Intentional contact is what the organism moves towards during the contact sequence. It is the figure of contacting (thus, for me at this moment, it is the sentence on the computer screen, whilst the reader is on my horizon). It is the expression of a deliberate choice which organizes the direction, time, and fashion of contact. From this point of view, it is representative of the *ego* function of the self.

We take for granted those forms of contact which are always present in the ground and towards which our attention is not directed (thus, in my case, I am in contact with the chair on which I am sitting, with the air I am breathing and with the process of breathing itself, and with the automatic motions of the sensory-motor processes which enable my hands to move across the keyboard). "There is, in sum, a kind of contact which we do not need to verify each time it takes place and which constitutes the set of automatically presupposed securities which form the ground of the self" (Spagnuolo Lobb, 2001b, p. 94. Translated from the Italian by A. Spencer). Those contacts that are taken for granted express the *id* function of the self.

Acquired contacts, instead, involve the personality function of the self, and describe the person "*Who I have become*" (thus, in my case, I am a native speaker of Italian, I am in my family home, I hear my children playing in nearby room with a fatherly ear, I have a history of relationships with my patients, and a broader personal history).

Intentional contact is the figure being created through the contact process, whilst taken for granted and acquired contacts are the ground (and the support) of that process. In underlining the role of figure and ground in the contact process, we should recall Laura Perls' distinction between the functions of contact and those of support:

74

The contact functions ... take place against a background of organismic functions that are normally unaware and taken for granted; yet these latter provide the indispensable support for the foreground function of contact. They comprise hereditary and constitutional factors (primary physiology, etc.); acquired habits that have become automatic and thus equivalent to primary physiology (posture, language, manners, techniques, etc.); and fully assimilated experience of any sort. Only what is completely assimilated and integrated into the total functioning of the organism can become support. (Perls, 1968, pp. 43–44)

Let us now take a look at the stories of some patients, considering how the three types of contact (i.e., intentional, acquired, and taken for granted forms of contact) are disturbed during panic attacks.

I was running an errand when I suddenly realized that I was far from home. The ground beneath my feet seemed to give way and my mind emptied. I was unable to breathe and was terrified that I was about to die.

I was having a relaxed chat with some friends when suddenly, as if something had clicked inside me, I felt as if I was no longer inside the situation. I felt lost, as if I was looking on from outside. I was gripped by a powerful sense of vertigo and terror.

I was driving to work, stuck in a queue at traffic lights. Everything seemed normal. However, at a certain point I was suddenly overcome with anxiety. I felt bottled up, with no way out. I felt a sudden rush of heat, which tightened my throat. It was as if I was suffocating. I was terribly afraid of dying.

A common process and rhythm can be observed in all these accounts. The normal continuum of experience is abruptly interrupted, suddenly and unexpectedly fractured. What is happening is a sudden loss of ground, which makes it impossible to follow through contact intentionality. It is the loss of the familiar, the loss of that which we take for granted as belonging to us and to which we belong. In panic attacks, contact intentionality is blocked, not by any obstacle to the procedure, but rather by the falling away of what normally sustains us and what we assume will be there of the ground.

To understand this experience we might picture an athlete running an obstacle race. What stops him from proceeding is not an obstacle, but the ground suddenly giving way beneath his feet. The ground that shatters is made up of taken for granted and acquired contacts, which sustain the figure as it forms. A figure, as a creative synthesis of the self, can only form if a set of contacts makes up and maintains the ground for long enough for the contact sequence to be completed and for the organism to withdraw, as excitement grows.

In general, there are three ways a figure can be prevented from forming. In the first case, contact is interrupted because the organism–environment field is unable to sustain the creative excitement (this is the neurotic form of contact interruption, which leads to the loss of the ego function). Secondly, contact can be interrupted by an interference in the field (for example, while I am kissing my wife, I am suddenly attacked by my children, who interrupt our kiss by pinching me). In the first case, contact intentionality remains, but contact is interrupted unawares by the organism's inability to complete the sequence as a result of insufficient support. In the second, the sequence is interrupted because a new and more urgent need for contact emerges and the organism's intentionality changes. There is, however, also a third possibility, which is what happens during panic attacks. If the ground shatters, the self involved in the contact suddenly finds itself as if suspended. The figure lacks a ground. Sense, excitement, and action cannot be sustained. The result is a sense of extreme danger, of imminent death.

In these cases, the ground suddenly gives way. Immediate support interventions in such cases need to reconnect the organism with its ground—to place the individual's feet back on the ground, to make him or her sit down and breathe deeply, to provide fresh air, space and time, to lead him or her back to familiar places and people.

This is a typical characteristic of the first panic attack and of the unexpected attacks that follow. These experiences lead the individual to be timorous and cautious in his or her contact habits, to have less faith in those contacts that were previously taken for granted. "Can I trust my body? My sense of orientation? The force of gravity? The people around me? The brakes of my car?" All of these things should be habitually and normally relied on. These experiences lead to a fear of panic attacks and consequent evasive behavior, the individual seeking to avoid the situations in which previous attacks have occurred.

The hypothesis that we are here proposing is: The fundamental and specific characteristic of a panic attack is that the ground suddenly becomes figure as a result of its collapse. The contact figure that was being formed consequently dissolves.

76

After the first attack, the fear that the ground might dissolve means that what is normally ground (acquired and taken for granted contacts) becomes a constant figure. "Am I breathing alright? Can I see my points of reference? Is there someone here who is familiar to me? Can my legs and my heart support me? Am I reasoning correctly? Will I be able to find my way home?"

It is sometimes possible to identify whether the id functions or the personality functions are primarily involved in the collapse of the ground.[1] Let us examine, for example, two brief dialogues with a patient, Antonella:

"I was on business in an area where my company is investing a lot of money. Some people, who are benefiting from our activities, had a go at me in the street. This made me absolutely furious—it was so unfair! I started to shout at them: 'You should be ashamed of yourselves!' I was really angry, out of my mind. Suddenly, my head started spinning. I felt everything spinning around as if a flying saucer had suddenly landed on top of my head. I was terrified, bewildered and overcome by a terrible fear that I was about to die."
"How did your body feel at that moment?"
Antonella (surprised): "I didn't feel anything ... I could only feel my head. What strange questions you ask."
"Strange?"
"Yes ... I don't know ... I never feel anything with my body. I don't know what to say ... I can only feel my brain."

In this experience of panic, the perception and expression of anger are not supported by the body, and it is the id function that, suddenly, does not provide a sufficient level of support for the ego function.

The same patient later recounts another episode:

"I had just entered a very important and difficult meeting. I had only found out a few moments beforehand that I would have to replace my director. As soon as I opened my mouth, I made a mistake, taking as given a decision that still had to be discussed. Everyone was instantly at my throat. I felt paralyzed, as if I was in an elevator that had sud-

---

[1] It is nonetheless worth recalling that the two functions of the self cannot be clearly differentiated. They are profoundly and reciprocally implicated in each other. For example, to assume a certain role involves an adjustment of bodily support, which can prove highly relevant, while a change in the id function can have a significant impact on the way in which the individual occupies a certain role.

denly plummeted to earth. For a moment, I didn't feel like I was anyone anymore. I thought I was about to lose control and die. Soon after
that my anxiety diminished and I was able to speak normally once
more."

"Was this particular role difficult to keep up?"

Antonella: "Yes. I realize now that my problem was that I was behav-
ing as if I was the boss."

"Would it have been different if you'd opened by saying that you
weren't the boss but were doing your very best to represent him well?"

Antonella: "Certainly. That would have made me much less anxious.
I'll have to remember that."

In this example, it is the personality function that did not offer a sufficient level of support to the contact intentionality. The role has not been assimilated and cannot support the ego function. The organism finds itself suspended and flung into an alien situation.

The experiences, which characterize derealization and depersonalization, can also be understood as eclipses from the ground of the taken for
granted and acquired contacts which render things, other people, and ourselves familiar, noteworthy, and meaningful. In cases of derealization,
things are suddenly perceived to be distant, unreachable, unreal, and confused, their meaning and consistency appearing mutable. They seem somehow alien or artificial, as if they were part of a play. The familiar frame of
reference, the relationships that form the ground of the individual's intentional contact with things, thus becomes problematic. In normal intentional
contact it is not necessary to give a meaning to things, to check up on their
solidity and reliability: All of this is taken for granted.

In depersonalization, the subject feels cut off from him- or herself. The
individual's own voice seems foreign, the body loses its familiarity, and its
movements acquire a strange fluidity, as if a new kind of force were needed
to move it. The body is not supportive, or, alternatively, it provides support
in a strange manner: "I become foreign and unfamiliar to myself, in a world
that is strange to me."

In some cases, the loss of the support provided by the personality function can be so severe that the subject begins to suffer from episodes of temporal–spatial disorientation (always concomitant with the panic episode),
which, in the exceptional case of one patient, lasted for up to an hour:
"When my anxiety reaches its peak, I no longer know why I am in a certain
place, or what day it is. I don't recognize places and I can't remember my
way home. My mind gets like a jigsaw puzzle that is missing pieces. Every-

thing gradually becomes confused. For a terrible moment everything seems to be slipping away from me, as I reach out desperately for any point of stability. Last time, it took me almost an hour to get my bearings."

In panic attacks, the blocking of creative excitement and the consequent interruption of figure formation are not the only causes of anxiety (as is the case in neurotic anxiety). Anxiety is caused by the interruption of creative excitement while the ground is, at the same time, giving way and becoming problematic.

This problematizing of the ground recalls certain characteristics of psychotic experience, as described above. Notwithstanding this, from a phenomenological perspective, there are some important differences between these two kinds of experience. First of all, the loss of continuity, consistency, and tenacity of the ground, experienced during panic attacks, is a transitory phenomenon. Fragmentation begins and ends at clearly definable moments and constitutes a brief interpolation into a temporal and experiential continuity that is never actually lost: "It seemed like an infinity, but the attack only lasted 10 minutes, even if they were the longest ten minutes of my life."

Another fundamental difference is that subjects suffering from panic attacks deem their experience of acute anxiety abnormal and pathological: "It isn't really the world that grows strange. It's I, myself, who, for a certain period of time, feel that the world has become terrifyingly alien." As another patient recounts: "It isn't that I really believe that gravity is going to be suspended, that I'm about to be sucked off the earth and into space. It's just that I am sometimes gripped by a sudden and irrational fear that such a thing is about to happen." In this case, therefore, the ego function remains intact and consistent and identifies the experience as his or her own.

Furthermore, as far as countertransference is concerned, we can observe that, during panic attacks, the "fracturing" of the ground does not preclude our viewing such strange and disturbing experiences together, from a shared perspective. It is fairly easy for us to share in a world where such experiences are possible. The same thing can also be said of psychotic experiences, but only to a much lesser extent. Sharing in these latter cases is a final goal to which we aspire. A far longer and more complex journey lies ahead of us if we wish to share in the world of psychotic experiences.

Conversely, it is easy to trace some continuity between what is experienced during a panic attack and the "normal" experience of each and every one of us. We need only be abstracted momentarily away from our ground of taken for granted and acquired certainties. A colleague of mine, who had never suffered from panic attacks, told me about an experience of hers, which was particularly interesting from this point of view. During a period when she was particularly overtired and overloaded with stimuli, and when a lot of the previously consolidated aspects of her life were rapidly changing (i.e., her relationships, emotional attachments, place of work, and home), she underwent an acute, yet very brief, episode of derealization and spatial disorientation. For a moment, all her habitual points of reference disappeared and the prospect of panic opened up. That which enabled her to ease her own anxiety and renew her own ground was her ability to read the experience as being "normal," given the situation in which she found herself at that moment. The personality function of the self thus intervened to provide the necessary ground, on the basis of her own acquired and assimilated clinical experience.

3.3 Panic Attacks and the Modalities of Contact Interruption

> *Being-in-the-world itself is that in the face of which anxiety is anxious. Being-anxious discloses, primordially and directly, the world as world.*
>
> (Heidegger, 1927/1962)

We saw in the previous paragraph that panic attacks share the collapse of the ground as their distinctive, common, fundamental, and constant characteristic. At the same time, the very intensity of such attacks makes any differences between patients appear less relevant. Nonetheless, we wish at this point to focus on a factor that tends to be underestimated (Pavan, 2002, p. 70). In addition to these common characteristics, there are also some important differences between panic experiences. Panic can be expected, feared, remembered, reelaborated, and overcome in a number of different ways, and even during the attacks themselves panic can manifest itself in various forms.

This is the issue being explored in studies looking at the phenomenology of panic attacks in different cultural contexts, where panic attacks can take on very different forms (Amering & Katschning, 1990; Schmidt & Warner, 2002, pp. 2–3). For example, in some contexts panic attacks can assume predominantly somatic characteristics (to give just one example of the findings of the many studies in this field, the "sore-neck syndrome" found among Khmer refugees; Hinton, Um, & Ba, 2001).

In addition to such variations between the manifestations of panic in different cultures, significant divergence can also be noted between the experiences of subjects living in the same context. These personal differences appear to be connected to the way in which individuals make contact. For example, the kinds of panic attack experienced by subjects with retroflective tendencies tend to share certain characteristics, as do those experienced by introjectively inclined subjects, and so on. Such considerations are of particular significance from a therapeutic point of view. Instead of considering a unique form of support for those suffering from panic attacks, it is necessary to consider that the various different forms of contact interruption require various different forms of support. Furthermore, our research gives rise to one particularly interesting observation: Panic attacks can only take place when the individual's habitual form of contact interruption becomes impossible in a field in which an insufficient level of support is available.

This phenomenon confirms the findings of previous research, which suggested that the collapse of the ground was a typical characteristic of panic attacks. Indeed, each individual's personal way of interrupting contact constitutes a structural part of the ground, which contributes to forming the contact figure. If such an interruption (which automatically structures perception, action, and experience) is impossible, a fundamental part of the ground (which makes the normal, secure, and [neurotically] stereotypical way of experiencing things) will be missing.

Panic, therefore, is also a form of laceration, an opening out towards a new kind of contact with the environment which cannot yet be sustained because the exposure to that which is new is too much for the individual to deal with. It rubs too much salt into the wound of his or her personal history. In this sense, panic attacks might even be described as a "satori" moment without the support of a Zen master, or as manifestations of what Carlos Castaneda terms "stopping the world." The veils (i.e., forms of contact interruption), which creatively protect us from perceiving what we do not usually perceive, are lifted, but we lack an adequate degree of support to cope with what is revealed.[1] The following description should not be read

---

[1] Castaneda's apprenticeship with the "brujo" Don Juan can be read as a training manual on how to escape from the limitations imposed by our own forms of contact interruption, by our own personalities: "You are like a horse with blinders, all you see is yourself apart from everything else" (1973, p. 33. Translated from the Italian by A. Spencer). This kind of schooling is often traumatic. In his short stories, Castaneda often recounts episodes of panic, which usually coincide with the opening out of a new and richer perceptive dimension. From our point of view, it is especially noteworthy that these narratives of the deconstruction of references were particularly popular in the 1960s and 1970s, a period when an analogous process was taking place in society (see chapter 5).

as in any way exhaustive in classifying the irreducible complexity and uniqueness of the experience and, even less, of the individual people who suffer from panic disorder. Indeed, any single form of contact interruption can only take place with the complicity of all the others, which are always more or less evidently present. The following distinctions have arisen from the observation that experience (i.e., what takes place at the contact-boundary between organism and environment) varies according to the moment at which contact loses its spontaneity. It thus proves useful to dwell on the relationship between the type of panic experienced and the interruption of the emerging contact, in order to detect the various nuances of such experiences, and to provide a point of reference for the therapist so that he or she may provide specific support.

3.3.1 Retroflection

> *As the various forms of contact interrup-*
> *tion emerge, feelings of profound and intense*
> *anxiety are released in the patient.*
>
> (Salonia, 1992)[1]

Let us now consider a number of panic episodes experienced by individuals with a retroflective modality of contact interruption.

Paolo is 44 years old. He is self-employed, a self-made man, and successful. He is divorced with a 4-year-old daughter. He suffered his first panic attack at the age of 35, shortly after getting married, when he was on holiday at the seaside. Paolo was not a very strong swimmer, but he felt quite safe snorkeling. He was swimming in the bay near the boat, together with several other people. This was a common activity for him, which he usually enjoyed. However, on that day he suddenly felt he was too far away from the others and was terrified to realize that reaching them depended not on his actions alone, but also (and, at that moment, above all) on the water current. His sureness that he would be able to reach the others disappeared in an instant, leaving him prey to a terrible and burgeoning panic, which was so overwhelming that he could not even scream. His struggling and thrashing attracted the attention of one of his companions, who swam over to his aid.

After this first episode, "the sense that I was not in control of everything

---

[1] Translated from the Italian by A. Spencer.

gnawed inexorably away at me. I knew that everything I could do, even if it was a simple matter of stepping outside the house, was no longer under my complete control." The disorder gradually began to limit Paolo's movements, to such an extent that for a while he found it very difficult to leave his house, notwithstanding the pharmacological remedies he had been prescribed.

Paolo suffered from panic attacks in contexts in which he felt that the situation was not under his control. For example, he was afraid to take the train because it would not stop at his command. He did not like driving on the motorway because he knew that it would only be possible to leave it at specific, predetermined exits. He was afraid of flying. Only if he felt that the situation was absolutely under his control was he able to respond to any of his own needs: "If I don't feel well, I have to be able to get back home." Home came to be the only place where he felt safe and in control. When he came to feel that he was lacking in control even here, Paolo reacted by managing his everyday routine in an obsessive manner. Keeping the house tidy, doing small-scale repair work, and planning shopping became his way of effectively controlling the environment and containing his anxiety.

Interestingly, for a while Paolo was able to fly on tourist planes flown by a friend, as opposed to those belonging to the big airlines. Thus his anxiety did not stem from flying itself, but rather from his lack of control over the route and times of the flight. In Paolo's case, then, panic is closely linked to experience and to an awareness of not being able to control the environment.

In anxiety, the environment is perceived as being other than the self, "beyond control" (to quote Paolo). This triggers a profound sense of danger—of being at the mercy of something uncontrollable, which will pay no attention to one's own personal needs. During panic attacks, the organism is perceived as impotent and vulnerable, and this fragility cannot be displayed because it leads to an unbearable sense of inadequacy and shame.

This case study provides us with a telling example of the retroflective modality of contact interruption falling into crisis: "The concrete environment of the retroflective individual consists in himself and himself alone" (Perls et al., 1951/1994, p. 236). Paolo's anxiety attack is a response to experiential evidence of an environment lying beyond the control of the organism.

The organism all at once begins to feel tiny in the face of a vast and uncontrollable environment. The organism–environment field is transformed from the retroflective "big" Organism–"small" environment model to a situation wherein a "small" organism is faced with an Environment that has suddenly grown vast.

In his panic, Paolo reverts to his earliest techniques for creatively employing contact interruption as a self-protective mechanism. He is once again small and vulnerable in the face of an environment that cares nothing for his welfare and does nothing to provide for his needs. The fact that Paolo's anxiety is so strong that he believes his life is at risk may well stem from the fact that retroflection had been the contact interruption modality on which his "survival," such as it was, had depended right from the very beginning. Retroflective contact interruption had right from the start served a self-protective purpose in that period of life in which Paolo had been unable to openly manifest his own fragility and satisfy his own needs within the environment.

To summarize, the impossibility of redirecting the activity inward and replacing himself with the environment as the target of his activities, that is to say, of retroflecting, can trigger panic when retroflective contact interruption constitutes a significant element in the ground.

The extent to which the environment can be controlled seems to be a central concern of subjects with a propensity for retroflection. The situations to which the individuals are afraid to expose themselves can be varied. For example, one patient was afraid that his car would cease to obey his commands—to brake and turn at his will. Another feared that the law of gravity would be suddenly suspended and he would go floating off into space.

An intense fear of physical illness is common. It is important to underline that the anxiety of these subjects consists not only in the fear of having to count on someone else at an hour of need, but above all, in the perception of their own bodies as alien and out of their control. Indeed, panic arises not when help is unavailable, but rather when the subject becomes aware of (or imagines or remembers) something unusual in his or her bodily sensations, senses the danger that the consequences of this may be beyond his or her control, and is afraid of having to rely on someone else. The body is often already an alien environment in itself.

To make this point clear, it is worth examining the experiences of Antonella, a 34-year-old woman whose life had offered her no opportunity to live through and contain her own ill-being in the context of a significant relationship. Her anxiety and fear had not been sufficiently recognized, taken in, and contained, with the result that Antonella had fixed them into her own ground, so as not to contact them. Throughout her life, she had lacked the environmental support (above all from her mother) that would have enabled her to elaborate and assimilate these feelings. Every time she got scared, she believed her emotions to be abnormal, infantile, and pathological. She consequently desensitized her body to these sensations. For various reasons, at a certain point these protective mechanisms ceased to be effective and Antonella began to experience sensations that frightened her with an increasing regularity. She attributed these feelings and panic episodes to a range of terrible illnesses. However, she was in fact merely undergoing the "reawakening" of her body to legitimate feelings of ill-being and fear, feelings with which she had to familiarize herself and which she would be able to reappropriate with the support of a therapeutic relationship. Up to that moment, such feelings had been alien.

In such cases, the psychotherapist's job at the early stages of therapy can be pretty frustrating, as it is difficult to make the patient perceive the therapist as a source of possible help. We are often left with the feeling that we hold the remedy to all the patient's problems but that it would be inconceivable for the patient to reach out and grasp it. That which should console the therapist (especially after sessions that have concluded with the patient "informing" him or her that their meeting has been of no use whatsoever), is that for such a patient to recognize the therapeutic relationship as a trustworthy environment is a final goal, not a preliminary given. There is often a tense atmosphere at the beginning of sessions, a sense that the patient is almost challenging you. It is important to manage anxiety by giving ground to the body, sitting comfortably on an armchair, and breathing deeply. I always remember the tranquility of my own therapists and how they gave me the time I needed. Sometimes the psychotherapist may feel afraid of not being strong enough to deal with the patient's problems. This anxiety stems from both the therapist him- or herself ("Will I feel up to doing my job without the gratification of being regarded as an effective therapist by my patient?") and the patient ("There's no environment other than myself. And if there is, I can't trust it. And if I can trust it, it's of no use to me"). Furthermore, panic attacks have left these subjects feeling "small" in the midst of a traumatic and inevitable world. It is therefore natural that they will wish to avoid a relational position in which the subject is "small," as is the characteristic situation in therapeutic relationships.

I will now record a brief exchange with Antonella, the patient I described above, as an example of this kind of situation.

One Friday, a year into her therapy, Antonella asks me, "If possible, I'd prefer that we only meet on Monday next week and skip the other appointment. There are only three days in between, so the appointments are too close together. It's no use. There isn't enough time for important things to happen for me to tell you about. If it's okay with you, let's make our next appointment Monday next week."

It is frustrating to hear that she is so oblivious to the aspect of our work which goes beyond simply updating me on her symptoms. Her therapy is at a crucial stage and we are touching on some very delicate moments of her story to which no one has yet paid any attention. I feel tempted to give up on her and let her do what she wants ("If you aren't up to understanding that our work is useful ... If you can't see what I'm doing for you"), yet I also sense that she is giving me an opportunity to fully occupy my therapeutic role in relation to her, so I answer: "We can fix an appointment for next Monday if you want. However, I don't think what we do here is limited to you updating me on how you're getting on, even if that is a very important part of it."

She, too, grasps the moment: "Anyhow, you do think it would be useful if we meet up again on Monday?" I reply, "Yes, of course."

Antonella, who has been absolutely serious so far, looks me in the face and smiles. We both share in a pleasant sensation. I feel that there is a recognition on her part, that a need, which she was unable to fully feel or express, has been perceived. In this moment, Antonella perceives me as "Other" (in fact, I feel that I am being observed as such) without being overcome with anxiety. She realizes that I could represent an environment that is at once out of control and nurturing. This experience is the antidote to what happens during a panic attack, when the "uncontrollable" is not supported by the "nurturing."

The next time I see her, on the following Monday, Antonella says: "I've thought a lot about our chat on Friday." She utters the word "chat" with a little smile, giving me to understand that the term is inappropriate, that she is deliberately winding me up and does not really want to trivialize our work together. "It'll seem strange to you, but after almost a year of therapy I've understood for the first time that there really might be a psychological explanation for my problems. You've told me that lots of times, but I only really understood it on Friday." In this session, for the first time, we discuss her relationship with her mother as representing a context into which she could bring neither her difference nor her ill-being. It was an emotionally charged session for both of us. I felt as if had finally, at least temporarily, come to represent a nurturing environment for her.

We can thus conclude, with regard to retroflective contact interruption, that panic attacks occur when the impossibility of structuring the field in the habitual manner (big Organism–small environment) leads to an experience of the environment as uncontrollable, for which there is insufficient support (small organism–big Environment). This experience is so traumatic because it carries the subject back to an earlier, primary anxiety, to that aspect of their personal history that is usually evaded through retroflection. Panic attacks take place when this protective mechanism cannot be activated and the field is suddenly restructured in a way that puts to rout the self's habitual modality of creative-adjustment. After this experience the subject tries to repair the damage done by restoring control (through retroflective interruption), but at this stage the environment has already been clearly "seen" and this form of interruption is no longer reliable. Therapy consists in looking for a new creative-adjustment, which makes it possible to contact the other, providing support for the individual's anxiety about his or her lack of control. From this perspective, panic attacks represent a precious opportunity to open the way for new contact modalities, which had been crystallized through original interruptions, and for a new perception of the world and of the individual's future prospects.

3.3.2 Projection

> There are no fearless people, only fear-
> less moments.
> (Hoeg, 1996)[1]

Let us now briefly examine the case of Carlo, a 24-year-old man who had suffered from panic disorder with agoraphobia. His modality of contact interruption was predominantly projective.

Until he turned 19, Carlo had always been quite shy, but nevertheless capable of being lively and expansive, and even of becoming a leader in contexts that were familiar to him. He had attended high school in his small provincial town, close to home and to the local church hall, where he spent his free time with his friends. Carlo began to suffer from anxiety when, after finishing school, he found a job outside his hometown, traveling about 40 kilometers by train every day. As he traveled away from home, Carlo experienced an almost incessant sense of danger. He only managed to cope with his anxiety because a work colleague always sat near him. One day, when this colleague had to work late, Carlo had to travel home alone. As he walked to the station, he was gripped by a sense of danger: "I'm scared. I might meet someone who wants to hurt me." Amidst unknown faces and

---

[1] Translated from the Italian by A. Spencer.

noises, which seemed to be intensifying, Carlo felt that, as well as finding his bearings by looking ahead of him, he also had to watch his back, to run away. His anxiety continued to escalate until it developed into a panic attack. From then on, for over two years, Carlo was unable to leave his house without being accompanied by somebody he trusted.

As in all cases of panic disorder with agoraphobia, Carlo experienced anxiety when he found himself exposed to an environment in which he felt unprotected. In this particular case the environment was not only considered dangerous—it also appeared to be intentionally threatening. Danger took on the form of other people with malevolent intentions. The environment is not "dangerous and disinterested." The extent to which it can be controlled is not a primary concern. The environment in this case is "dangerous and potentially interested" in Carlo, potentially threatening and powerful. Panic arises from the experience of being exposed to a situation in which someone might specifically and intentionally threaten the subject.

The organism is perceived as small and, although full of energy, at risk of losing its strength or, at any rate, of being overcome. Carlo looks to his home as a place where he feels protected from potential threats. In his imagination, he often feels as if he has been unwillingly thrust into an unwinnable battle.

Carlo's experience can be connected to contact interruption through projection:

> [The subject] feels the emotion but it is free-floating, unrelated to the active sense of the self that comes in further outgoing behavior. Since the emotion does not spring from himself, it is attributed to the other possible reality, the environment; he feels it "in the air" or directed against himself by the other. (Perls et al., 1951/1994, p. 234)

Patients with projective tendencies, who suffer from panic attacks, seem to have certain characteristics in common with regard to their relationships with their mothers. I once had direct contact with the mother of one such patient, whom we will call Antonio. This lady was always formally very respectful of the boundaries of therapy. About once a year, she had her son ask if she could speak to me, to find out how the therapy was going. Antonio had a powerful sense of affection and gratitude towards her. She was a "great" mother, much respected and a very powerful force at home. The son was unable to perceive the aggressiveness of his mother's behavior. Towards her, he could only behave in a manner that was obliging, passive, flexible, and submissive. He was blind to her limitations, and this was not just a result of his respect for her. He was gradually overwhelmed by a powerful fear of his mother's aggression, of which it was only possible to make the patient aware with a great deal of difficulty. This kind of fear impedes the motor functions, making the muscles grow tense and rigid. It is a powerful and static form of tension. When I met Antonio's mother for the first time, after several months of therapy, I felt very anxious. I was aware that a simple gesture on the part of this powerful, diffident woman, who was rushing me and did not seem to see me, could destroy my relationship with her son. I understood how the environment in which Antonio lived was replete with tension and how it was difficult for him to attain awareness of this atmosphere and to react to it. The impossibility of attributing to oneself what is being felt by oneself leads to catastrophic contortions of the imagination: "The brooding is full of highly colored thoughts. This is the activity possible to the self in the rigid framework of shutting out the environment [and] inhibiting the motor powers" (Perls et al., 1951/1994, p. 235). I feel that my own body can now immediately understand his experience: His tendency to avoid opening out his hips and thorax, his hunching over into himself, the way he moves his hands without moving his arms, his caution in resting his feet on the ground, always trying to lay down firm roots. A great deal of my therapeutic work consisted of defending the therapy taking place from the attacks made by his mother every time her son took a step towards autonomy.

During therapy with these patients, a great deal of attention was paid to developing awareness and, then, the patient's ability to regulate the aggression present in these relationships. It was always difficult for the patients to perceive their own aggressiveness and to express it in a functional manner in the relationship. It was always very easy to slip to one extreme (being unaware of aggression) or to the other (expressing aggression without taking the environment into account). For example, Antonio got very frightened when, during a basketball game, he argued and ended up fighting with an opponent. This was an absolute novelty for him, and it scared him. He had never before experienced his *own* aggression, and the aggression he had experienced (i.e., his mother's) had been destructive. Every time aggression emerged and was expressed, initially in a manner that was not regulated by its context, Antonio's mother grew very anxious, underlining the seriousness of such behavior and calling into question her son's mental health and the efficacy of his therapy. Anger was read within Antonio's context as madness or sickness: "When I get angry, my mother gets scared and tells me that instead of coming here I should have my head examined." At such moments, it is vital that the therapist stays calm about the patient's anger and tries to provide the patient with a "key" for reading what is happening as a series of "experiments" through which his or her natural aggression is seeking to adjust and regulate itself.

The other major area we concentrated on was that of sustaining the patients' perception of the complexity of the world in all its various nuances, in all its richness and variety. In such cases, the therapist will come across a lot of stereotypical preconceptions and fixed notions about people, places, and contexts. This stems, on the one hand, from the individual's limited experience of the world (of which he or she is unaware) and, on the other, from a self-protection mechanism. Namely, if the individual does not face up to the real world, his or her ideas of it (i.e., his or her projections) will not be thrown into crisis.

My experience of working with Carlo was very different from that of working with the previous group of patients. I feel calm right from the beginning of the therapy, aware that Carlo is feeling very small and needs to reappropriate his own energies and resources. In order to fully experience himself, he needs to be able to breathe in a relaxed manner, to feel supported by the seat he is sitting on or the floor he is standing on, to empty his mind for a little while. I feel as if I am building up a safe place for him, almost a nest. When he becomes aware of this, he never rests for long in the safe environment provided, not because he interrupts contact with me, but rather because when he feels safe he also feels energized, which leads him to act. Sometimes he seems like a spring that cannot stretch out and release its energy because it lacks a stable base to rest on. He needs time to get to know and to appropriate his own strength, and it is often necessary to defend the time he needs for himself, the time he needs to grow from his rather invasive environment. During our work on his body, his voice and his energy stretch my powers of containment almost to the limit. I feel that he is confronting me as an equal. It is a pleasing sensation, which enables Carlo to combine relaxation with force, in a context in which he does not feel threatened.

Whilst in the case of retroflection, it is pretty clear that panic attacks occur when it is impossible to retroflect and when there is insufficient support to sustain this new restructuring of the field, in projective experience it is more difficult to trace a connection between the impossibility of interrupting contact and the panic attack.

In the case of Antonio, as in those of the other patients in this group, the climate in which he grew up was characterized by a significant and potentially destructive level of maternal aggression, not directed at Antonio himself, but nonetheless always present in the air: "It's as if the air at home is charged with the kind of electricity you feel before a thunder storm. It's as if the smallest spark could give rise to a full-blown tempest." Antonio was thus unable to express his own energy in this environment, and reacted creatively by projecting his own aggression outside himself. Instead of attributing it to his mother (how could he have dealt with his own fear and anger?), he attributed it to the world outside his family, a fantastic and rigid, dangerous and fixed world, a world devoid of subtleties and nuances, since it derived not from his direct experience of the world, but from his fantastic projections onto it. Antonio projected his perception of the tense and threatening atmosphere of his family and his consequent emotions onto the world, so that the outside world, for him, assumed these characteristics.

Projection had served Antonio well in protecting him within his family life (i.e., by resituating the danger outside its limits). However, it represented a considerable obstacle to his making contact with the rest of the world. In order to do so, he would need to stop projecting and to learn to perceive, on the one hand, the complexity of the world, and on the other, his own fear and potential aggression. These factors explain the fact that all the subjects in this group began to suffer from anxiety and panic attacks during adolescence, that is to say, at the moment when they began to go out into the world into situations not protected by the family context.

We can hypothesize that in such situations panic attacks take place when projection is no longer a viable protective measure. As long as the subject is at home, he or she can project the family's tensions out onto the world (thereby defining the home as safe and the world as dangerous), but when he or she is out in the world projection becomes impossible and with it and the habitual modality of contact interruption. He or she consequently feels threatened and fearful, but is unable to keep the threat at a distance.

When he has panic attacks, Carlo does not project (if he were able to do so, he would attribute his sense of danger to some other place). Rather, he finds himself face-to-face with the no longer functional effects of his having projected. Panic emerges when projection no longer suffices to make the environment secure. Carlo lacks new tools for facing the world and lacks the support necessary for him to deal with this experience. He (at last) feels the fear of being exposed to potential dangers and his excitement grows exponentially without being supported. Carlo returns to his original, primal situation, without being able to interrupt contact. He instinctively seeks out his habitual mode of interruption. He moves back in with his family, leaves his job, refuses to leave home without a family member, seeks out a safe and beneficent place from which he excludes all that which he conceives of as dangerous and threatening. At the same time, fortunately, he seeks out a new potential creative-adjustment. It is at this point that his therapy begins.

3.3.3 Introjection

> *And the inanimate things*
> *that I created before*
> *come to die again*
> *in the breast of my intelligence.*
> *Avid for my asylum and beneficence,*
> *they beg for wealth*
> *from a beggar.*
>
> (Merini, 1998)[1]

Simona, whose modality of contact interruption was predominantly introjective, presents us with a third type of panic attack. Simona is a 42-year-old woman who had two panic attacks during the advanced stages of her therapy (i.e., after five years). She had begun therapy in order to help her along the difficult path towards autonomy. Although she had been married for several years, she was still very much involved with her birth family and above all with her mother, who had great difficulty in conceiving of her daughter as an autonomous being with any aims in life other than to look after her parents. Simona was much entangled in her mother's agenda, which had been reinforced for her by the sudden and traumatic death of her brother. This event further crystallized Simona's relationship with her family, loading her with an even greater sense of duty in taking care of her parents. Not even Simona's suffering from a severe illness and her husband's considerable support during this period changed the situation. After this series of events, Simona began psychotherapy and gradually developed an awareness of her situation, beginning to grow personally and to be "born back into life." In the same period, however, she had to deal with the death of her parents and the sudden death of her husband. These bereavements, particularly the loss of her husband, turned her life upside down. Now that Simona was without any family, she asked herself what reason she had for continuing to live. She found a great deal of support, in addition to her individual therapy, in group psychotherapy and in a network of close friends who constituted a very important part of her life.

On the basis of these relationships, Simona found a meaning for her life. When she was with this important network of people, everything went on as normal. However, when she found herself alone, she felt uncomfortable and succumbed to an acute sensation of meaninglessness.

---

[1] Translated from the Italian by A. Spencer.

Simona had her first panic attack one summer when she was on the beach with friends. She suddenly found herself asking why she was there, what she could possibly have to do with these people and their conversations. Suddenly, everything around her seemed alien and distant: "What's the point of being here? I could just as easily be anywhere else. Everything is indifferent, desolate, and meaningless. Everything becomes frightening." At this moment Simona felt short of breath and her anxiety evolved into panic. This episode occurred in a particularly significant moment in Simona's life and her therapy. The very meaning of existence, for Simona, had been living for her mother and her family, without ever having had the possibility (or being aware of the need) to consider her own needs and organize her own life around them. In her relationship with her husband she had had, instead, the healthier experience of being able to be conscious of her own needs and to orient herself accordingly. The loss of both of these forms of belonging had, naturally, turned Simona's life on its head. It is worth noting that panic struck, not immediately after her bereavement, but over a year after her husband's death. Panic began at the very moment when Simona was beginning to look towards the future once more. After the period of mourning, she was faced with the need and, ultimately, the chance to discover a meaning for her own existence that did not consist in assuming (without assimilating) the meaning, needs, and desires of someone else.

This took place during the fifth year of her therapy, in a period of relative calm after the various emergencies she had been through, and when her therapy itself was proving capable of managing the anxiety of differentiation. We can thus observe that not even the sweet milk of therapy can provide a meaning for life per se.

Simona suffered a panic attack when she was unable to introject, and suddenly she saw the world as desolate and meaningless. She lacked the orientation provided by introjection, which usually supported meaning for her. In that period, Simona had made some significant progress in her search for a form of nonintrojective contact, orientated by her needs. She had discovered that the right way to avoid introjection lies not in isolation, but rather in mastication and assimilation. In fact, on the one hand, what she was experiencing was a sense of the risk of solitude: "If I think I am alone, I feel physically maimed, like a trunk without arms, hands, or legs. I grow breathless. If I feel the other, I can feel that I am touching it and my whole body lies in that." On the other hand, Simona expresses her aggression with increasing vigor in relationships. Her aggression makes her more lively and attractive. It emerges, in some sense, in a form that is already regulated within the relationship. This kind of aggressive recovery is phenomenologically different from what we

93

saw in cases of projection, where there is quite a long period of experimenting, during which anger can be disproportionate to the situation. This may be caused by the introjective subject's more accurate perception of his or her environment. It requires a different therapeutic procedure: Whilst the expression of aggression can be sustained in cases of introjection (since we know that the subject "sees" his or her environment), in cases of projection we need to pay more attention to sustaining both the patient's experience and his or her perception of the environment.

This sense that objects and life itself are losing their meaning is common during the panic attacks experienced by patients with an introjective modality of contact. Another characteristic shared by such patients (in contrast to groups tending to alternative modalities of contact interruption) is an increased level of depression. It is a well-known fact that there is often a comorbidity between panic attacks and depression. However, it would seem that this relationship between the two disorders is particularly close when patients employ an introjective modality of contact interruption. Indeed, when the protection afforded by introjection is lacking, together with adequate support for contact, the subject experiences a sense of desolation and loss of meaning, which is typically characteristic of depression. The dreams of one patient in this group, a painter, presented a fine illustration of such an experience. Recurrently and for a period of almost three years (during which she also went through a period of profound depression), she dreamt that she found herself in unknown, desolate, colorless, pale, and lifeless landscapes, alone or surrounded by indifferent strangers, wandering aimlessly without any points of reference and without understanding what she was doing there.

Another patient in this group permitted me to observe a number of aspects of the specific support required in such situations. Elisabetta is a 36-year-old woman who approached me for therapy after going through about 12 years of individual and group therapy based on a body therapeutic approach.

Elisabetta told me that she had first gone into therapy at the age of 22, when she began to experience panic attacks with agoraphobia, powerful anxiety, and bouts of depression, during a period in which she also felt profoundly disorientated and uncertain with regards to the direction her life was taking. During her childhood, she had suffered from a serious lack of parental care, both as an outcome of their physical absence due to their work commitments, and as a result of their relational absence—their incapacity to recognize their daughter's feelings and needs. In addition to this lack of communication, there was also a very tense atmosphere in her family, which sometimes erupted into violent episodes, from which Elisabetta was not protected. During her previous course of therapy, she had developed a number of important affective relationships and, from a professional point of view, had begun to work freelance. Her periods of anxiety and depression progressively diminished until they disappeared altogether, and Elisabetta developed strong ties to her therapy group, establishing deep friendships with some of its members. She had finally discovered a world that was completely different from that of her childhood and finally felt herself to be recognized and valued as a human being in her own right.

Elisabetta described her previous therapeutic experience as enriching and positive, as having "saved her life." Although often frustrating, the therapy directed and stimulated her towards autonomy and strength, enabled her to express her own anger and enter into conflictive relationships without always feeling dependent on others.

Shortly after concluding her individual therapy, Elisabetta went into business partnership with another member of her therapy group. Unfortunately, their relationship proved more difficult than she had expected and Elisabetta soon discovered that her friend was a very different person in this context than he had been when she had first known him. She felt as if the world that had saved her was at risk of shattering. She was terrified by the thought that it might have all been nothing but an illusion. She began to suffer from episodes of anxiety and panic attacks once more, again needing someone to accompany her when she ventured out of the house. Eventually, she asked if she could go back into individual therapy. Her therapist refused her request, encouraging her to try to manage on her own without asking for help, to not let herself be beaten, to not be "a softy." She felt as if her disorder and her request for help had been seriously underestimated. Her symptoms intensified and Elisabetta no longer felt able to cope with her job. She resigned and looked for a new therapist.

In this case, it is quite evident that the remission in the patient's symptoms and her developing autonomy were not due to the fact that Elisabetta was pushed into coping by herself. Rather, she drew on a strong sense of belonging, which provided a sense of security, enabling her to move in the world (see the paragraph on the life cycle below). Unfortunately, this kind of belonging was more introjected than assimilated. In fact, when the world in which Elisabetta was finally able to really take part (in the group and in the world of therapy) fell into crisis, she relapsed into her disorder.[1]

---

[1] The following passage from Perls, Hefferline, & Goodman sheds a great deal of light on this point: "The anxiety is 'tolerated' not by Spartan fortitude—though courage is a beautiful and indispensable virtue—but because the disturbing energy flows into the new figure... A bet-

The next course of therapy, instead of directly stimulating her to become independent, sought to support Elisabetta in constructing the network of affiliations, of "belonging" in her world, since this is the basic terrain that can nourish the spontaneous development of autonomy. Furthermore, a great deal of attention needed to be paid to making sure that different networks of belonging (including those pertaining to therapy) are masticated (not just introjected) so that they become a stable, fluid, and fully assimilated ground. It is, paradoxically, this very stability of the ground which makes it possible for the ground to enter into crisis without breaking up and to grow by modifying its own networks of belonging.

3.3.4 Confluence

> *Everyone has gone away.*
> *And I remain*
> *With a tiny lantern*
> *In my hands.*
> *Every now and then*
> *I am a tree*
> *Putting down roots*
> *Into the earth.*
>
> (Yanez, 1998)[1]

Let us now consider therapeutic experiences with patients who have a confluent modality of contact interruption.

Federica is a 35-year-old woman who has been suffering from panic attacks for about three years. At this point, she had been in psychotherapy for about four months, after a number of psychopharmacological treatments and other nonconventional therapies, applied in a sporadic manner and leading to only a temporary relief in her symptoms. Federica works as a paramedic, but is not very satisfied with her job, because "it is undervalued and people don't appreciate the qualifications it requires." She is married and has a son. Her marriage is evidently very disturbed. Her husband is very violent, both towards Federica and towards her son. Notwithstanding

ter meaning of 'security' would be the confidence of a firm support, which comes from previous experience having been assimilated and growth achieved, without unfinished situations ... The secure state is without interest, it is unnoticed; and the secure person never knows it but always feels that he is risking it and will be adequate" (Perls et al., 1951/1994, p. 9).

[1] Translated from the Italian by A. Spencer.

the seriousness of certain episodes, Federica is quite calm in talking about this situation and is unwilling to call this relationship into question. She is an only child and it is difficult to gather and define her relationship with her parents. It appears that her relationship with her mother is still very close, whilst her father is very distant. He seems to represent a horizon, viewed from afar and desired, yet perpetually distant.

It is difficult for me to give a detailed, linear, and continuous account of Federica's biography, since she is unwilling to provide what I would consider to be a meaningful description of events in her life. During our dialogues, everything was hazy and confused, fuzzy around the edges and difficult to single out, as if immersed in a thick fog. Every speech she made opened up and branched off along thousands of different passageways, each possible and equivalent, all potentially interesting, yet all of which eventually petered out into nothingness. During my sessions with Federica, I often struggled to remain lucid and aware. I repeatedly felt as if I was sinking into a swamp out of which it would be difficult for me to extract myself. Federica took every single thing I said as being equally permanent, which left me feeling that I was not being sufficiently incisive in the dialogue and that anything I had to say was indifferent. Together with this, it felt as if every time we met we were back to square one, as if what we had experienced during the previous sessions had vanished without a trace. I am aware (with occasional irritation) that Federica is trying to grasp hold of me, but without actually seeing me and without moving, as paralyzed in a specific position in which she perceives neither her own body nor her environment. Perls, Hefferline, and Goodman's description of confluence provides us with a fine outline of this kind of contact modality:

> The patient sees that nothing new will occur, but in the old there is no interest or discrimination. The archetypal distances are unaware suckling or clinging to warmth and body-contact that are not felt but whose absence makes one freeze ... In the framework of muscular paralysis and desensitization, satisfaction is possible only in random spontaneity and independent of the ego-surveillance altogether (hysteria). (1951/1994, p. 232)

The symptoms, too, are hard to define, obscure, and variable. In addition to panic attacks that clearly correspond to diagnostic criteria, there is also a continuum, almost a flood, of psychosomatic disorders (gastrointestinal symptoms, tension headaches, fevers, autonomic and sleep disorders, dyspnea, and swooning fits that do not culminate in the loss of consciousness).

Federica had her first panic attack during a refresher course for her job, which was taking place quite a long way from her hometown. Federica's memories of what happened are hazy:

> I didn't like the people who were there, although some of them were pretty important in my sector. I didn't feel at ease and I didn't know anyone. I was there to do a course, which, once again, undervalued my skills. Suddenly, in the middle of all those people, I felt terribly confused and disorientated. My throat seemed to close up and I felt as if I was suffocating. I almost fainted. Luckily, there were a lot of doctors present, who immediately came to my aid.

On another occasion:

> I was at work and one of my patients was arguing with me. My boss arrived at that very moment, surely aware that I was having difficulties. He told me off in front of everyone. I felt as if I was about to die and I didn't know where to look. I was confused. My throat suddenly seemed blocked up and my heart started beating like crazy. I felt as if I was suffocating and I fell to the ground in what was almost a faint.

If we take a closer look at the first attack and at those that followed, we can see that they all appear to be determined by a particular moment at which Federica comes "unstuck" from her context. A sudden lack of identification and resonance with her environment leaves her disorientated and confused. In therapy, Federica is gripped with anxiety every time a boundary between us is marked out, every time a difference is highlighted, which makes it difficult for her to connect her experiences and thoughts to me and to our conversations. In these moments, I can feel that some energy is finally building up between us. However, whilst for me the experience is invigorating, for Federica it is frightening.

It seems, then, that in Federica's case panic attacks strike when a boundary suddenly emerges where previously there was "no self-boundary" (Perls et al., 1951/1994, p. 231) and when a sufficient level of support is lacking. When the subject's habitual modality of contact interruption (confluence) becomes impossible, the risk of panic attacks emerges.

I wish to underline the fact that, in contrast to cases of introjection, confluent subjects do not experience a sense of solitude and meaninglessness (although these individuals, too, feel as if they are coming "unstuck" from one's context during the moment of anxiety). The introjective mode is probably marked by a greater degree of consistency and continuity of the horizons of meaning (although these are introjected). The perception of their fragmentation by introjective individuals is therefore particularly acute. Federica's state of mind is far more confused, as she desperately reaches for a foothold. She cannot be said to suffer from a sense of solitude, since she has no clear experience of a differentiated "Other" to whom she can connect and relate. Here, the establishment of a boundary does not result in the overturning of meaning, but rather in the terror of ceasing to be.

Another confluent patient "fell" into panic at moments in which she did not feel "anchored" in her context. This sensation brought on a terror that the continuous flow of time, the ongoing passage from one moment to the next, could be interrupted. Feeling "anchored," for her, meant "feeling like part of a unified whole"—being in contact without perceiving boundaries and differences. Her problems began when she moved to a city in the North of Italy, very different from the province in Puglia where she had been born and, at the same time, began a job that was much less satisfactory than her previous one. In this new context, she no longer felt her "normal connection with others." From then on, she was almost compulsive in seeking out help from many different quarters (from priests, doctors, psychotherapists, and various kinds of healers). She experienced a brief moment of relief when she was actually speaking to them, but remained empty, confused, and desperate after each encounter. She had been in therapy for several years. Unfortunately, the relational boundaries in this relationship had not been clearly maintained. The spatial and temporal boundaries of the sessions had become increasingly vague and she had come to confuse therapy with friendship to an extent that the therapist eventually decided to interrupt the treatment, suggesting that she resume with another therapist. The patient was unable to "assimilate" this decision and was devastated by the event, which she viewed as an abandonment. The development of her next therapeutic relationship was naturally much problematized as a consequence of this, as the patient alternated between a paralyzed and nonbeneficial clinging on and the terror of being abandoned once more. Her panic attacks, which had previously been contained through her confluent relationship with her therapist, intensified once more in the absence of a relational "anchor" to support the patient. This patient found herself in a highly vulnerable state, in which her habitual neurotic adjustment could not act (since her fear of another abandonment and "failure" inhibited her from anchoring herself through confluence), and she had yet to acquire a new, healthy way of making contact. For therapy to be effective, we needed to build up a novel therapeutic relationship able to sustain the patient's contact needs and to help her learn how to perceive boundaries and differentiate herself.

3.4 From *Oikos* to *Polis*: Panic Attacks and the Life Cycle

> *Anxiety individualizes Dasein and thus discloses it as "solus ipse." But this existential solipsism is so far from the displacement of putting an isolated subject-Thing into the innocuous emptiness of a worldless occurring, that in an extreme sense what it does is precisely to bring Dasein face to face with its world as world, and thus bring it face to face with itself as Being-in-the-world... In anxiety one feels "uncanny." ... But here "uncanniness" also means "not-being-at-home."*
>
> (Heidegger, 1927/1962)

Whilst the habitual modality of contact interruption and its impediments can shed light on the onset of each individual panic attack, the consideration of the life cycle can help to broaden our horizons with regard to panic attacks at any specific stage of the patient's life.

From an epidemiological point of view, the peak period for individuals to have their first panic attack is between late adolescence and the age of 35 (DSM–IV). Nowadays, this is the period of the life cycle during which subjects normally break away from their birth families and acquire an increased level of independence. It is a period during which developing new affective and social networks of belonging is of preeminent concern, whilst existing affiliations are being replaced and dissolved. At present, this transition is more precarious than ever, since both the individual's roots in his or her own family, and the new networks of relationships he or she is seeking to establish, are increasingly uncertain and tenuous (see chapter 5 on this point). For this separation to take place, the birth family needs to constitute a stable ground (an affectively present and spatially and temporally constant "home"), which is also flexible (i.e., which will allow the subject to deconstruct his or her previous networks of belonging to make way for the new).[1] The new environment, "outside" the birth family, should offer points of reference to which the individual can relate. There should be new, consistent, and open networks of belonging, which the subject can identify with or differentiate him- or herself from (see chapter 6).

---

[1] On the relationship between the home and the various aspects of the life cycle, see Giovanna Giordano's original and in-depth study (1997).

The passage from *oikos* (a space belonging to the few, to the home, to intimate friendship) to *polis* (a space belonging to the many, to the city, opening out into the world) would seem to be a key factor in the onset of panic disorder. This crucial passage involves a profound restructuring of the subject's affiliations and ground, exposing the subject to solitude and vulnerability. While chapters 2, 5, and 6 deal with the social aspects of this issue, we will here focus on its clinical relevance.

Belonging is a significant element in the ground in which the individual puts down his or her roots, which provides sustenance and security at the most basic, fundamental level (Perls et. al, 1951/1994). When the subject breaks away from his or her family, this ground has to be broken down and reconstructed. Its instability exposes the organism to the risk of its sudden collapse, and this leads to panic attacks. Patients suffering from panic attacks are suspended between past affiliations, which no longer offer any support, and future affiliations, which have yet to become supportive.

The postmodern difficulty in finding support in the polis is therefore particularly connected to, and evident during, those stages of the life cycle in the course of which individuals are in the process of abandoning their existing networks of belonging and increasing their autonomy.

It appears likely that panic attacks strike at the very moment when the subject's autonomy increases in disproportion to the support provided by his or her networks of belonging or, to put it another way, when the individual's movement away from the oikos receives insufficient support from the polis.

To illustrate this point, let us now examine the case of Laura, a 45-year-old patient who had begun therapy after suffering from a period of intense and undefined psychological ill-being with a significant and variable somatic factor. During the period in question, she was having a hard time differentiating and separating herself from her birth family, with whom she was still living. She was determined to find her own house and her own direction in life, which had so far been dominated by taking care of the rest of her family. However, she was not yet sure where she wanted to live ("I don't know which city to choose, or if I'd maybe prefer living in the countryside"). She was also lacking an affective point of reference ("I'm in a relationship with a man who is already in another relationship. We meet up when he can, but I can never predict when I'll see him"). Her professional situation was also uncertain, as she had so far dedicated all her skills to the family business. She therefore lacked the social, professional, and affective support needed to sustain her transition to autonomy. She had her first panic attack after the first few sessions of psychotherapy. Although this was later in life than is the norm, it was clearly explicable in terms of the peculiar phase of life that she was going through. Laura was very frightened by this intense and sudden attack. However, my ability to contextualize this event within the important transitional period she was going through provided her with a useful point of reference that was of significant support.

Panic attacks during therapy can be, as in this example, a sign of growth and, in particular, of a potential for increased autonomy (i.e., it is a sign that previous networks of belonging are dissolving and are therefore incapable of providing sufficient support). In such cases, particular attention needs to be paid to the new networks of belonging that appear on the horizon. At this stage, therapy needs to be perceived as a particularly significant form of belonging. Laura often asked me for explicit or implicit reassurance that I would be there for her, that I intended to help her, that I was not going to leave her alone. At that point it was essential to confirm my presence and my confidence in my ability to help her, without worrying too much about her becoming "dependent" on me and her often pressing need to be able to talk to me. It was important for her, for example, to be allowed to speak to me on the telephone between sessions, even though she only actually took advantage of this possibility once. *(without support)*

The onset of panic attacks often coincides with dramatic changes in the individual's networks of belonging. Such transformations usually take place for one of two reasons (or a combination of the two): They may either result from a loss that is independent of the subject's intentionality, or the subject may grow away from their acquired networks of belonging.

In the first case, it may result from a dramatic change of context (in the case of one patient, moving to another region), the loss of a significant affective connection (for one patient, the loss of a parent; for another, the death of a relative), or from the discovery of a profound affective solitude (to quote one patient: "I realize now how alone I am. Notwithstanding my parents and my husband, I am alone and have always been so").

In the second case, panic attacks are a symptom of a rapid (indeed, over-rapid) evolution taking place. For example, Laura had panic attacks as she was seeking to differentiate herself from her family. Another patient, Antonia, a 36-year-old woman, suffered panic attacks when she began to differentiate herself from her husband. Antonia's husband's serious family and health problems had dominated their lives as a couple for over 10 years, with the result that she had always taken care of him without being able to express her own needs within the relationship. When her husband's problems began to clear up, their equilibrium as a couple was altered. Antonia began to request more support and there were moments of conflict. The panic attacks she suffered at this stage marked [the breakdown of her previ- in Summary ous modality of belonging, in a context lacking in the shared ground needed to offer a sufficient level of support.] Significantly, Antonia had a birth family that was very much present and able to offer her practical and emotional support. However, the support they provided was rooted in the previous status quo, and when she began to feel and express her own needs, her family belittled them as "weaknesses to be overcome." Their aim in supporting her was to make her "go back to being like she was before." Therefore, Antonella was lacking in affiliations that could support her intentionality to differentiate herself, to be autonomous, and to find a new way of belonging.

The support provided by one's networks of belonging can often be least forthcoming in the most precocious stages of life. Marco is a young man who, since childhood, has always excelled in sports. At the age of only 15, he was already a freestyle motocross champion. He is an only child and his parents split up when he was 19. With regard to their divorce, he told me:

It was no problem at all for me. I was already very autonomous. I was happy and extroverted, with loads of friends and a girlfriend. And also, deep inside me, I'd always known I shouldn't get too attached to my family. The fact that my father had been abandoned at birth and had grown up in an orphanage had always made me tell myself: "Marco, you can manage without your parents. Don't get too attached to them." After their separation, I got on with my life without any changes, except I didn't talk to my parents. That wasn't because I was angry with them. It was just that I didn't have anything to say to them.

He finished secondary school in the same period:

It was the end of an era. I didn't know what university course to sign up for, so I decided to take a year out. Up to that point, I'd been able to pursue my sporting interests and dream about doing it professionally, knowing at the same time that there was always school to fall back on. This gave me a sense of security. After I finished school, I felt an enormous gulf open up.

A few months later, when Marco was far from home for an important competition, he had a major panic attack. He was devastated by what had happened, but he did not tell anyone for several weeks—until his anxiety had grown so intense that he no longer felt able to leave the house.

Since then my life has become hell. I don't know myself any more and I don't understand what is happening to me. No one has been able to explain it to me. I want to do billions of things, but every time I set foot outside the house I get ill. I wasn't scared of anything. I was fearless. Now I'm scared of everything. It's unbearable!

In Marco's case, two fundamentally incompatible circumstances have occurred concomitantly. On the one hand, his level of autonomy has undergone a powerful growth spurt, on the other, he has lost his acquired modality of belonging. Panic brings to light the insufficiency of the support afforded by Marco's networks of belonging and the impossibility of adapting them to his new conditions and requirements. When I met him for the first time, three years after his first attack, I was struck by the profound suffering caused by the limitations that his situation imposed on him. His deep and somehow "ancient" solitude was striking, as was the courage and tenacity with which he faced up to this experience. However, what struck me most of all were the bewilderment and anxiety which stemmed from his inability to understand what was happening to him. Panic, three years after his first panic attack, was still a figure without a ground. A few simple reference keys, which helped him to read his own story and to form a cognitive and emotional ground for his anxiety, enabled him to breathe easily and to begin to calm down.

The most disorientating and shocking aspect of panic attacks is often their unpredictability. It is bewildering for individuals to suddenly experience the loss of autonomy caused by panic attacks in a period of their life cycle when their level of autonomy is increasing: "What's happening to me? I thought I'd made all the right decisions, but instead I'm feeling terrible. I'm walking on eggshells and it's terrifying." In fact, the onset of panic disorder often leads to a considerable and abrupt diminishing of the patient's independence, which often seems like a frustrating "regression": "Something suddenly snapped and I regressed. I can't do things by myself now that I used to take for granted." Patients may be further confused by the apparent contradiction between their yearning for autonomy and their need to seek assistance in therapy. We often come across introjective subjects (typical of what Christopher Lasch describes as the *The Culture of Narcissism*, 1978) who strive for self-sufficiency: "You've got to make it on your own," "The most important thing is to feel well within yourself," "I mustn't need anything." At this stage, it is important that the therapist remembers that our aim in helping these patients to become more autonomous is not that they become completely independent. Instead, we wish to help them find a way to deconstruct existing networks of belonging in order to build up new ones.

To push a patient towards autonomy prematurely (e.g., by encouraging them to move around unaccompanied) is to collaborate with a narcissistic trait that often exacerbates their problems. Whilst for the patient, the figure is his or her loss of autonomy and efforts to regain it, the therapist's figure should be the fragility of the patient's networks of belongings (i.e., his or her ground). While the patient may worry about the new affiliation he or she is developing with the therapist, the therapist, who sees the ground as well as the figure, can be confident that autonomy will result spontaneously from the construction of a healthy, consistent, and flexible form of belonging. A new figure of autonomy will gradually emerge from this work on the ground of belonging that is being deconstructed and on the new ground that is being constructed in its place (and which is the product of therapeutic belonging; see section 3.5). It is difficult for the patient to enter into relationships in which he or she experiences a sense of dependence once more. However, the therapist's work consists in giving time and support to the patient in retracing those kinds of belonging in a new way, with the support of the therapeutic relationship.[1]

Autonomy is not opposed to belonging. It is rather nourished by belong-

---

[1] The fracturing of the continuity of experience, which takes place when panic attacks occur, has something in common with catastrophic phenomena as described by Réné Thom (cf. Arnol'd, 1990): Let us suppose that a system can be described with a given number of variables. If at least one of those variables exceeds its critical value, the system suffers a brusque transition from one condition of stability (S1) to another (S2). Phenomena of this kind are called catastrophic because small changes to one variable can cause relatively big changes to the state of the system as a whole. In general, it is impossible to recover the system's precatastrophic state (S1) by returning the variable to its critical value. To regain state S1, the whole system has to pass to a state S0, which may be very different from both state S1 and state S2. This kind of irreversibility, known as hysteresis, is common in nonlinear systems.

We might adapt Thom's terminology (without any pretence that catastrophe theory can describe the phenomenology of panic attacks), using the term hysteresis to refer to the panic attack, after which, to return to his or her previous level of autonomy, the patient must first return to an even earlier state, retracing for a certain period of time his or her earlier relationships of dependency.

To provide a simple illustration, we might consider the position of an object on a table. The object's position in space can be described with three variables. If the object is at the edge of the table, a small variation in one variable (a small longitudinal shift along the surface of the table) can cause a swift and dramatic transformation of the object's position (the object falls vertically to the floor). A longitudinal identical shift in the opposite direction will not return the object to its previous position.

ing. Belonging and autonomy should not be seen as two diametrically opposed polarities to be weighed against each other, with the augmentation of one always being at the expense of the other. They should rather be conceived of as Cartesian axes, which intersect to open up quadrants, in which there are the various combinations of the two elements.

Autonomy is a figure that stands against a ground of belonging.

Clinically speaking, when dealing with patients suffering from panic attacks in our contemporary context, it is important to work on constructing and deconstructing networks of belonging before urging the patient towards autonomy. As Giovanni Salonia has underlined (see for example chapter 2 of this volume), in another historical context the required specific support might be very different. For example, in a context characterized by secure, clear, and rigid networks of belonging, it might be more important to sustain the deconstruction of affiliations and to encourage autonomy right from the beginning, without worrying about sustaining the ground of present and future belonging networks. The spirit of the "new" schools of psychotherapy in the 1960s, with their strong emphasis on the independence and self-sufficiency of the subject, can be understood from this point of view (Salonia, 1999).

This consideration of the movement towards autonomy brings us to one of the key issues in patients suffering from panic attacks: solitude. The fragmentation of networks of belonging, the process of differentiation, and leaving the oikos all leave the individual at risk of a solitude that is not only painful but also unsustainable and terrifying.

A patient called Clara, who had her first panic attack after five years of therapy, provides us with a case in point. For various reasons, Clara's ground of belonging had been rather fragile throughout her life.

Clara's first two panic attacks occurred on occasions when she was particularly exposed socially. Clara had taken on a number of high responsibility roles at work, at a point in her life when she was feeling particularly "big" and autonomous. In that period, I had to go away for about twenty days and, for the first time since we had begun therapy, Clara told me that it did not bother her that there would be two weeks instead of only one between our meetings. In fact, however, she was (or, rather, we were) abandoning her therapeutic belonging too hastily and, during that period of particular well-being, she had her first panic attack whilst giving a public presentation.

Our analysis of these episodes helped Clara to attain an awareness of her relationships of belonging in therapy and at work. In so doing, she was able to identify her need for support during moments of social exposure:

I've worked out that, if I want to be less anxious, I've got to stop telling myself "you've got to do it alone." That only makes things worse. Instead, I need to share my projects, my perception of things and my professional values with some of my colleagues. This will help me feel calmer and stronger, even when the people I confide in aren't physically present.

The following statement reveals another yet more important development in her awareness:

I thought that therapy was something that had to finish at a certain point and afterwards I could get along alone again. However, it isn't quite like that. Therapy has to end, but that doesn't mean that I'll be alone. You'll always be inside of me, and I'm starting to believe that I'll always be inside of you. Of course I'll have to cope on my own ... But even that means something new to me now because I'm discovering that there are a lot of other people whom I can ask for help, not just you, and they often answer me.

For the next few months, Clara did not suffer any panic attacks. Even so, she then began to suffer from an intense sense of anxiety and ill-being which only struck in the evenings and which sometimes led into a full-scale panic attack during which Clara was afraid she was about to die of a heart attack. This form of panic was phenomenologically very different from that which had preceded it.

In a moment of profound insight, Clara captured the central feature of this new disorder: "I'm terrified of dying ... No, that's not it ... In fact, I think what I'm really terrified of is dying alone." (ad leaving s alone)

Clara's therapy was now geared towards dealing with her fear of death on two fronts. Firstly, she was afraid of losing people dear to her. In particular, she was very much surprised to realize that she was suffering as a result of her fear of losing her parents. This anxiety was a sign of a new elaboration of her sense of belonging to her family. Secondly, she discovered that her panic in the evenings was linked to a sense of distance from her husband, in a period of solitude and little intimacy between the couple. "I'm not afraid of suffering a stroke at work, even if the idea comes to mind or I deliberately try to think of it. I'm scared of dying in my bedroom." She gradually realized that her fear was transforming itself: "I'm increasingly less afraid that I have heart disease. Instead, I feel as if my heart is swollen from crying."

Clara made another significant step forwards during a period in which she was very isolated in her professional life, which opened up an acute and overwhelming awareness of the solitude in which she had spent her life. In a moment she suddenly and intensely relived and grew aware of the solitude of her childhood, the emotional distance of her mother, and the absence of her father. At this point Clara was able to sense and articulate her fear: "I'm so alone that I'm going to die." Her fear of death was no longer figure for her. Solitude became her new figure and this opened up new and fecund potentials for her work and for her personal growth.

Over the following months, a number of other profoundly painful memories of traumatic childhood experiences resulting from insufficient parental protection emerged, which had until now been removed. In this way, Clara passed from fear of her future to pain for her past experiences. Her fear was incomprehensible, devoid of history and reason, suspended like a figure with no ground. Her pain was, instead, rooted in the experiences that she was gradually recovering. On the one hand, it was tied in with the trials and tribulations of her personal history. On the other, it was concretized in the suffering, tears, and the new breath of life which accompanied these discoveries. We can see here how our work with the personality functions and id functions of the self rebuilt and provided a ground on which Clara could rest.

The lack of support, which resulted from the absence of stable and significant networks of belonging at that moment, recalled her whole history of solitude and the shortage of nurturing relationships. Clara's working skills and her capacity to stay physically alone (functions that were both disturbed by her panic) deteriorated even further the more she sought to recover her autonomy through self-sufficiency and independence. They improved, instead, as Clara gradually laid down roots in her networks of belonging at work, in her relationships with her partner and her family, and in her therapeutic relationship.

Solitude and isolation are often the ground against which the fear of dying emerges so devastatingly during panic attacks. This terror cannot be eased medically (these patients have often undergone a long series of medical analyses, health checks, and trips to the emergency room). They can only be dealt with by working on the issues of solitude, which constitute the more or less rigid ground. Marco, a patient suffering from panic attacks, put his finger right on the point with the following illuminating synthesis: "A panic attack is basically an attack of acute loneliness." It is interesting to note that the two main fears in panic attacks are the fear of dying and the fear of going mad. These are, in effect, the two ways in which an individual can "drop off the edge" of human belonging and community.

The experience of solitude acquires different nuances, depending on the contact experience of the individual within relationship. When the individual's experience of contact has been predominantly retroflective, solitude is accompanied by a fear of being "small" and inadequate. Such individuals often experience a profound and unsustainable shame when they are exposed to another's gaze. In projective cases, when the subject feels alone, he or she feels endangered by a world that is as threatening as it is alien. This sense of being "small" and terrorized can, in extreme cases, lead to paralysis or impulsive actions. For introjective subjects, solitude can lead to the loss of meaning, of priorities, and of any taste for life, with a consequent sinking into depression. When the individual's experience of contact has been confluent, solitude is accompanied by a sense of nothingness, disintegration, and bewilderment. Subjects grasp desperately and randomly at any stable point.

Being alone in the face of the world's complexity is an experience that needs a ground—the support of intimate (oikos) and of social relationships (polis). The presence and the assimilation of such relationships enables the subject to breathe freely and to cope with the precariousness of his or her individual life:

> At the Lars Olsen Memorial Home, after three weeks in isolation, the world ceased to exist. In the end, I seemed to be lacking in even an interior reality. If man is totally isolated, he ceases to exist.
> It is therefore impossible to be alone. Each man has to be with other men. If a man is completely alone, he ceases to exist. (Hoeg, 1996, p. 237. Translated from the Italian by A. Spencer)

3.5 Specific Support: Building Up the Ground

> *New life springs from the collapse of the* status quo.
>
> (Goodman, 1968)

In Gestalt psychotherapy, each intervention is founded on the analysis of the contact sequence and its interruptions. The aim is to renew awareness and to support contact intentionality towards a new creative-adjustment (Salonia, 1989, p. 55; Spagnuolo Lobb, 1990, p. 13; Perls et al., 1951/1994). Our practice with patients suffering from panic attacks is no exception.

We are not, therefore, putting forward "techniques" to be reproduced, since specific support can only arise from an authentic relationship, from the unique and creative contact established between patient and therapist.[1]

[1] It is worth, at this juncture, underlining a number of convergences and differences between the Gestalt approach presented here and the strategic models which have dedicated a great deal of attention to anxiety disorders in recent years (Nardone, 1993; Nardone & Watzlawick, 2005; Rovetto, 2003). We should particularly recall three areas of common ground:

1. The attention paid to *how* instead of *why*. Both approaches place more emphasis on the process, that is, *how* the disorder proceeds, than on the recapitulation of *why* it developed in the first place. This is because reconstructing the various stages that have led to the disorder does not, in itself, represent a solution to the problem. Notwithstanding this, personal history remains very important in Gestalt therapy as an element in the specific support provided to the patient. This is not so much in order to establish a rational chain of cause and effect as to boost the ground that sustains the patient.
2. A pro-active attitude. Both approaches look to the future instead of the past, although with different eyes. The strategic approach looks forward to a future in which there will no longer be any symptoms. Gestalt therapy, instead, looks to the "next" as the time in which the patient, with adequate support, will give expression to his or her impeded intentionality and, in so doing, will be able to establish a better oriented and more nurturing form of contact with the world.
3. Action. Both approaches propose active forms of intervention. In the strategic approach tasks are "studied" strategically by the therapist so as to obtain a predetermined effect of which the patient remains in the dark. In Gestalt therapy, by contrast, the proposed action is born spontaneously from the moment, is co-created and developed during the session, so as to support the intentionality towards which the organism is moving.

Let us now move on to the differences between the two approaches. The clinical treatment of panic attacks is emblematic of the difference between approaches primarily oriented towards the resolution of symptoms (as is the case with the strategic approach) and those focused on the evolution of the individual and his or her way of being in the world. In the first case, the therapeutic intervention is aimed at diminishing the intensity and the frequency of the symptoms. To realize this end, techniques are employed to distract the patient's attention from his or her anxiety, augmenting his or her sense of control over the situation, and seeking to diminish physical reaction to anxiety-provoking stimuli. The therapeutic relationship is a brief (sometimes very brief) period of consultation aimed at shifting panic back to the ground. One of the problems with this kind of relationship is that it runs the risk of not noticing its own failings because a patient, who is not getting better or who is relapsing, may find it difficult to admit to failure or express criticism within a relationship where there is little space and little support for his or her own experiences. It is possible to reestablish the *status quo ante* the emergence of the disorder. The subject can recover his or her autonomy, but it is difficult to create a new way of being autonomous.

Gestalt psychotherapy, instead, which considers the panic attack as an opportunity and a request for evolution at a delicate stage in the subject's life, offers a relationship that builds up the ground until the patient is able to know, face, deal with, and ultimately integrate and dissolve his or her anxiety. A new way of being autonomous arises from a new experience of belonging. Therapeutic success consists in the growth of the patients in the various areas of their life and in the gradual disappearance of symptoms. The advantage of strategic the-

Indeed, the clinical examples we will present here do not follow a set course defined *a priori*. They do not follow a plan or apply protocols. Instead, they are examples of unrepeatable experiences, which can only provide a limited amount of orientation and direction.

The therapeutic relationship provides the ground that enables the patient to work through and overcome his or her sense of solitude. Fear, like any other emotion, is not an intrapsychic phenomenon and does not belong to any single subject. The experience is always one of contact at the organism–environment boundary. Fear, for example, is the result of a lack of environmental support. In this holistic and relational sense, it is not correct to say: "This child is afraid," since we are making an unjust and artificial scission. We should rather say: "This child in this situation, with the support available to him, is afraid." The question: "How can we make his fear go away?" (or, worse, the imperative: "You mustn't be afraid!") becomes: "What environmental support does he or she need and how can he or she assimilate it?" This question encapsulates the basic direction in which our interventions move.

Let us therefore focus our attention on some important points that the therapist should bear in mind when dealing with patients suffering from this disorder.

3.5.1 The Therapist's Ground

> *No organism is self-sufficient.*
> (Perls, 1969)

The anxiety that the patient experiences during a session is often very intense. His or her sense of worry and urgency can seem palpable and destabilizing. Above all during the first sessions, the therapist may end up feeling short of breath and overwhelmed by the air of emergency. In order to cope with the impact of this anxiety, the therapist must be calm, feeling him- or herself to be supported by a ground that makes it possible to deal with a relationship so strongly characterized by anxiety and the lack of support. On the

rapy is the brevity of the intervention (for example, 10 sessions might be booked *a priori*). The main risk it runs is that, in not taking the evolving meaning of the symptom into account, such interventions might make the subject miss out on a crucial opportunity for growth. The limitation of the Gestalt approach is that it usually takes more time for the symptoms to disappear and requires a greater level of commitment on many levels. Its advantage is that it can open up a whole new world for the subject, through a profound and creative restructuring of his or her relationships and of his or her life.

one hand, he or she must be able to rely on the support provided by his or her own breathing, from the body's rootedness and comfort (we might say that, for a certain period of the therapeutic relationship, at least, the therapist has to breathe for both him- or herself and for the patient). On the other, he or she must have faith in his or her own knowledge of the phenomenon and in his or her own skills and therapeutic experience. The first of these forms of support derives from the id function of the self, the second from the personality function. Furthermore, it is important that the therapist can receive supervision during the period of therapy and that he or she is aware of this (on the importance of the "third person" in therapy, see Salonia & Spagnuolo Lobb, 1986, p. 11).

Another telling point, to which significant attention is rarely paid, is that the therapist is participating in the same field as his or her patient (i.e., is living in the same world during the same historical period). The therapist too encounters fragmentation, uncertainty, and fear, sharing some of the patient's difficulties in building up a secure ground and secure networks of belonging. It is important for the therapist to be aware of the problematic nature of his or her own ground, firstly because this awareness enables him or her to "meet" the patient on common ground and, secondly, because it aids him or her in seeking out contextual support and relational networks which will help him or her to put down stable roots and deal with uncertainty (on this point, see also chapter 6).

3.5.2 Support During Acute Episodes

> An enormous bird was swooping down
> upon him. Someone thrust him to the ground.
> The point of a lance pierced his breast.
> All of a sudden, sweating, trembling, in fits
> of convulsions, he awoke amidst the mirages.
> (Said Bahaudin Majrouh, 1995)[1]

It is rare, but not impossible, for a panic attack to occur during the therapy session. When this happens, the patient will need to be supported on various fronts:

1. By drawing attention to the various support functions of the body: Support the patient's breathing (give him or her space, provide fresh air, encourage him or her to breathe out), allowing freedom of movement (including allowing the patient to leave the room). Help the patient to

---

[1] Translated from the Italian by A. Spencer.

112

(handwritten: VW, holding here; breathing, with me)

feel rooted (draw the patient's attention to his or her feet resting on the ground or to his or her body resting on the chair).

2. Supporting the maintenance of contact: The patient will feel catapulted into a state of fear (as if the ground beneath his or her feet has given way). The therapist will represent a point of stability to which the patient can cling. Contact can be through the eyes or the voice. It can also be kinesthetic, for example, holding the patient's hand or asking him or her to look into your eyes or to breathe more deeply).

3. Circumscribing the experience within temporal boundaries: Reassuring the patient of the fact that this disturbance has a beginning and an end, and that it is possible for patient and therapist to get through it together.

Next, it is important to consider the exact significance of a panic attack *(handwritten: talking about dad brother...)* occurring during a therapy session. In order to gauge this, we should consider the precise stage of the session at which it occurs (Salonia, 1992). For example, a panic attack at the beginning of a session could be a way of introducing the disorder into the therapeutic relationship, whereas a panic attack at the end of the session might mark the patient's difficulty in separating him- or herself from the therapist.

It is also worth bearing in mind the stage in the therapeutic process as a whole at which the panic attack occurs. Is the therapeutic relationship providing an insufficient level of support, leaving the patient overexposed to anxiety? Or, on the other hand, is the patient's trust in the relationship such that he or she believes it can support all the anxiety of an acute episode? If the panic attack occurs at the beginning of the therapeutic process, does it mean that something is impeding the construction of a good sense of belonging in the therapeutic context? If it occurs at the end of the therapeutic relationship, does this mean that patient and therapist are growing apart too rapidly?

All of this enables us to locate the symptom within a meaningful context and to connect it to the history of the therapeutic relationship. It is a way to provide a ground for episodes that occur during therapy.

At other times, instead, emotions emerge and are experienced that are so intense that the patient is afraid of being overwhelmed by them. It is important to specify that what happens here is not panic. However, the fear can be as great and the kind of support analogous to that described above. This kind of episode usually occurs at relatively advanced stages of therapy. What the patient is experiencing is not anxiety but emotions so strong that he or she feels unable to deal with them. These feelings are therefore always on the brink of becoming acute anxiety. Without an adequate degree of support, they may evolve into a panic attack.

113

These emotions are often historically and semantically connected to the panic experience, or they may recall such experiences in their intensity. Once again, the support provided in these situations should consist in rooting the subject in his or her body and in the contact taking place in the "here and now" of the relationship.

One example of the kind of support that should be supplied during panic attacks is provided in Giuseppe Sampognaro's *Mille Mondi*, a novel in which the main character suffers from panic attacks.

"I don't know what's happening. I just know that my sense of suffocation is overwhelming right now. What I'm feeling now is scarily similar to what happens when I have those goddamn crises, which suddenly come upon me for no apparent reason ... Christ, Aldo, I feel awful ... as if I'm going to faint ... help me ... I'm falling down into an abyss ... Do you know what panic is, Aldo? No, what could you know about it? You couldn't possibly know anything about it ... It's a no man's land you have to cross, and you know that you're going to be all alone in the world and that no one will take pity on you... . It's a vacuum, an overwhelming sense of emptiness in life, which grows inside you. It's the laceration of my soul which I felt when my parents went off to work early in the morning and I lacked the words to hold them back."

I'm losing myself ... I'm losing myself ... but I can feel that Aldo is holding me back.

"Look at me," he orders me, "and hold my hands."

I cling onto them, reeling, his strong hands my only hope of salvation. My fingers are slippery and unsure of themselves, but I don't let go... .

"Now look around you and tell me everything you can see in this room."

But what is he saying. I don't understand. He repeats, forcefully: "Tell me what you can see around you!"

I put my trust in him. I put my trust in him because this is the only way to prevent my being sucked away into the abyss. I fearfully remove my gaze from him. I see a table, a diary, and a box of tissues. I tell him that there's a table with a diary and a box of tissues on top of it. I raise my eyes. There is a Monet print on the wall.

"What do you see in that painting?" he asks me, and I force myself to understand and pronounce the word "nymphs."

"What color are they?" he asks me.

Like a fool, I answer "blue," because I can really see the blue that dominates Monet's painting and I'm already feeling better. I grow in-

114

terested in the wrought iron coat hangers, then in the brass umbrella stand. Gradually, I list all the objects I can see around me, and I grow calm, because I know what they are and I can say all their names. I look at Aldo and, continuing to grasp his hands, I thank him. (Sampognaro, 2000, p. 112. Translated from the Italian by A. Spencer)

3.5.3 Building the Ground

> *I'm a feather lost in the universe ... My feet never touch the ground.*
> (Michele, a patient suffering from panic attacks).

> *I'm terrified that the force of gravity will stop working and I'll be sucked out into space.*
> (Antonio, a patient suffering from panic attacks).

Panic attacks strike like lightning, dazzling the patient. Their bodily manifestations tend to occupy all the patient's attention and are often the only figure he or she is able to construct. Providing a ground to this figure, without being blinded by it, is a key element of the support provided by the therapist.

The therapist's capacity to perceive and stay in touch with the ground is vital in any relationship with patients suffering from panic attacks, since this capacity is a necessary prerequisite for the opening out of the field to other significant elements. Suffering panic alone (without such a broadening of the field of perception) is unbearable. One patient, who was suffering from panic attacks and had already undergone a significant period of therapy, described to me the terror he experienced upon looking into the eyes of another, severely disturbed patient:

"He had the same eyes as my brother, and I felt the same overwhelming fear I had used to feel when, as a little girl, I saw the madness in his eyes." As she told me this, I perceived no terror in her expression, so I asked her why things had changed. "There's no difference ... They're still the same eyes" (pause). "In fact, now I think about it, the experience in itself is identical. It's what's around it that is different. I really was terrified for a moment, but that terror immediately situated itself amongst other things, within a kind of 'network' of meanings and experiences ... This made it possible for me to breathe."

We have already considered various examples of this process in this chapter (section 3 and 4). We will therefore now limit ourselves to summarizing the most significant aspects that favor the construction of the ground in therapy.

3.5.3.1 Words as Ground

> *I had seen how the world appeared to her, as if I had seen it with her own eyes. It was enormous and oppressive. In the midst of all this chaos, she was seeking, with words, to dig out tunnels of order.*
>
> *Putting things in order means recognizing them, knowing that in an infinite and unknown sea there is one island you have already visited. She had pointed these islands out to me. She had built up a network of familiar people and objects with words... . Words recall and stabilize things that are far away. With her lists she reassured herself that what she had once known would return to her.*
>
> (Hoeg, 1996)[1]

Words, by shaping and outlining the chaos of nascent experience and rendering its freshness *sayable*, are a fundamentally important element in supporting every *Erlebnis*.

Often, at the beginning, panic attacks are devastating because they cannot be defined and lack the significant points of reference that would make it possible to circumscribe and name the experience.

The patient is profoundly disorientated and is further terrified by the incomprehensible nature of what is happening to him or her. The therapist should bear this factor in mind, be it implicitly or explicitly expressed, and support the patient as he or she seeks to define the experience, encouraging questions and offering reassurance wherever possible. For example, an awareness that his or her fear of going mad or dying is a "normal" symptom of acute anxiety can help the patient to contain his or her anxiety (as, at

---

[1] Translated from the Italian by A. Spencer.

the end of the day, it should also help the therapist). Notwithstanding this, words, to be useful, must give voice to a shared and shareable world, where both therapist and patient can rest and play with an equal degree of dignity, whilst, at the same time, retaining their diverse and clearly defined roles and competences.

One example of lacking support on this level is provided, once again, by the novel *Mille Mondi*:

> After he had exposed the problem, he limited himself to sentencing me to "PAD: panic attack disorder with agoraphobia and claustrophobia."
> And when I, frightened by the word "panic," asked him to help me understand better, he froze me to the spot with a sentence that seemed even more peremptory and mysterious.
> "It's an alteration of the limbic system, probably caused by a dysfunction of serotonin receptors." He said all this without raising his eyes from the letter-headed sheet of paper on which he was scribbling a series of equally incomprehensible words with a glittering and creaking fountain pen.
> I was no wiser than I had been before, but his obscure definition and grave composure disturbed me even further.
> He didn't give me a chance to come back for further explanation.
> (Sampognaro, 2000, p. 62. Translated from the Italian by A. Spencer)

Sometimes the patient will refer to their symptoms as panic attacks right from the very beginning. In such cases, it is important not to blindly accept the label (is it just a diagnosis imposed by others and not fully "chewed" by the patient? Is it a name that has simply been applied in order to calm anxiety generated by the indefinite?). An overhasty diagnosis is often a response to the patient's need to escape from uncertainty and the unknown. The specific support provided by the therapeutic relationship in contexts such as these consists in dwelling on and "chewing" the indefinite, elaborating on it together in order to reach a shared understanding based on the description and the phenomenology of the experience. Otherwise, there is a risk that the patient may remain isolated. If language (including technical language) is the fruit of a shared process of elaboration, it will become a common ground within which therapist and patient can move together, and this stage constitutes an important part of the ground on which the therapeutic relationship rests.

> *The chain of his experience in time had broken up. The links constituted by individual instances had become disjoined from one another. Each passing moment connected him to nothing, to no one. He was tightly chained. To himself.*
>
> (Said Bahaudin Majrouh, 1995)[1]

Every experience is a figure that stands out against a ground. Every episode of panic has a "before" and an "after" which are often not recounted by patients because the intensity of panic tends to cancel out everything else. Recovering this experience enables us, from one point of view, to delimit temporal boundaries around the experience, and, from another, to recover the continuum within which this experience, often perceived as a schism, as something "other," is actually situated.

Owing to this preliminary work, which is sometimes slow and difficult (the patient often has difficulty in recovering the before and after), the causes that triggered the episode gradually emerge (these often vary from one attack to another). This, in turn, builds up the patient's faith that the panic attack is not a completely unpredictable flash of lightning out of a clear sky. It comes rather to be seen as the result of experiential circumstances, which formulate a pathway to panic.

The recovery of the patient's awareness of the other emotions that accompany the terror of panic is an important step forward. These emotions will be perceived more clearly as this awareness becomes more sustainable. This stage enables us to open out the field to other experiences with which it is of fundamental importance that we work. The story of Clara, who passed from the "terror of dying" to the terrible awareness of "being so alone that she was about to die," is a case in point. Often, in fact, together with terror we will encounter pain, but this latter emotion will only emerge when the therapeutic relationship is mature enough to sustain the patient's anxiety and support his or her solitude.

---

[1] Translated from the Italian by A. Spencer.

"Where does this little shred of certainty come from, this sensation that I am more than just a ghost?" he asked himself, flabbergasted ... The names that I attach to things are unraveling, slipping away like sand between my fingers. Names and words are empty. Once upon a time things and names were related, woven together in an infinite web of relationships. A staircase connected two floors. A wall surrounded a garden. A chair pulled up to a table. But now, see how they ignore each other, how they lie suspended in the anticipation of a meaning that never comes.

(Said Bahaudin Majrouh, 1995)[1]

The panic experience, which the patient brings with him or her into therapy, is an incomprehensible event with no ground. When the therapist begins to understand the patient's personal history and to meaningfully locate the disorder within that context, he or she will identify the direction in which the therapeutic process should move to establish a ground of perceptible support for the therapeutic relationship.

The life cycle of the patient and his or her changing networks of belonging (cf. section 3.4) provide us with a precious key for reading the symptoms in connection with the patient's life. We can thus gradually locate panic within the subject's biography, so that it becomes a figure that emerges naturally, even obviously, from his or her life experiences.

A turning point in therapy is when the patient arrives at the conclusion: "Now I understand it isn't so strange that I'm suffering from panic attacks!" At this moment, panic is no longer a suspended figure without meaning. It is instead recognized as an expression of the individual's personal history and life experience.

When this happens, the patient's fear that the symptoms of anxiety are signs of a physical threat or illness diminishes. Symptoms at last come to be viewed as expressions of ill-being in his or her life as opposed to a physical emergency. At the same time, the patient's sense of therapy as a

---

[1] Translated from the Italian by A. Spencer.

meaningful and profitable undertaking will heighten. A coherent, less fragmented figure begins to emerge in the frame as symptoms acquire meaning and legitimacy.

3.5.3.4 The Functions of Self: The Id Function and Personality Function as Ground

> *He savored the elixir of feeling lost: Everything that was going to happen could not but be a surprise. He could attach no meaning to the things that were essential to him ... He could feel them slipping away, but made no despairing efforts to clutch onto them. Instead, he touched his body, looked around him, and said to himself, "I am here and now," without falling prey to panic.*
>
> (Goodman, *The Empire City*, 1959)[1]

The id and personality functions of self support the formation of the contact figure (see section 3.2 on this point). During panic attacks the support provided by those two functions is partially lost. During therapy, it is important to renew the patient's awareness of and the functioning of this support: bodily awareness and support (id function) together with awareness and assimilation of roles and allegiances (personality function).

When a patient recounts a panic episode, it is sometimes possible to identify which function was lacking most. Such is the case with the experience of Antonella, described above (although, as we have already noted, the two functions always have a reciprocal relationship and are inseparable).

The id function of self can be restored by drawing the patients' attention to their perceptions of their body, thereby revitalizing their awareness (for a deeper exploration of this point, see for example Kepner, 1987; Frank, 2001). A desensitization of the body and an interruption to the fluidity of its gestures and rhythms can often be noted in subjects suffering from panic attacks.

Sometimes the body seems to be suspended in space or trapped, instead of resting on a chair. The resulting impression is that the organism feels un-

---

[1] Translated from the Italian by A. Spencer.

able to rely on any resting place, that the body is braced against the sudden collapse of its support and therefore stands guard, cautious, and vigilant.

It is necessary to pay particular attention to the patient's breathing, as this is one of the fundamental bases of the organism's self-support and a site *par excellence* of organism–environment contact: "I felt as if my breathing was regular as clockwork once more, measuring out the brief period of time we had to be together" (Hoeg, 1996, p. 149. Translated from the Italian by A. Spencer). The breathing of patients suffering from panic attacks is lacking in fluidity, continuity, rhythm, and harmony. The patient will be partially aware of this and will often complain that his or her breathing is labored and provides no satisfaction, a never-ending, irritating, or painful struggle for air, which is often attributed to a bodily illness.

Breathing is never entirely satisfactory. Specific support in such cases should consist in helping the patient to achieve awareness of the way he or she interrupts the spontaneous flow of breathing, of feeling, and ultimately of the emotions which accompany this interruption. The patient seeks satisfaction by trying to breathe in more deeply, but, as Isadore From has illustrated,[1] it is the patient's expiration, not his or her inhalation, which has been interrupted. The organism holds his or her breath after breathing in. It is only through breathing out that the rhythm and fullness of breathing can be restored. Sometimes anxiety is so strong that the patient is unable to breathe out. In such cases, it is necessary to give the patient time to gain awareness of his or her breathing and to trust in the therapeutic relationship.

The interruption of breathing is a manifestation of an interruption to the spontaneity of contact. When contact is fulfilled, the experience is concluded and the organism can be observed to encounter a sense of closure and satisfaction. The breathing cycle can, in this sense, be seen as punctuating occurrence. A deep breath affords closure to an experiential phenomenon. For example, it is noticeable that when patients are talking, they often pass from one subject to another without breathing out. It is only by breathing out that they will really be able to "turn the page," so to speak. It is necessary to take the time to breathe when saying goodbye—and if we breathe deeply separation becomes easier and more beneficial. After a scare, we "breathe a sigh of relief." Breathing enables us to savor sublime moments with our whole bodies.[2]

---

[1] By oral communication.

[2] This way of blocking our own breathing was probably advantageous during our evolution. It is, indeed, characteristic of the situations of "inhibition of the action" described by Henri Laborit (1986). Action inhibition is the way organisms react to situations of danger in which they can neither fight nor flee. In such situations, it can be useful for the animal to

Amongst the various experiments that can take place in the course of a therapeutic session (Polster & Polster, 1973), it is sometimes useful to offer the patient some experiences of "grounding" (Lowen, 1975). Such activities increase awareness, vitality, and bodily rootedness. Particular attention needs to be paid to when and how these exercises are introduced, since there is always a risk that they will simply reproduce the organism's fixed and stereotypical modes of contact yet again. For example, a patient might employ them retroflectively to gain autonomous control over moments of acute anxiety (whilst in this case, the technique should serve as a vehicle for the relational support provided by therapy). Another subject might introjectively use the technique as a task imposed by the therapist, rather than responding to his or her perceived needs (whilst in this case, it should arise from the patient's own sensations and needs and be employed creatively).

Turning to the personality function of self, specific support should here consist in sustaining the assimilation of experience through the narration of oneself (the personality function is a verbal copy of self; Perls et al., 1951/1994). In this way, the patient's life story acquires meaning and continuity. It becomes a narrative that belongs, at a deep level, to the subject, a story that comes to be revitalized and inhabited. This process necessitates a therapeutic ear willing to respect the experience narrated without distorting it—able to respond to and provide names for the experiences that gradually emerge during the relationship (for a more detailed study on this point, see Franta & Salonia, 1981). It is only possible for the therapist to listen in this way if he or she is genuinely interested in the uniqueness and worth of the

---

impede its motor functions, including breathing, so as to faint and play dead. In extreme cases, this mechanism can afford a chance of survival. It is clear, therefore, that in dangerous situations it can be useful to stop breathing after breathing in, rather than after breathing out, as this provides the body with a greater reserve of oxygen, therefore allowing a longer period of inhibition.

A physiological relationship has been observed between respiratory parameters and panic attacks. For example, panic attacks can be triggered by air that is particularly high in carbon dioxide. I do not believe that this experimental situation is correct for studying panic attacks because a situation of carbon dioxide increasing is a situation of real danger for the organism, and what is triggered is a panic phenomenon (which happens when the organism has to face a real danger) and not a panic attack. I believe that these observations can be better understood when considered in the light of phenomenology, in an attempt at a reciprocal and more rounded reading of symptoms, seeking to further the quest for more effective clinical approaches. For example, the difficulties in breathing, which can be observed in patients suffering from panic attacks, cannot be explained only in terms of an ahistorical biological correlation, attributed to a blind genetic predisposition. The interruption of the breathing cycle must also be viewed, as we have already noted, as a constituent part of the panic interruption that typifies the collapse of the ground.

individual who emerges from the narrative. Erving Polster hit the nail on the head when he wrote that "every person's life is worth a novel" (Polster, 1987). In this way, the individual can integrate and distinguish between his or her roles and affiliations, bringing up to date his or her notions of *"Who I am"* and *"Who I have become"* through life experiences—the creative-adjustment which takes place between roles and intentionalities. During the life cycle's most crucial moments of transition, the subject's notion of *"Who I am"* undergoes some major restructuring, moving between *"Who I was," "Who I am becoming,"* and *"Who I will be."* The therapist's feedback on, and recognition of, these transitions plays an important role in "giving body" to this process. The more this assistance is rooted in the relational trust between patient and therapist, which has built up over time, the more fruitful and effective it will be. For example, one patient, who had always felt herself to be lost in the midst of multiple interruptions to her networks of belonging (in her family, emotional and professional lives) felt enormously relieved and bolstered when she suddenly found the words to describe herself as "at the crossroads" of these various narratives: "A half-caste! There it is at last! That's who I am!" This insight was instantaneously accompanied by a new perception of herself and of the world: "I feel as if I've established a point of stability, without losing any 'bits' of myself and without limiting my potential."[1]

3.5.3.5 The "Next" as Ground: The Unfolding of Intentionality

> When the future closes its doors, or opens them only to present itself as uncertainty, precariousness, insecurity, and agitation, then "the worst has already happened."
>
> (Galimberti, 2004)[2]

It may seem paradoxical, but the ground is made up not only of the past, but also of the future. As a perceived horizon, the future, too, provides roots

---

[1] In building up the ground during therapy, we should bear in mind that when individuals have been suffering from panic attacks for a long time, the attacks themselves (together with all the strategies and limitations which come with them) have become part of the ground of the subject's life. Panic attacks sometimes become the "traveling companions" through which the subject defines him- or herself. In this case it is, naturally, important to respect this part of the subject's experience and, at the same time, to support new creative-adjustments that will bring the personality function of the self up-to-date.

[2] Translated from the Italian by A. Spencer.

and support. The figure created in the present acquires direction not only from moving in response to stimuli and needs, but also by moving towards the creation of a form or shape—a *Gestalt*. The "next" is the point towards which the organism's intentionality moves. The unfolding of intentionality and new projects forms part of the ground in the present, to which imagination, prediction, hope, desire, expectation, possibility, and dreams all contribute.

The subject's personal horizon emerges as a figure against the ground formed by the perception of the future, which is shared on a social level. Representations of the future have taken on previously unheard of contours over the last decades (see chapters 2 and 5). As several authors have noted, we have passed from a vision of "future promise" to one of a "future threat" (Benasayag & Schmit, 2006). Once again, we come up against the sum of two kinds of vulnerability: In his or her uncertainty as to the horizons of his or her own biography, characteristic of certain stages of the life cycle, the subject is afforded no support by the profound and disturbing collective scenarios prevalent at a social level.

Panic can indeed be overcome, in part, through a construction or reconstruction of the future horizon and, in particular, of the future plans and networks of belonging towards which the individual is moving and which have yet to be defined, acquired, or consolidated.

It is common, as we have already seen with regard to the life cycle, for the individual to "trip up" and fall into panic at the very moments in which he or she is moving towards new networks of belonging. When this happens, support should come not only from the preacquired networks of belonging with which a new creative-adjustment is being sought, but also from the subject's capacity to "look-towards," maintaining contact with the next step in the direction of which his or her life is tending. Panic, inasmuch as it represents an interruption of this movement, can cause disorientation. For example, one patient began suffering from panic attacks again when she decided to get married. Once again, she only felt safe when she got home. "Why am I getting panic attacks again? Could it be that I don't really want to get married? Does this mean that my fiancé isn't giving me enough support—that he isn't the right person for me?" These doubts express the sense of disorientation which panic has once again created: "If I can't keep on in the direction in which I'm going, does that mean I'm going the wrong way?" This is clearly a very important question, but it is important to carefully avoid being too "interpretative," as it is possible to come up with an infinite number of suppositions that provide no direction. This patient told me "I feel like a point at the crossroads of an infinite number of lines." In this case, it was very important to bring a halt to the thousands of questions that were disorienting the patient and to stick with what she was feeling: "I understand that there are many questions, but hold it just a moment ... What are you feeling?" After a pause, the patient started to cry: "I feel really sad to leave my family ... but I also feel that my life is with Fabio." After she had got these sentences out, we were able to start elaborating on the feelings arising from breaking away from her birth family but also, and above all, to start "building" the horizon towards which she was moving. What would be their relationship as a couple, but also, and more importantly at that moment, what would be the relationship between the couple and their birth families and with the broader environment of their circles of friends?

Giving legitimacy and consistency to the scenarios through which the subject is moving and to his or her future is part of the specific support needed by subjects suffering from panic attacks. The loss of this support opens the door to depression, which is by no coincidence a common stage in the development of untreated panic disorder. Naturally, this does not mean that every horizon should be supported in a rigid and uncritical manner. Indeed, projects may well be modified as therapy proceeds. It means, instead, that we must sustain that the "next," which the patient brings with him or her into therapy, exists and is legitimate. Only after this ground has been acquired can we begin to discuss the projects themselves. In fact, patients suffering from panic attacks often come to therapy terrified by the fact that they need to reconstruct their whole lives, their personality, that they need to change all their relationships, be they emotional, professional, or friendships. In these phenomena, we can perceive a vulgarization of psychology, which appears, in many cases, as a social introjection. According to such a "psychology," if you are unwell it means that all your life choices are wrong and need to be changed. This generalization is often incorrect and it obscures the dignity and functionality of the creative-adjustment that has taken place. The subject feels unable to count on what he or she has built up so far, and unable to trust in his or her own planning and decision-making capacities. This can lead to a worsening of symptoms or an implicit or explicit delegation of life choices to the therapist. These patients, for whom everything is questionable, need support to help them, in turn, to recognize the support afforded to them by all that they have built up, are building and wish to build up in the future. Panic is overwhelming and disorientating. The patient's suffering is so extreme that they seek out an immediate solution. They are willing to follow any road, just so long as it leads to change.

Life choices will, obviously, be discussed. However, the therapist should not lose sight of the "next" towards which the organism was tending when he or she was interrupted by panic attacks. Panic attacks do not necessarily mean that the organism is going in the wrong direction. To get out of panic, the individual needs to feel that he or she is heading in a particular direction, tending towards a particular "next."

The impetus towards this future horizon, "which already lives in us" (Salonia, 2000, p. 108), is powerfully evoked in this poem by Nazim Hikmet (1995, p. 25. Translated from the Italian by A. Spencer):

> *The most beautiful of all seas*
> *Is the sea we are not sailing on.*
> *The most beautiful of our children*
> *Has yet to grow.*
> *The most beautiful of our days*
> *Are those we have yet to live.*
> *And that*
> *Most beautiful thing I wish to say to you*
> *I have yet to say to you.*

3.5.3.6 Therapeutic Belonging

> *Finally I can carry you with me ... and*
> *I'm not scared anymore.*
> (A patient suffering from panic attacks)

The process of rooting and building up the ground is not a purely abstract procedure. Rather, it takes place within the therapeutic relationship. Although this will be obvious for any Gestalt psychotherapist, we wish to underline that the work done on the therapeutic relationship and on therapeutic belonging is a determining factor in the therapeutic process when dealing with patients suffering from panic attacks.

We feel confident in maintaining that the development of this disorder is extremely sensitive (perhaps more so than in other clinical situations) to the development of the therapeutic connection.

On the other hand, as we have observed, panic disorder is the expression of an inconsistency in networks of belonging and, therefore, of an insupportable solitude that is gradually revealing itself. It becomes clear that an authentically and emotionally therapeutic relationship should constitute a specific remedy for this condition.

126

The complex process whereby, through a combination of boundaries and warmth, the therapeutic relationship develops has already been documented elsewhere (Spagnuolo Lobb, 2001b). We will therefore limit ourselves here to a few examples that should illustrate the importance of this fundamental element.

Patients suffering from panic attacks will improve significantly when they feel able to carry the therapist with them from one session to another. In order for this to happen, the patient needs to experience contact with the therapist and to assimilate this novelty. There are no shortcuts here. It would be useless (indeed, downright foolish) to dilate the boundaries of therapy, passing beyond its limits. Neither is it possible to keep a safe distance without getting personally and authentically involved. It is necessary, instead, to respect, support, and get across the protective mechanisms that the patient has established in the course of his or her lifetime (modalities of contact interruption), which impede him or her from risking a new involvement. There is nothing specific about this: It is rather the methodology and horizon of Gestalt psychotherapy in general. Notwithstanding this, such considerations should be particularly present when dealing with patients suffering from panic attacks: "How do we two belong to each other? Will you take me with you? What impedes you from doing this? In what way is this place present from one meeting to another? How do you lose me? What are your feelings for me? Do you think you disappear to me when you walk out of the door? Do I disappear to you?" Obviously, these questions will not be asked explicitly. However, the therapist should hold onto them as fundamental hermeneutic keys to understanding what is going on during therapy.

Patients who perceive that there is the possibility of an authentic personal relationship with the therapist (who is recognized as something more than just an aseptic screen) and grow to trust that they will be seen and loved with full respect to their boundaries and given all the time they need (not abandoned, confused, or invaded), will gradually begin to have a sense of belonging within the therapeutic relationship. They will then, perhaps surprisingly, begin to feel less alone. Where there was panic, therapeutic belonging will gradually emerge, weaving together a network strong enough to provide a persistent ground upon which the patient's experiences can be founded. This should not entail creating a dependency. Dependency on a substance or on another person is characterized by a lack of evolution and growth. The nourishment provided by the individual or substance depended on cannot be assimilated, and it is for this reason that the subject is unable to do without it. In the therapeutic relationship, instead, belonging is the *humus* in which autonomy puts down its roots and from which it progressively grows.

For the same reasons, group therapy can often be particularly useful, since it favors the building up of networks of belonging, in this case between equals, and rapidly leads its participants to elaborate on related issues.

It is healthy for the patient to carry the therapist with him or her only once the relationship has passed through and overcome the various relational risks. The therapeutic relationship should have passed beyond the risk of confusion or nondefinition of boundaries which characterizes confluence ("We are one"; "He's so much more than a therapist"). It should run no risk of slipping into the introjective tendency of maintaining the connection on only one behavioral level. ("He told me to carry him with me, so that's what I'm trying to do"). Neither should it risk becoming too invasive, as is the case in projection ("He wants me to carry him with me, but why?"; "I always carry him with me, even when I don't want him"). Nor should the therapeutic relationship risk being conceived of retroflectively, the patient perceiving the therapist's presence in his or her mind as responding to a need of the therapist, rather than of him- or herself ("He needs me to carry him with me"; "I certainly don't need to carry anyone with me!").

One patient who was suffering from very severe and, initially, almost incessant panic attacks, gradually began to recover as she began to trust in her belonging to the therapeutic relationship being established. Panic reappeared or worsened every time she came to doubt the authenticity or reliability of the relationship: A period in which the therapist was absent, a change to the schedule of her sessions, an expression or gesture which could be interpreted as a rejection, sometimes even just the lingering thought that therapy must come to an end. A lengthy period of elaboration upon these experiences, of exploring and gradually getting over the patient's fear of trusting another person, and of overcoming the pain of separation, eventually enabled us to reconstruct, in the patient's belonging to the therapeutic relationship, that basic level of faith without which "no individual can bear such direct contact with all the complexity of the world" (Luhmann, 1979. Translated from the Italian by A. Spencer). This process brought us to an encounter that was intense, rich, and profoundly poetic. To quote the patient:

> "I've subjected you to no end of tests. I've spied on you, trying to catch you. I've studied your every gesture and your every word. I took your

silences as devastated refusals. But then I came to understand that those were the spaces where you were waiting for me. I fled from any confirmation of your presence, because that flung me into the abyss of uncertainty that you would be absent. I dreamed a million times that you wouldn't be there when we were supposed to meet. I lost the use of my legs, my hands. There was no way out. But in the end, I took your eyes away with me."

On another occasion, she grasped another essential aspect of this process, namely reciprocity:

"I'm always really attentive to you, since I know that I can't carry you with me if you're not carrying me with you!"

The above speech fully and dramatically illustrates the fact that the therapeutic relationship is not "other than" or set apart from "real" relationships. It is rather, and in every possible sense, a real, authentic, and profoundly reciprocal relationship, even if the participants' levels of responsibility are, obviously, unequal (on this point, see Spagnuolo Lobb & Salonia, 2003).

Sometimes it takes a long time to establish belonging within the therapeutic relationship:

I never think about our meetings. My life is separate from my therapy. I didn't choose to come here. It's my symptoms that are obliging me. As far as I'm concerned, therapy is like taking medicine. I take it with an ill will. I knock it back and then try to forget about it.

Shortly, the same patient conceded:

"Therapy isn't something I carry with me, because I'm afraid to do so. I'm not a cold person, but I do my best to be one in this relationship."
Therapist: "How do you feel if you don't carry me with you?"
"I'm always alone. I have no point of reference. I'm always alone and I'm always scared."

and the therapists (mine) ! ✫

It is vital to work on the patient's evasions of therapeutic belonging in order to open the way for the construction of new relational grounds that will be able to support the subject.

Sometimes the patient's sense of belonging can follow a kind of evolutional shortcut, whereby the patient falls in love with the therapist. Panic in these cases will melt away as if by magic. The patient's love for the therapist immediately remedies the collapse of the ground, since it builds up a relational ground that constantly accompanies the patient and leads to a shift in the therapeutic focus (Salonia, 1987, p. 74). One patient who was suffering from the limitations that, in her opinion, the therapeutic relationship was imposing upon her powerful affection, exclaimed: "My anxiety has completely passed away. But sometimes I almost miss the panic attacks I used to have!"

At this juncture, the central focus of attention is no longer anxiety, but rather the regulation of distances ("I want to be with you always"), the limits of the setting ("If only we could have more time"), the authenticity of the relationship ("I bet if we'd met somewhere else you wouldn't have blinked an eyelid"), and the humiliation generated by the disparity of therapist–patient love ("I will never accept being loved as if I were a child! I don't give a damn about you as a doctor! You're a freak of nature: half man, half pill!"). The patient's love is an authentic and rich ground, which enables certain vital and creative parts of the self to emerge and to be integrated. This is a phase the evolving therapeutic relationship needs to get through and elaborate upon, as the patient's life and other relationships are gradually transformed.

The warmth of the therapeutic relationship requires particular attention when the patient has a history in which boundaries have repeatedly been confused (as is the case in borderline subjects, for example). Such cases may include complex family situations, the loss of clarity or the reversal of roles, and disturbed relationships within the family, involving parental confusion on a cognitive, emotive, or sexual level. Patients, who have been through these kinds of experiences, may be confused by the warmth that naturally develops during the therapeutic relationship. Therapeutic belonging should not be forced in such cases: It develops principally (and, in many cases, exclusively) through clarity.[1]

The following example is illuminating on this point. During a session with Isabella, a patient whose family life had been characterized by confusion and invasiveness on various levels, I felt a great deal of sympathy for her and was moved by the potency and the pain of her history. She realized this and said: "I can feel you drawing me to you and it makes me furious! It's like when you're a child and they say: 'You're so lovely I could eat you up!'"

Soon afterwards, as she continued to tell her story, she came to define

---

[1] I wish to thank Giovanni Salonia and Margherita Spagnuolo Lobb for clarifying this point by underlining the centrality of confused relational boundaries to borderline cases.

one highly relevant aspect of her experience in very clear terms. I was aware of a high degree of clarity in our dialogue. At this point, she told me: "I feel myself being drawn to you, but in the sense that you really understand what I'm saying. And that's fine by me."

Only after boundaries had been clearly established and she had come to trust that they would be respected, was this patient able to play on the regulation of distances and warmth. This was a very important step forward, inasmuch as our relationship was now ripe to provide a location for, and the words to express, warmth. This experience was of fundamental importance, insofar as it enabled the subject to combine the clarity of boundaries with her emotions and affections, absorbing the therapeutic relationship into herself and carrying it away with her.

my need for warmth before she has built in boundary (cf a desire, longing or more 'healthy' version)

3.5.4 Pharmacological Support

> *Contrary to the dictates of the advocates of simplification, there is no distinction between art and science.*
>
> (Morin, 1987)[1]

One final element of support, which needs considering, is the possibility of psychopharmacological therapy. This kind of therapy can be usefully considered as a support not only for the patient but also for the psychotherapist–patient "couple."

Pharmacological products can play an important role when the patient's symptoms are so acute that they are creating a major disruption to his or her life and especially when they are making it difficult for the patient to carry forward his or her projects. Pharmaceutical products can provide a significant level of relief very quickly and are therefore an important resource, worthy of consideration.

To generalize to the point of exaggeration, there are two diametrically opposed notions commonly held about the use of pharmacological products: The first sees them as a cure in themselves, the second as completely useless. The first of these ideas would seem to be correct, if we bear in mind the symptoms alone. Similarly, the second might be upheld if we only consider the disorder of which the symptoms are a manifestation. For a broader perspective, we need to take two phenomena into account. Firstly,

---

[1] Translated from the Italian by A. Spencer.

pharmacological therapy significantly improves the patient's symptoms. Secondly, if we rely on pharmacological therapy alone, symptoms usually reappear when the treatment is interrupted. In other words, the major limitation of pharmaceutical treatments is that they have no impact on the relational dynamics and the personal history from which panic emerges.

There is, however another risk, namely that the patient may feel so much better due to the relief offered by pharmaceutical products that he or she will see no need to go through a psychotherapeutic process that could play a vital role at that particular stage of his or her life:

> The patient's state of anxiety indicates that he or she is desperately seeking a new aim for his or her life. This existential problem is not simply a biological dysfunction, nor is it simply a question of inadequate behavior. We find ourselves facing another dimension of life, and we might therefore suspect that effective pharmacological therapy might reduce the patient's chances of solving his or her real problems. (Wulff et al., 1986. Translated from the Italian by A. Spencer)

It is therefore a fundamental task and a major responsibility of those prescribing pharmaceutical products to define and make clearly explicit both their limitations and their potential. The patient must know that panic is not just a meaningless "accident," but a pathway to be followed. To neglect this enterprise, however painful, is to run the risk of lacking the awareness necessary to steer his or her life in the right direction.

We have argued that pharmacology can provide support for the psychotherapist–patient "couple." This is because, under the right circumstances, being able to "trust" the management of symptoms to a third party (the doctor in charge of the pharmaceutical part of the treatment) can be a great relief, as therapist and patient proceed with the difficult process of the reconstruction the ground.

For this to happen, there must be a dialogue between the two professionals, medical doctor and psychotherapist, who need to have a shared vision and to be mutually respectful of their respective skills and of the boundaries between their professions. If, instead, the patient receives, even implicitly, contradictory or even directly conflicting messages, her or she may become yet more disorientated and anxious.

Pharmacological prescriptions should lie on a relational horizon that determines their meaning and has a profound impact on compliance and on the final results of therapy (for a detailed study on this point, see Argentino, 2001, p. 159).

In conclusion, in cases of panic disorder, psychotherapy and psychopharmacy working in synergy is of evident benefit to the patient, as long as the relationship between the two is clear and there is a good level of awareness of the advantages and limitations of both.

3.5.5 To Conclude

> *I will consider here the idea that therapeutic co-creation works on an improvisational basis: it cannot happen as the result of premeditated, known, schematic, and knowledgeable processes, but only when there is a person-to-person encounter, where the partners put their knowledge in the background and become instruments of the relationship itself. Improvisational co-creation demands that the partners are present and live at the contact boundary: it is similar to the sophisticated ability of the jazz player who has all the musical knowledge in her blood and is able to be fresh, strong, contactful, and unique in her playing.*
>
> (Spagnuolo Lobb, 2003)

Panic attacks are a field phenomenon. Although this phenomenon manifests itself in individual suffering, it is the expression of a relational and social fabric that is unable to provide the ground necessary to withstand the complexity of life. To read and treat panic attacks, we need a perceptive ground able to respond to this field. The patient needs to (re)build and assimilate the grounds that will support him or her. Panic attacks are a terrifying opening out onto life, a precious opportunity to restructure and give new meaning to one's personal history. The opening of a pathway towards feeling at home in the world. The therapist supports the patient through presence, creativity, and skill, by carefully balancing boundaries with warmth, by instilling faith in the potency of the encounter. The therapist, too, must be rooted in his or her own ground of assimilated networks of belonging and open to the novelty and creativity of the polis.

He or she must therefore command many resources: The capacity to knowingly touch upon the anxiety that is a constituent part of being, to support it through the settled ground of assimilated contacts from his or her own history, and to creatively transform it through an opening out towards life and towards the other, in a new and continuous co-creation of experience and meaning.

Yet these resources are anchored in their turn in the network of nourishing relationships that support the therapist in his or her caring role.

The limitations of an individualistic vision and of a purely "technical" approach, which does nothing to nourish belonging, is that it leaves the therapist alone. Without this support, the therapist remains breathless and disorientated in the face of such overwhelming symptoms.

Now, more than ever, it is essential to view clinical phenomena as a personal figure that emerges against a collective ground. Having passed beyond the euphoria and blindness of the narcissistic era, we therapists can finally come to realize that we should not only consider the patient as an isolated individual. We should also bear in mind the whole fabric of relationships in which he or she is immersed—a living, breathing network that nourishes the patient and in which we will inevitably come to participate.

Even though, as Gestalt psychotherapy has always emphasized, this has been true in every historical moment for every patient, it is nonetheless more evident than ever today, in this period of fragmentation, chaos. and, indeed, panic itself, these "acute attacks of solitude," in which the unbearable inconsistency of the individual's various connections becomes devastatingly apparent.

References

American Psychiatric Association. (1994). *Diagnostic and statistical manual of mental disorders* (4th ed.). Washington, DC: American Psychiatric Association.

Amering, M., & Katschning, H. (1990). Panic attacks and disorders in cross-cultural perspective. *Psychiatric Annals, 20*(9), 511–516.

Argentino, P. (2001). Psicofarmacoterapia gestaltica [Gestalt psychopharmacotherapy]. In M. Spagnuolo Lobb (Ed.), *Psicoterapia della Gestalt. Ermeneutica e clinica* (pp. 159–179). Milan: Angeli.

Arnol'd, V. I. (Ed.). (1994). *Bifurcation theory and catastrophe theory.* Berlin & London: Springer.

Ballerini, A., & Callieri, B. (Eds.). (1996). *Breviario di psicopatologia. La dimensione umana della sofferenza mentale* [A breviary of psychopathology: The human dimension of mental suffering]. Milan: Feltrinelli.

Benasayag, M., & Schmit, G. (2006). *Les passions tristes: Souffrance psychique et crise sociale* [The sad passions: Psychic sufferance and social crisis]. Paris: Editions La Découverte.

Borgna, E. (1989). *I conflitti del conoscere* [The conflicts of knowledge]. Milan: Feltrinelli.

Borgna, E. (1995). *Come se finisse il mondo* [As if the world was ending]. Milan: Feltrinelli.

Borgna, E. (1997). *Le figure dell'ansia* [The figures of anxiety]. Milan: Feltrinelli.

Castaneda, C. (1972). *Journey to Ixtlan: The lessons of Don Juan.* New York: Simon and Schuster.

Cavaleri, P. (2003). *La profondità della superficie* [The depth of surfaces]. Milan: Angeli.

Frank, R. (2001). *Body of awareness: A somatic and developmental approach to psychotherapy.* Cambridge, MA: GestaltPress.

Franta, H., & Salonia, G. (1981). *Comunicazione interpersonale. Teoria e pratica* [Interpersonal communication: Theory and practice]. Rome: Las.

Galimberti, U. (1991). *Psichiatria e fenomenologia* [Psychiatry and phenomenology]. Milan: Feltrinelli.

Galimberti, U. (2004, June 1). Noi, malati di tristezza [We, sufferers from sadness]. *La Repubblica,* p. 37.

Gerdes, T., Yates, W.R., & Clancy, G. (1995). Increasing identification and referral of panic disorder over the past decade. *Psychosomatics, 36*(5), 480–486.

Giordano, G. (1997). *La casa vissuta* [The experienced house]. Milan: Giuffrè.

Goodman, P. (1959). *The empire city.* Indianapolis, IN: Bobbs-Merrill.

Goodman, P. (1968). Growing up. In P. D. Pursglove (Ed.), *Recognitions in Gestalt therapy* (pp. 107–111). New York: Funk & Wagnalls.

Heidegger, M. (1962). *Being and time* (J. Macquarrie & E. Robinson, Trans.). London: SCM Press. (Original work published 1927)

Hikmet, N. (1995). *Poesie d'amore* [Love poetry]. Milan: Mondadori.

Hinton, D., Um, K., & Ba, P. (2001). A unique panic-disorder presentation among Khmer refugees: The sore-neck syndrome. *Culture, Medicine, and Psychiatry, 25*(3), 297–316.

Hoeg, P. (1996). *I quasi adatti* [Borderliners] (B. Berni, Trans.). Milan: Modadori.

Kepner, J. I. (1987). *Body process: A Gestalt approach.* Cleveland, OH: Gestalt Institute of Cleveland Press.

Laborit, H. (1986). *L'inhibition de l'action: Biologie comportementale et physio-pathologie* [The inhibition of the action: Behavioral biology and physiopathology] (2nd ed.). Paris: Masson.

Lasch, C. (1978). *The culture of narcissism: American life in an age of diminishing expectations.* New York: Norton.

Lowen, A. (1975). *Bioenergetics.* New York: Coward, McCann, & Geoghegan.

Luhmann, N. (1979). *Trust and power: Two works by Niklas Luhmann* (H. Davis, J. Raffan, & K. Rooney, Trans.). Chichester & New York: Wiley. (Original works published 1973 and 1975)

Majrouh, S. B. (1995). *Il viandante di mezzanotte* [The Midnight wayfarer]. Milan: Luni Editrice.

Merini, A. (1998). *Fiore di poesia* [The flowers of poetry]. Turin: Einaudi.

Muñoz Molina, A. (2002). *Sefarad: un romanzo di romanzi* [Sefarad: A novel of novels] (M. Nicola & C. Stella, Trans.). Milan: Mondadori.

Morin, E. (1987). Le vie della complessità [The ways of complexity]. In G. Bocchi & M. Ceruti (Eds.), *La sfida della complessità* (pp. 49–60). Milan: Feltrinelli.

Moustakas, C. (1994). *Phenomenological research methods.* Thousand Oaks, CA: Sage.

Nardone, G. (1993). *Paura, panico, fobie* [Fear, panic, and phobias]. Florence: Ponte alle Grazie.

Nardone, G., & Watzlawick, P. (2005). *Brief strategic therapy: Philosophy, techniques, and research.* Lanham, MD: Jason Aronson.

Pavan, L. (2002). *L'identità fra continuità e cambiamento. Psicopatologia dell'attacco di panico e delle psicosi acute* [Identity between continuity and change: The psychopathology of panic attacks and acute psychoses]. Milan: Angeli.

Perls, F. (1969). *Ego, hunger, and aggression: The beginning of Gestalt therapy.* New York: Random House. (Original work published 1942)

Perls, F., Hefferline, R., & Goodman, P. (1994). *Gestalt therapy: Excitement and growth in the human personality.* Gouldsboro, ME: The Gestalt Journal Press. (Original work published 1951)

Perls, L. (1968). Two instances of Gestalt therapy. In P. D. Pursglove (Ed.), *Recognitions in Gestalt therapy* (pp. 42–63). New York: Funk & Wagnalls.

Polster, E., & Polster, M. (1973). *Gestalt therapy integrated: Contours of theory and practice.* New York: Brunner/Mazel.

Polster, E. (1987). *Every person's life is worth a novel.* New York: Norton.

Pursglove, P. D. (Ed.). (1968). *Recognitions in Gestalt therapy.* New York: Funk & Wagnalls.

Rovetto, F. (2003). *Panico* [Panic]. Milan: The McGraw-Hill Companies.

Salonia, G. (1987). L'innamoramento come terapia e la terapia come innamoramento [Falling in love as therapy and therapy as falling in love]. *Quaderni di Gestalt, 4,* 74–99.

Salonia, G. (1989). Tempi e modi di contatto [Times and modalities of contact]. *Quaderni di Gestalt, 8–9,* 55–64.

Salonia, G. (1992). Tempo e relazione. L'intenzionalità relazionale come orizzonte ermeneutico della Gestalt Terapia. *Quaderni di Gestalt, 14,* 7–21 (Successively published 1993 as Time and relation: Relational deliberateness as hermeneutic horizon in Gestalt therapy. *Studies in Gestalt Therapy, 1,* 7–19)

Salonia, G. (1999). Dialogare nel tempo della frammentazione [Dialogue in the time of fragmentation]. In F. Armetta & M. Naro (Eds.), *Impense adlaboravit. Scritti in onore del Card. Salvatore Pappalardo* (pp. 571–585). Palermo: Facoltà Teologica di Sicilia.

Salonia, G. (2000). La criminalità giovanile fra vecchie e nuove regole: Verso l'integrazione dello straniero nella *polis* [Juvenile delinquency between old and new rules: Towards the integration of the foreigner into the *polis*]. *Quaderni di Gestalt, 30/31*, 100–109.

Sampognaro, G. (2000). *Mille mondi* [A thousand worlds]. Verona: Positive Press.

Schmidt, L. J., & Warner, B. (Eds.). (2002). *Panic: Origins, insight, and treatment*. Berkeley, CA: North Atlantic Books.

Spagnuolo Lobb, M. (1990). Il sostegno specifico nelle interruzioni di contatto. *Quaderni di Gestalt, 10–11*, 13–24. (Successively published 1993 as Specific support in the interruption of contact. *Studies in Gestalt Therapy, 1*, 43–51)

Spagnuolo Lobb, M. (Ed.). (2001a). *Psicoterapia della Gestalt. Ermeneutica e clinica* [Gestalt psychotherapy: Hermeutics and clinical practice]. Milan: Angeli.

Spagnuolo Lobb, M. (2001b). La teoria del sè in psicoterapia della Gestalt [The Theory of self in Gestalt Therapy]. In M. Spagnuolo Lobb (Ed.), *Psicoterapia della Gestalt. Ermeneutica e clinica* (pp. 86–110). Milan: Angeli.

Spagnolo Lobb, M. (2003). Therapeutic meeting as improvisational co-creation. In M. Spagnuolo Lobb & N. Amendt-Lyon (Eds.), *Creative license: The art of Gestalt Therapy* (pp. 37–49). Vienna & New York: Springer.

Spagnuolo Lobb M., & Amendt-Lyon, N. (Eds.). (2003). *Creative license: The art of Gestalt therapy*. Vienna & New York: Springer.

Spagnuolo Lobb, M., & Salonia, G. (1986). Al di là della sedia vuota: un modello di coterapia [Beyond the empty Chair: A model for co-therapy]. *Quaderni di Gestalt, 3*, 11–35.

Spagnuolo Lobb, M., & Salonia, G. (2003). Presentazione [Preface]. In P. Cavaleri, *La profondità della superficie* (pp. 9–13). Milan: Angeli.

Wulff, H. R., Pedersen, S. A., & Rosenberg, R. (1986). *Philosophy of medicine: An introduction*. Oxford: Blackwell Scientific.

Yanez, C. (1998). *Paesaggio di luna fredda* [Cold moon landscape]. Parma: Guanda.

4. The Words of One Who Asked for Help

by Cristiana Filippi and Michela Gecele[*]

4.1 Preface

What follows is a somewhat revised and corrected version of the feelings and thoughts, which I vented in writing shortly after my first experience in psychotherapy. *I had interrupted my therapy (after four months of biweekly sessions) because I felt that it was useless and, sometimes, even counterproductive.*

I had sought specific help about a year after I had begun suffering from symptoms of general and sometimes acute anxiety, with two or three episodes that came very close to spiraling into a panic attack.[1] After various

---

[*] The first three paragraphs of this chapter, written by Cristiana Filippi, are an account of her experiences when she sought help for panic attack disorder.

We wished to include the testimony of someone who had suffered from panic attacks and who had gone through psychotherapy in order to give some space to those who occupy the other part of the therapeutic field. This voice has as much right to be heard as any other in this volume, since it provides us at once with feedback on, and an interrogation of, the therapeutic relationship—an "other" voice for both the therapist and the therapeutic relationship. From another point of view, considering that this text was not written for therapists alone, this testimony may prove a useful point of confrontation and support for those about to begin, thinking of beginning, or who are already in the course of, a therapeutic relationship.

We have not included these reflections with the intention of upsetting the balance of the therapeutic relationship by overindulging and giving too much space to the expectations and the needs of the patient as opposed to the role and the skills of the therapist. Our intention was merely to fully bring out all of the resources present in the relational field.

This introduction, the final paragraph and all the notes on the text (except for those explicitly attributed to Cristiana) were written by Michela Gecele.

[1] (Note by Cristiana) For what it may be worth, here follows a brief summary of the events and changes which had characterized my life during the 12 months (before and after

attempts at *self-analysis* and *self-therapy*—during which I sought out support and comfort from friends and family, read various texts on the subject, conducted web-based research, joined a mailing list, and a forum for people suffering from panic attack disorder (PAD), depression, and obsessive–compulsive disorder (OCD), in addition to dabbling with tranquillizers—I had finally decided that the moment had come to seek out specialist help.

Unfortunately, the 40 or so psychotherapy sessions that I had experienced up to that point had not produced the effects I had been hoping for. So, a few months later, before starting up again with another therapeutic experience, which would this time prove fruitful (see the epilogue), I sought to shed some light on *what had gone wrong*, in part so as to prepare myself for the possibility of trying again. I came to the conclusion that this "failure" did not stem alone from the fact that there was not much "feeling" between the therapist and myself. Therapy had also been impeded by the existence of a kind of reciprocal misunderstanding (resulting, I believe, both from my inability to express myself and from my therapist's inability—or so I felt—to *draw me out*) as to *the primary needs and expectations which should, in my opinion derived from my direct experience, be cultivated and drawn out, in such a way as to instill a productive and trustful relationship.*

My intention now, without any pretence, is simply to provide professionals with the point of view (and the initial expectations) of someone who, suffering from acute anxiety or PAD, sought the help of a psychotherapist. I ask forgiveness, in advance, for the anger that still comes across sharply in what I have written and that I have deliberately avoided "filing

---

the emergence of my psychic disorder) between my 34th and 35th year of life: Preparation of my master's thesis (September 1999), a trip to the United States and Canada (October 1999). During that holiday, I followed a course of antibiotics for an acute dental abscess, which led to physical weakness and fainting fits. On the return trip from the holiday: Alone on the plane, suffering since the previous day from dizziness and vertigo (later diagnosed as the consequence of cervicalgia). Upon returning to Italy, I received news of a recent death of a close family member (an aunt). Little possibility, therefore, of receiving sympathy for my own anxieties and fears. A series of medical examinations seeking to ascertain the cause of my sense of vertigo (with the temporary diagnosis of a more serious illness, which proved inexact, but led to closer and more serious diagnostic examination). Beginning of a two-year part-time contract as a grant-recipient (November 1999). Completion and consignment of master'sthesis (December 1999). House-hunting and marriage-planning. Choice of house and furniture. Completion of academic degree (January–February, 2000). Another death in the family—a cousin (April 2000). Final preparations for marriage (Spring, 2000) and marriage itself (June, 2000). Living in temporary accommodation while waiting for house to become available (June–October, 2000).

down." This is not just because the anger was a constituent and authentic presence in my state of mind when I first poured out these words, but also because I still feel the need to recognize the legitimacy of that anger today. It is indeed partly due to these feelings of anger that I have been spurred on to continue seeking out the means to attain to a more balanced state and an increased level of well-being. Here, then, are my reflections, divided up under a number of key headings, just as I originally scribbled them down, imagining that I was writing an "open letter" to my psychotherapist. The actions that followed were the fruit of that expressive act. In the epilogue to this chapter, I will return to my present condition, including a few considerations on my second psychotherapeutic experience.

4.2 Letter to My Therapist
(Three Months After the End of My First Period of Psychotherapy)

4.2.1 What Happened to the Reassurance and Satisfaction That I Was Expecting?

Three months have passed since our last meeting and I have realized that, perhaps because I am still unwell, I often find myself recalling our sessions and trying to understand what mistakes we had made, what went wrong and why, and who might be to blame?

First of all, what most often springs to my mind are the understanding and sympathy I felt were lacking on your part.

The first thing I expected from psychotherapy (and I have since been able to verify that this expectation is common to many patients suffering from acute and generalized anxiety and panic attacks) was a *site* of reassurance, welcoming, and sympathy, which would be able to contain and manage *the waves of anxiety that swept over me*. In other words, a place that would calm me and help me to trust in the fact that I would be first supported in overcoming what I was going through. I realize such a powerful request for trust and support must be terrible for a psychotherapist who, perhaps, wishes to avoid being treated as an emotional crutch, and who does not want the patient to develop an excessive degree of dependency on him or her.[1] I would suggest that, in order to fully understand the kind of

[1] From the point of view of the clinical classification system outlined above, the experiences described by Cristiana in this last sentence could indeed be described as retroflective. We might, however, view them in another light, considering the relational beauty of the em-

request being put forward, the therapist should view anxious patients—and especially patients suffering from panic attacks—as children, inasmuch as, like children, they are unable to make full use of the intellectual and cognitive tools at their disposal at this particular stage of their lives. Instead, they employ these faculties in a mistaken manner so that, instead of calming and containing the powerful and irrational fears they are experiencing, they tend to magnify them. I feel qualified to posit this suggestion on the basis of the many testimonies I have gathered (on the internet, in books, and in conversation with friends), as I sought to find common ground with others so that I might face up to and share the distress I was experiencing and to avoid feeling too *different*. Amongst these testimonies, I found the following useful summary that mirrored my own experience:

> I have been very much changed over these last two and a half years. My whole life has changed, as if I had gone back to being a child. I need to know that there's someone always at my side, on whom I can rely. In moments of acute crisis, I have the same terror in my eyes as a child who has just awoken from a nightmare. This happens when a child is afraid of something that is new and unknown. I just about manage not to collapse into a sobbing and desolate heap, but I feel my heart beating fast and I'm short of breath. I undergo a terrible anxiety that I'm going to fall down into an abyss.

Like a child, I too felt that I needed a trustworthy *adult* at my side, someone who would be able to take my hand and lead me, gradually, away from my current state of bewilderment and towards a greater level of awareness. In addition to all this, people suffering from anxiety know that there should be a logical explanation for what they are going through, which should calm them down, but they also realize that they are unable to identify and take advantage of this explanation. They realize they cannot convince themselves of the efficacy of such a solution alone. Their fears are thus augmented and tend to include the fear of going mad and not being able to cope and react as they once did.

Another testimony:

> At 31 years of age, I am no longer able to be the strong person I always used to be, an unstoppable young woman, with a solution to every

pathetic attitude towards her therapist, who is viewed above all as "another human being," both at the moment of their meeting and in its aftermath.

141

problem. Now, I always need someone to hold my hand: my husband, my mother, some charitable friend ... I feel bewildered and unable to cope with things if nobody helps me. I need frequent encouragement. I always ask the same questions, so as to always receive the same answers. I feel like a broken record, going on and on forever—just like my nephew used to be, when he was only three! But now that he's eight, he goes out on his own to buy bread, while I don't feel capable of doing anything anymore. I'm scared to leave the house, to go to the cinema or the supermarket, to walk the streets... . I'd like to have a child, but how can I possibly take on the role of mother when I'm stuck being a little girl? How can I take care of someone else when I feel as if, once again, I myself need to be taken care of and fussed over?

This general sense of bewilderment is exacerbated by the sensation of not recognizing yourself any more—of perceiving yourself as changed, impotent, unable to face up to even the most everyday aspects of life. I was never particularly courageous, but I was not particularly disturbed at having to fly (the limited kind of fear that I did feel was surely common to many people). I drove a car by myself, by day and by night, in the city and cross-country. I felt calm about doing things by myself. In contrast, now—although I try really hard not to let it bring me to a halt—a lot of situations scare me and I face them, despite myself, in a state of anxiety, which eventually wears me right down. In my case, it is not so much a question of the fear of dying as it is the fear of suffering (and I think this distinction is fundamental). Nearing desperation, my ever more catastrophic thoughts crowd in on me, and nothing seems able to calm me. It is purely, almost tangibly, anxiety.

The pain resembles a terrible oppression, a purely cerebral kind of pain, an unjustified sense of bereavement accompanied by an inconsolable sadness. A sense of infinite loss: The loss of the part of me that was once strong, active, and able.

I had already sought out explanations for this disorder by myself—by attributing the causes of my ill-being to significant changes in my recent life. Namely, I had to cope with: Finishing my studies at 35 years of age (having thereby spent 80% of my life to date studying); not knowing if the final results of all my toils would enable me to find a suitable job; preparing to begin life as a couple (with no previous experience of living as a couple); leaving home (with a certain sense that I was *abandoning* my parents, who were already elderly); moving house (to a different area and thus having to update all my paperwork), away from the house where I had been born and where I had spent all my life. Despite desiring these changes and their undoubted positive aspects, I believed (and continue to believe) that all of these circumstances were possible sources of stress. I sought confirmation of this on the Holmes–Rahe scale, which I had found in several psychology textbooks. And when I started my sessions with you I thought, upon referring this information to you, that you would support me in this and share this experience with me, at least in the most general sense. But you just could not *acknowledge and respect my point of view*. Indeed, I remember that you almost "told me off," advising me against either consulting further books during our period of therapeutic consultation, or leaping to overhasty conclusions by myself.[1]

What I needed to find, first of all, were reassurances and support, even though, at the same time, my awareness of this need irritated and frightened me (see note 1). This is why, although asking for help, I was worried by the idea that I did not know for how long I would be needing such assistance. For this reason—although I knew that nobody, including you, could really tell me "look, you will only require so many sessions"—I needed to believe that the support, which was so essential for me at that moment, would be drawn out only as long as it was *absolutely, strictly necessary*. At the time, I felt the same fear of dependency and the loss of self-sufficiency with regard to psychotherapy as I had felt towards pharmacological treatment, which I was seeking to avoid. I was frightened that such relief as this kind of treatment could afford would disappear as soon as I stopped taking the medicine.

It was not so much that I did not want to trust in you. It was rather that I needed to learn to believe in myself once more.

4.2.2 The Examination

Another constant factor in our meetings, often accompanied by a certain degree of anger, was my experience of feeling that I was taking an exam: that I had to perform certain tasks I was unable to perform. Indeed, I went

---

[1] Reading these and other statements leads me, as a therapist, to ask myself what we can possibly "draw" from the experience narrated to us, without, to this end, accepting the patient's anger and criticism towards my colleague as a pertinent evaluation. This chapter should be an opportunity to explore at length what happens during therapeutic sessions, giving weight to the patient's experiences (even when they result in criticism of our own professional practice) without taking it as the only measure of the therapist's skills and of therapeutic progress.

to almost every meeting, not with curiosity, interest, or positive expectations, but rather with a sense of apprehension and anxiety which accumulated until they were not dissimilar to the anxiety for which I had sought psychotherapeutic assistance in the first place. My experience was "scholastic" in nature. The emotions aroused in the course of my psychotherapeutic sessions were similar to those I experienced at school: My worries that I would not know where to begin and where I would end up when I had to speak. This led me, foolishly, to try to draw up an introduction prior to the sessions, as I was walking to your office. My long silences echoed your equally silent air of expectancy. I lived through those moments like an unprepared student who has run out of things to say during an oral exam. My inability to produce dreams led me to feel, upon perceiving your disappointment, that I was somehow, on an unconscious level, refusing to participate and contribute.

I underlined these points to you on several occasions, but I realize only now that my sense of "failure" did not only stay with me, but contributed to the preexistent sense of *being blocked* of which I was already victim. With your comments and silences, together with a behavior I perceived as a "snub," you intensified the sense of ill-being and failure which I was already going through on my own account, further diminishing my self-esteem. I can still hear your exhortations of "So?"; "Come on—pull yourself together!"; "Is it really possible that nothing is coming into your mind?"; "Finally, we are getting somewhere!"; and so on, echoing in my mind. I still recall my sense of impotence, inadequacy, frustration, and guilt. I already felt guilty because I viewed myself as being someone who was not able to cooperate, who perhaps did not even want to cooperate, who was not even willing to make an effort for her own good. I can guarantee to you that all this is very oppressive, and especially so in the cases of those who suffer from internal conflicts but feel unable to express themselves with awareness and clarity. And it is for this very reason that, in such cases, one goes to a psychotherapist in the first case: Because it should provide clarity, help you to know yourself, to bring out what is making you suffer, to pull that which is hurting you to the surface.

Perhaps you wanted to spur me on? Perhaps you wanted to "pick away at me" and draw out a reaction? All this may indeed be, but the only long-term effect was to make me want to give up the sessions. You just cannot expect somebody who, at that particular moment of his or her life, is unable to work, who cannot apply him- or herself, and who is experiencing irrational fears, to be able to cope with certain things. It is absolutely necessary to provide constructive stimuli and certain starting points, instead of assuming (or appearing to assume) prematurely that the patient can cope by him- or herself—to leave them with the incredible burden of *abandonment*.[1]

Also this I asked of you. I told you that I could not manage on my own. However, instead of helping me to melt down the obstacles you yourself had outlined to me, you simply threw it at me, as if it was none of your business. As a consequence, I not only felt even more trapped in the prison of my own mental block, of my own limitations, but I also felt increasingly culpable for this fact.

Even now that several weeks have passed, I still believe that I made the best decision, even though it did nothing to resolve my problems of anxiety and anguish. The only positive thing I can see in the whole experience has been my capacity to "listen to my sensations, my experiences, my intuitions, and my reflections." Notwithstanding your attempts to discourage me from abandoning my therapy, because it would be a bad choice and could have negative consequences (ah! the sense of menace and foreboding which came across in your words), and notwithstanding your willingness to keep an open door for me if I ever changed my mind, I instead trusted my own sense that interrupting the sessions was the right choice for me.

If, as is probably the case, one of the causes or components of my states of anxiety lies in the generic "fear of performance," I think it would have been better if you had borne this in mind right from the beginning, so as to avoid further exacerbating the problem.

4.2.3 The Half Full Glass

Another fairly obvious observation I would like to make concerns my need to sense your capacity to appreciate my abilities and skills, which, in that moment of crisis, I was unable to recognize by myself. If, as I have learned through my research into the topic, the anxious person suffers, amongst other things, from insecurity and low self-esteem, one of the therapist's tasks, above all at the beginning of the treatment, consists in making the patient aware of his or her positive qualities.

It is very improbable that an individual will be completely devoid of

---

[1] As I will suggest in more detail in my closing comments, whilst valuing and welcoming Cristiana's comments, I cannot but underline the fact that the very manner in which she herself closed the therapeutic relationship suggests that therapy was of some support to her. It supported her in her very need to close the relationship (or, at least, it did not impede her). It supported her in her capacity to "look elsewhere," to identify a better direction in which to proceed.

abilities, however he or she may feel that to be the case during moments of anxiety. It is therefore necessary, partly in order to gain the patient's trust, to break through the barrier of this insecurity, showing faith in their abilities. This will, in addition to its long-term effectiveness, have an immediate effect on the unpleasant sense of impotency the subject is experiencing (nay, suffering). This will serve, on the one hand, to break the vicious circle that is carrying the person into an ever deeper state of demoralization and depression and, on the other, as a therapeutic agent in itself *hic et nunc*.

This component was lacking in my therapeutic experience, even though I sought on many occasions, perhaps mistakenly, to make you aware of my need. My request that you should help me learn to see the *glass as half full* went unheard and undervalued. This discouraged me yet further and intensified my sense of oppression. When I go back over our time together I am still unable to identify any valid attempts on your part to deal with this need. There was only one occasion when you *really tried*. This was during a session in which I was describing and recounting examples to illustrate my *happy and playful side*. However, even on this occasion I did not come away without a certain sense of reproach. I can remember feeling abandoned and reproached by a sarcastic comment on your part immediately afterwards, which can be summed up as followed: "Thank God for that! I thought you would never stop whining!" This, I must say, completely ruined the positive and therapeutic effect that I could have gained from the exchange. Not only were neither your tone nor your expression constructive, but you also muttered a rather mean comment: "Can you only manage to be cheerful when you're drunk?" These were your very words when I told you about my "wild nights out" with my friends.

What you could (if not necessarily what you should) have said, sweetly but firmly, was something like the following: "I was sure that you had a joyful and cheerful side, capable of being positive about things. I am really pleased that you, too, as you describe these episodes to me, cannot only remember them, but you can also be aware of them and consider them as a treasure from which you need to draw more often. It reflects well on you."

4.2.4 Symptoms

Symptoms. Do you remember them? I do not imagine you remember my particular symptoms very well. I described them to you the first time we met, trying to let you know what I was going through physically and psychologically. You listened for a little while, but soon interrupted me, telling me you did not think it was useful to dwell on them. You argued that there is not always an obvious correspondence between a particular symptom and its cause. Despite believing that, in reality, the mind often expresses itself through the body (and that is hardly surprising), at first this seemed to me to be a reasonable belief that I could share. This was partly because I saw this attitude as a means of shifting attention away from the physical detail that tends to obsess individuals suffering from acute anxiety attacks. It was clear to me that you were not following the practice adopted by many other specialists who seek to "deconstruct" the symptom. That was fine with me, or so I thought, above all because I had already attained to a good level of awareness that my physical symptoms did not derive from organic causes I needed to worry about, nor would it be impossible to eliminate them in what I hoped would be the near future. What I was not yet ready to accept were the symptoms themselves—their power over my psychoemotional state, their inevitability. In short, my big problem was that I was neither able to control nor, most importantly, prevent my symptoms. My conviction and faith in your approach were consequently short-lived. I still had an urgent need to describe and discuss my symptoms. I needed to express them a little more in order to confront them and be reassured that they were common to patients suffering from this kind of psychic disorder.

Often, in fact, like many patients suffering from PAD, depression, and OCD, I found myself asking friends and relations for reassurances or comparisons, beginning always with the words "But does the same thing happen to you?" or "Have you ever?" If this was not enough (and it rarely was), I went in search of documentation in books and online, reading long lists of symptoms associated with specific disorders so as to identify what was happening to me—so as not to feel like some kind of alien. Often none of this was enough. The descriptions and the lists, however long, could never provide a satisfactory description, could never fully capture the symptoms that emerged so suddenly. There were only generic states of tension, alert, pins and needles, and so forth.

What you rarely find in specialist, scientific descriptions are concrete examples presented by those who experience the symptom or sensation firsthand. You then lose yourself in an internet quest and the different documentation available. And you learn that pins and needles are not limited to the hands, but they can also be experienced in the lips or the tongue. You discover a description of a state of tension which resembles your own when you drive a car through the fog—the sense of disorientation, the fear of fainting, or being somehow lessened, as "your ankles feel as if they were tied and you feel everything give way. The feeling is so overwhelming that you have trouble staying on your feet, that you have to struggle to stay in touch with the world." Someone else writes that

> For a full two years my life has been a "nonlife." I now live only in the fear of suffering from serious illnesses. I have been suffering from a burning sensation on my tongue accompanied by nausea and vomiting for several months now. They tell me that it's a nervous problem, but I'm still stuck here, inert, unable to live and to think. It's some time since I've left the house or been able to work. I feel weak, powerless, susceptible to colds and bronchitis. Yet nothing came up during my clinical examinations. On Friday I'll undergo yet another mortifying trip to a gastroenterologist, who I know for sure will never be able to solve my problems with my tongue and my stomach. And I'll come back feeling even more depressed and discouraged than before, even less able to take control of my life. At 29 years of age I've gone back to being a child who measures time by meals and nightly sleep. Or rather, I feel like an old lady, with all the weight of experience on her shoulders.

Another person writes that they had also undergone a Holter and three ECGs, which found no trace of any anomaly. Yet I can empathize with this man—I really understand what he was going through. And what about the sense of your head being empty, that it is spinning? What can you possibly do about the palpitations in your vision which you experience even in moments of relative tranquility? And the fear does not go away even when you are in a peaceful state. It derives from anxiety and worry. That is why it can happen even when you are relaxed? And your head spins? It scares you because you are worried you might faint from one moment to the next. And this fear increases your anxiety and makes your head spin even more.

There are those who seek to provide themselves with explanations:

> What does my dizziness depend on? I tried with all my might to find an explanation, trying to imagine myself overloaded with work all day (as is often the case) and every day, without a break. Imagine what it is like when the thought of all this work never leaves you in peace. It is an important job on which your future depends ... Your mind is concentrated on that alone. No holidays, no distractions ... Night and day. After a few days, wouldn't your head spin? Of course it would! And doesn't anxiety do exactly the same thing, making us concentrate on a single, obsessive thought, without breaks or interruptions? ... Doesn't

this thought keep telling you that the worst could happen at any time? Your brain responds to this hyperstimulation. It gets tired and you find yourself with your mind suddenly "emptied out," devoid of energy.

This bloody anxiety never lets up. It depends on many factors, amongst which there are surely fear, feeling fragile, and worry about losing control. I knew that talking about it at every single session would have been useless, leading to a single-minded fixation with the physical manifestations of my condition. I was aware of this, but I still needed a bit of time (the first few sessions at least) to find a way to "banish" them from myself and to listen to them being narrated back to me. In that way, I could already have begun with you the process I am only just starting now—to realize of my own accord to what extent my symptoms were (and still are) derived from my thoughts alone and exaggerated to an almost comic extent. I needed to know—nay, I needed *to hear someone tell me*—that also "normal" people have unpleasant physical sensations (and surely I had done so in the past) without attaching such weight and importance to them. They manage to live through these situations and overcome them without getting so scared.

4.2.5 The Past, in Search of a Lost Cause

You wanted us to *go searching* in my past ... You wanted me to get angry with you so as to bring out the anger of my past. You wanted me to be made brutally aware of the mistakes I had made and the pain I had suffered, perhaps stemming from my parents. Yet I told you right from the beginning that I was scared, and continue to be scared of discovering who knows what—of unearthing some past *monster* inside of me. I was scared of having made some irreparable mistake. I was scared of being devastated at the discovery of a Cristiana too far removed from the person I knew—of finding a mother and a father who were lacking in affection for me, who were ever absent, or in some way different from the ideal I had built up around them, and which, as I have now realized with a considerable degree of sadness, was divorced from reality.

It is clear that there are going to be some more or less unconscious causes at the root of any series of panic attacks or of general anxiety disorder. My point is that whilst, on the one hand, it can "calm" the patient to know that there is some repressed cause of the symptoms being expressed through the body (as many sufferers from panic attacks often point out: "The soul and the psyche speak through the body"), which can reduce his

149

or her suffering once it has been brought to the surface, on the other hand, there can be a great fear (as there was in my case) of discovering whatever it is that has been repressed. The very fact that it has been repressed makes you doubt whether you really want to discover it.

Of course, in most cases there is nothing too monstrous lurking in the past of those suffering from anxiety and panic attacks. However, to arrive at the truth you need to have already attained a level of tranquility at which, with time, your desire, curiosity and, above all, your serenity and strength to deal with the "dark side" will begin to emerge.

4.3 Epilogue

I took another look at my writing, exactly three years after the end of my first psychotherapeutic experience (and about two years after the end of my second). Now, as I await the birth of my second child (and am again forced to take a break), I feel much stronger, although perhaps not as much as I could be, and sure of my own potential.[1]

Five months after the last session with my first psychotherapist, I met a new therapist with whom I worked for about nine months. We met once a week for two hours. This was because, to get to and from the sessions, I had to make a train journey of about four hours. A different school of psychotherapy, a natural empathy, and having been able to express my own reflections on my previous therapeutic experience during the first sessions made it possible for me to enjoy and benefit from these sessions.

First of all, I felt right from the beginning that this psychotherapist understood and was *receptive* to me. Not only did she give me the impression of being a *safe place* for me herself, but even her office, which I always visited in the morning, seemed warmer, more *human*, and full of light (whilst the office where I had attended my late afternoon sessions with the other therapist had been a cold and "ascetic" room inside a public institution).[2]

---

[1] (Note by Cristiana) In the intervening period of time, my life has undergone some further changes. I had a miscarriage during the 8th week of my first pregnancy (August 2001), but successfully gave birth to my first daughter, Martina, about a year later (July 2002). I left my job (after a few disappointments—October 2001) and found a part-time job as a consultant (which did not really satisfy my expectations or reflect my qualifications). I had to deal with my father falling ill (June 2003) and his death a few months later (October 2003). I have now found a new professional solution, which will enable me to stay closer to and look after my mother, who is almost 80. As I have already said, I am now expecting my second child.

[2] (Note by Cristiana) Although this might seem like a rather frivolous detail, I felt that it

Neither in this series of sessions were any promises made *that I would be cured, nor was I given any guarantee that my condition would improve after a total number of sessions.* However, I felt that this therapist was somehow more receptive to, and less dismissive of, my need, in some way, to *establish temporal boundaries around the process.* All of this was so effective that, at the end of this series of sessions, which I was forced to interrupt because of my pregnancy, I was really sorry to end the therapy, which I was increasingly *keen to pursue.* I had been reassured that there were no monsters lurking in my past from which I was seeking to escape. In the most natural and simple of manners, I was provided with the tools I needed to attain awareness of, and to reflect on, the relationships in my family (without being scared that the behavior of my parents and my brother would come under criticism) and on my own way of relating to events and changes in my life. Moreover, I must say that the tranquility with which I was able to face up to all of this derived in part, if not principally, from the prompts with which my psychotherapist was able to provide me. I always felt that she understood and shared in what I was going through, without needing to hear her explicitly tell me "I've been through that, too," or "I know what you're talking about, because I know the subject and some of my other patients have described similar experiences to me." First of all, it was useful for me to hear from her lips that it could be "normal to experience these kinds of disturbances during certain moments of transition in your life" and that such episodes often take place when "the emotions, which move at a snail's pace, need their own time to adapt to these kinds of changes." In this way, I felt that she shared[1] my opinions as to the causes of the ill-being by which I had been so suddenly afflicted.

As in my first period of therapy, I was unable to bring more than two or

---

was noteworthy in my case as it has always been very important to me to have places I could call *home, nest,* or *refuge* and because it is easier to feel at ease and, therefore, to be more open and uninhibited. Far be it from me to criticize or make suggestions about the interior design of a psychotherapist's office. I nonetheless feel that it is worth underlining the following small, but significant difference between my two psychotherapeutic experiences: During the previous series of sessions, the psychotherapist sat behind a desk on the other side of which I sat, on an ordinary chair. I believe that this may have been another factor contributing to my sense of being back at school during the sessions. During my second therapeutic relationship, instead, the professional therapist and I were positioned in a manner that gave a sense of greater *equality*. We both sat on armchairs, face to face, without any obstacles separating us.

[1] Here, as elsewhere in Cristiana's exposition of her experience, we can see the importance of sharing in support, which calls to mind both the clinical section above and the points that will be made in chapter 5.

151

three dreams to sessions. However, in this case, my therapist was very positive both as to their content (it was clear that something inside me was changing) and in her interpretation of them. In addition, I no longer felt that I was being blamed for the small number of dreams I was able to describe to her.

The long silences that had characterized my sessions with the previous therapist were replaced by a verbal fluency on my part, which sometimes approached logorrhea, balanced with a series of prompts from and exchanges with the psychotherapist. I did not need coaxing to speak, as I had now found a space in which I felt able to let my feelings pour out. For the first time, I was able to give voice to the thoughts and emotions I so urgently needed to express. After the relief of this initial, liberating outpouring, I was able to accept and recognize the utility of a few simple grounding exercises that the psychotherapist suggested we work on *together,* thus interrupting the flux of my verbal outpourings and beginning to rebuild my personal integrity.

I also found that, above all during the first sessions, time and space was made available for me to describe my symptoms, even though no attempt was made to analyze whether there was any possible correspondence between motivation, circumstance, and symptom. I was simply able to talk about them, because I felt that *I was being listened to.* My need to speak about my psychophysical symptoms thus gradually diminished, enabling me to overcome my sense of impotence and slavery to dizziness, the fear of fainting, tachycardia, etc. Now, when I experience such sensations, I am strong enough *not to dwell on them*: I feel them arrive, I live through them, and I pass beyond them.

I still cannot always manage to see the glass as half full, but my psychotherapist's support and the manner in which she underlined my skills (which I either did not recognize or was unable to appreciate) has helped me immensely. I will always recall the way she squeezed my hand and simply and spontaneously exclaimed "Well done!" when I recounted an experience in which I had made Herculean efforts to manage on my own. In order to begin to believe in myself, I really needed a *pat on the back.*

In conclusion, I would like to briefly compare the differing kinds of support that my family offered me during the two periods of therapy. I had never tried to hide the fact that I had sought psychotherapeutic help, especially from my husband (indeed, to do so would have been very complicated, especially during the second period when I had to leave home at 6:30 a.m. to get to the station on time). Whereas the dissatisfaction I was trying to hide during the first period of therapy, together with my scant improvement, tended to heighten my husband's already existent skepticism, the positive effects of the second series of sessions produced a change—even a new kind of serenity—in my husband. He no longer saw himself as excluded and threatened by a process that belonged to me alone. Instead, he shared in the comfort and support I was receiving, having, in some sense, found an ally himself in my therapist, even though they never met.

4.4 Some Notes in Conclusion

Going over Cristiana's experiences again, I feel that it is important to underline the significance of a few specific passages for the general message of this book and for our particular school of psychotherapy.

Some other therapists and some readers may not share my opinions and may find other passages in this text more significant. I am not, in fact, trying to exhaust the hermeneutic potentials of Cristiana's account. I only wish to open the way for its further examination.

As it will increasingly emerge as the main thesis of this volume, the themes of sharing, confrontation, and belonging are central to panic disorder. Our principal concern is with the support provided by the therapist and the therapeutic relationship between the therapist–patient duo. However, this is not our only concern. The patient's need to come face to face with other individuals suffering from the same symptoms and to share their experiences of solitude and the changes they have undergone, the separations they have experienced, and the difficulties of coping with certain moments of passage, emerges around the therapeutic relationship like a series of concentric circles. Only through comprehension, communication, and exchange can we "give weight" and legitimacy to the experience, to pass from the "constriction" of the symptom to the complexity of life.

This is what was lacking in Cristiana's relationship with her first therapist (as, perhaps, is often the case in the early stages of a single course of therapy). This relationship, up to a certain point, permitted Cristiana to get through part of her journey "alone." She was consequently able to differentiate herself and bring out and express her aggression (as she does in the letter we have just read). All of this is very important, in part because such a differentiation presupposes and involves a shared context—a relationship. As I said in my notes, it detracts nothing from Cristiana's testimony to outline how the relationship with the first therapist provided her with a sufficient level of support to help her, on the one hand, to break up her retroflective tendencies and, on the other, to better define the direction in which she wished to proceed.

hm... can't lose, can you?!

153

Cristiana's trust in the relationship, drawn in the field from the therapist was of central importance to her second relationship. From this perspective, it is worth reiterating the point Cristiana makes about time: "This therapist was somehow more receptive to and less dismissive of my need, in some way, to *establish temporal boundaries around the process*." The therapist did not give an answer as to "when," but she at least recognized the validity of the patient's question and supported her in the need that it expressed. She was able to be receptive to and to support the patient in the problem, because of her trust in the relationship. In other words, and in accordance with both the reality of this relationship and the central paradigm of Gestalt psychotherapy, it is the relationship which supports the need. Our trust and expectations are not, therefore, focused above all on either therapist or patient, but rather on the relationship.

It is through the relationship that we can face up to limitations—both our own as therapists and those of our patients—whilst always at the same time keeping our faith in the "next."

(handwritten annotation)

★ hmm... I am swaying to the reassurance offered by the second therapist; a rich of belonging, being attended to, "humanity" ct. first therapist 'held the space' or was just denigrating, shaming, irritated - but congruent!

two therapies afforded two different things - which is better? It is clear fo. the client, is this all that matters?

... And, role of shame/shaming in this book about panic!

my experience of confusion, not guilt, panic, elements of shame... more like 'neurotic' than 'psychotic' ... my and abuse experiences differ here - the ground doesn't give way for me;

154

5. Networks and Processes of Belonging: Between Roots and Intentionalities

by Maria Mione, Elisabetta Conte, Gianni Francesetti
and Michela Gecele

> *The individuation of one's self, the accep-*
> *tance of oneself as alone and separate is ori-*
> *ented, in a radical sense, towards the "deliv-*
> *erance" of the self, towards belonging to*
> *someone other-than-yourself.*
>   *It is a process of becoming a single-*
> *"for," for God and for man, becoming a*
> *"companion," a familiar.*
>
> Martin Buber, 1958/2004[1]

The experience of belonging, in all of its diverse clinical and social aspects alluded to elsewhere in this text, has recently been studied by various
authors. In our contemporary context, belonging has become a difficult, uncertain, and problematic field, which no one can take for granted. As a
topic, it bridges the boundaries between social, anthropological, political,
and economic, in addition to psychological disciplines (Salonia, 1999a;
Geertz, 1999; Giddens, 2000; Bauman, 2000).

It is interesting to note how all that has been said on the theme of belonging indicates a significant change in perspective, which we cannot but
view favorably. After the narcissistic emphasis, which stemmed from the
prevalence of individualism over belonging (Lasch, 1978), the common notion of identity has now begun to take the cultural and social background,
or "We," as its starting point once more. Identity is always viewed as the
result of a "We" (a figure emerging from meaningful relationships). However, in our postmodern climate, networks of belonging are in a state of crisis which makes the quest for identity ever more uncertain and tragic and
which foregrounds the need to form new connections, a new "community"
(Salonia, 1999a; Bauman, 2000).

We can define belonging as feeling part of a meaningful ensemble, of a
field perceived as a possible place and time for dialogue and for sharing

---

[1] Translated from the Italian by A. Spencer.

155

one's own subjectivity. It has already been noted in the preceding chapters that belonging has a significant bearing on panic disorder. We wish now to expand upon this theme with a more detailed consideration of its relationship to the founding principles of Gestalt therapy and we attempt to provide a reading of a number of significant changes in our present period from this perspective.

5.1 Belonging and the Figure/Ground Dynamic

From the point of view of the figure/ground dynamic, belonging can either appear as figure or as ground.

First of all, it can be part of the ground on which contact is based and from which it originates. In this case, networks of belonging established during the individual's history of acquired and taken for granted forms of contact (Spagnuolo Lobb, 2001) are the ground for the current contact intentionality. Contact intentionality can be realized due to the support functions that sustain the self's unfolding out into the organism–environment field.[1] Assimilated links of belonging (the being part of and the expression, for example, of your own family or network of social affiliations, with the resultant memories and perspectives) are a fundamental part of this ground, which, in a manner that the subject takes for granted, participates in the construction of contact figures and provides constant and flexible support. "If one is forced to become aware of these grounds of ultimate security, the 'bottom drops out,' and the anxiety that one feels is metaphysical" (Perls, Hefferline, & Goodman, 1951/1994, p. 232).

Belonging as ground enables us to locate ourselves in the world, to answer the question, *"Who am I?"* It thus enable the individual to individuate him- or herself and, in this way, to cope with new contacts (Bauman, 2001). Identity and autonomy, indeed, are the figure that is established, supported, and defined against the ground of assimilated networks of belonging.

More precisely, then, the question is not so much *"Who am I?"* as *"Who*

[1] "The contact functions ... take place against a background of organismic functions that are normally unaware and taken for granted; yet these latter provide the indispensable support for the foreground function of contact. They comprise hereditary and constitutional factors (primary physiology, etc.); acquired habits that have become automatic and thus equivalent to primary physiology (posture, language, manners, techniques, etc.); and fully assimilated experience of any sort. Only what is completely assimilated and integrated into the total functioning of the organism can become support" (Perls, 1968, pp. 43–44).

am I for you?" The answer to this question consists in a dialogue that, if it is assimilated, will constitute the individual's ground of belonging and that will nourish his or her identity (see chapter 3 for the implications of the consistency or fragility of this ground for those who suffer from panic attacks).

Secondly, belonging can be the figure that is completed when contact is at its fullest. From this point of view, belonging appears as the need to build up new networks of belonging, a need that becomes figure and organizes the field (and the relationships in the field), guiding the process of creative-adjustment. Contact intentionality and the organism's spontaneous impulses tend towards the satisfaction of this need. As, little by little, "the urgencies and resources of the field progressively lend their powers to the interest, brightness, and force of the dominant figure" (Perls et al., 1951/1994, p. 7), the person can, through contact with the novelty, deconstruct some of the ties of belonging present in the ground. Others will remain, in order to sustain the contact process that is in progress and aimed at introducing new networks of belonging.

Hence, for a new tie of belonging to form, the preexistent networks of belonging, which provide the necessary support for the contact process, must, at least in part, be deconstructed in order to allow the new figure to emerge (this is not always possible, as, for example, in cases of fundamentalism).

5.2 Networks of Belonging and Contact Sequence

Where networks of belonging remain in the ground, they delimit all the stages of the contact sequence in which the individual is involved. They are hence strongly connected to the id functions (i.e., the ground of forms of contact that are taken for granted) and personality functions (i.e., the ground of acquired contacts; Spagnuolo Lobb, 2001, p. 94). Every contact figure finds its *humus* and nourishment in this ground of assimilated networks of belonging.

When, instead, belonging emerges as a possible figure of contact, as a need, it triggers a contact sequence (and with it the ego function) that aims, at the moment of contact, to formulate a new tie of belonging. When this happens, belonging is transformed into "belonging with." There is a reciprocal exchange, a full and all-consuming being one for the other. This brings forth both potential horizons and ancient wounds. The potentially concrete nature of this becomes an existential tie, a life connection.

Belonging with, at the moment of full contact, is an uncompromising figure that (because of the strong degree of communion it connotes) is accompanied by a powerful sense of gratitude not only towards the other, but also for the relationship itself. It is similar to being before a painting that has particularly struck us: We do not simply rest our gaze, but the initial space opens out into another. A clear sense of gratitude emerges since, in the act of looking at the picture, our eyes do not just satisfy themselves with seeing, but they are able to establish meaning, by which we ourselves are built up in turn. "Every song of gratitude at once separates and unites. It separates by maintaining proximity and it unites by maintaining distance. It joins past and present, healing ancient wounds, and opening up new tasks. It gives birth once more to relationships and ties of belonging" (Salonia, 1999b, p. 134. Translated from the Italian by A. Spencer).

The brilliance of this "belonging to each other" restores the current of energy, which flows through the network that connects us—it restores the flow of life itself. The assimilation of repeated cases of belonging to each other enables us to contact the "deepest root" of belonging, the most fundamental and, potentially the most common source. In fact, as the Latin word for the verb *to belong* (*ad-pertinere*) reminds us, belonging is not so much a matter of possession, as of the extension and spreading out of "being-in-relation-to."

Furthermore, it is important to underline that the wider "world" is by no means excluded from the full and fundamental experience of belonging. Belonging is by no means self-referential or "autistic" in nature. It is rather a meeting place that liberates and opens up the world.

The "We" that, just for a moment, envelopes all of experience, is an all-inclusive We. Belonging is connection to context, to history. It constitutes reality itself and defines one dimension of ethics. These experiences become ground and support for subsequent experiences and connections, for new contact sequences that constantly occur, opening the way once more to a continuous process of renewal. Belonging, as we understand it, is a process of growth, which consists of a continuous and constructive interaction with the context. In this sense, it would be incorrect to define the rigid constructs of society and of closed groups or fundamentalist sects in terms of belonging.

5.3 Belonging and Generational Differences

Taking as a starting point both our own personal experiences and our reading of contemporary psychosociology, we have defined three possible modalities of experience with regard to belonging, all related to three different generations alive today (we interpret the gap between one generation and another as being a 10–15 year period). Naturally, we are thus rather oversimplifying in order to set a form to the free flow of experience. It is almost too obvious to note that not all the individuals belonging to a certain generation share the same characteristics. In order to highlight possible simplification, to problematize our concepts, and to avoid slipping into potential introjections, we need to put emphasis on another factor, which might be termed the mythological perspective—a vision of worldly time as being not linear, but circular. From this perspective, the three modalities of experience outlined below would seem to represent nothing more than characteristics that have always emerged along the road to relational, social, and political maturity across all the generations.

5.3.1 First Generation

This grouping would roughly incorporate today's "fifty-somethings," who already have a basis of acquired ties of belonging (personal history, family, culture, etc.). The idea that they share a world and belong to it (one world, *the* world) has been fully assimilated *a priori* and is taken for granted.

Although these individuals are the postwar generation, and were around in a period when all "rigid ground" seemed to be shattered, they nonetheless feel able to count on "secure grounds." The latter was defined by sociocultural processes marked by the construction of powerful networks of belonging: the labor, student, and women's movements, the endurance of the nuclear family within a network of relations and society, within which it was possible to identify with or differentiate oneself from others.

For this generation, also from a spatial point of view, cities, city squares, and places of work were meeting places where effective networks of solidarity could be developed, together with strong friendships and shared networks of belonging. These supported a sense of personal, social, and ideological identity, which was to be catastrophically lost by the next generation.

In this context, the need to construct relationships, the need to meet others, became figure: "The world exists for us. How can we, and how do we wish to, encounter it?" The safety and security provided by the ground acts as a springboard for relationships, which are sought out in themselves and for the novelty they can provide. In this modality of experience, belonging

159

is a particularly significant factor inasmuch as it appears as a contact intentionality. These individuals constantly favor the construction of new networks of belonging.

5.3.2 Second Generation

This kind of experience can be traced in the generation that is now between about 35 and 40 years of age. For this generation the ground ("I am part of a world—of 'our' world") can no longer be taken for granted: It needs to be defined.

Networks of belonging have been built up and assimilated on a more personal level for this generation, with a smaller quantum of networks of belonging being "taken for granted" than previous generations. Such ties of belonging are developed between individuals and small groups as opposed to collective ideologies and more broadly shared social objectives. These individuals have not grown up in a world functioning as a solid and persistent "ubi consistam." They have lived in small groups that have not met up with the end of changing society or for the sake of the encounter in itself. They have come into contact in order to reciprocally provide each other with *ground*.

Their experience of belonging to a preestablished world, where participation is taken for granted, has been problematic. The world of which they feel themselves to be a part is the result of a laborious day-to-day process of construction. These individuals are no longer part of movements that constitute a crucial part of their lives. They instead need to make a constant effort to develop and nourish their little niches of belonging, which are otherwise at risk of dissolving or breaking up.

A sense of nostalgia at not having lived through the big movements in the 1960s and 1970s (if not in the manner in which they have since become problematic and sometimes broken up) is a factor here, as is the difficulty of creating and sustaining relationships in an attempt to develop worlds that are shared. In the experience of this generation, "being together" is never something that is taken for granted. They always walk a razor's edge, at risk of being separated or lost at any moment.

The ground, which supported and was taken for granted by our first generation, has now become a problematic figure to be established and sustained.

It is easy to perceive a sense of solitude in this generation. Although they are competent at creating a new sense of belonging within each single

160

relationship, there remains a powerful sense that they are lacking in a ground of belonging that can be taken for granted. There is therefore a clear need to nurture the ground. The seeking out of relationships, which is instrumental in the construction of the "world" of the individual's ground, comes to take on more significance and value than the pleasure of the encounter *per se*.

5.3.3 Third Generation

As we move on to what we will call the third generation—that is, of individuals now between 20 and 25 years of age—we will formulate our description of this relational experience by drawing in part on the reflections put forward by other authors. As we lack any firsthand experience of what this generation has gone through, we will stick to the relationships that we have had with them, without trying to present a definitive account but, at the same time, without denying ourselves the possibility of putting forward a number of stimulating points that might give rise to a dialogue between generations. Only in this way can the possibility of a new meeting ground and new networks of belonging, based on the experience of this "third generation," arise. We are aware that the glass through which we are viewing this generation may be, in some sense, cracked (Diamanti, 2004), but this is the only instrument through which we can perceive their experience and sustain a dialogue whereby we will be able to affirm or correct each other's perceptions.

Reflecting on our own clinical and educational experience, then, we are left with the impression that in this generation—the children of a culture without limits[1]—the lack of strong networks of belonging, which would constitute a solid ground which they can take for granted, is accompanied by the risk of not perceiving the need for belonging in and of itself (of "belonging to" as a contact intentionality). These individuals are no longer part of movements that constitute a crucial part of their lives. They have no possibility of belonging anywhere, not even within casual networks where belonging is characterized by violence, or where violence is a means to acquire visibility and power (Russo, 2002).

[1] Serge Beaugrand relates the culture without limits to the concept of *sociopathology*. A Gestalt psychotherapist himself, this author first used this term in his clinical work with youths from 16 to 21 years of age to refer to a disorder that is specific to the youth of today—the children of a world "in which the primary value is overcoming every limitation," children of a "culture without limits" (Beaugrand, 1999, p. 135. Translated from the Italian by A. Spencer).

161

→ hm, yes and no - online belonging?

The lack of a sufficient sense of belonging to a world that is "ours," of "you and me" being intrinsically linked, is not alleviated by the quest for relationships "which are not only affective but are above all value-based" (Russo, 2002, p. 5). Such a quest may become a ground in itself, since the need becomes figure. There is therefore none of the contact motivation that could afford satisfaction. In this situation, it becomes very difficult to orientate oneself (to strongly identify one's own ground) in respect to oneself, to others, to time, and to limits. In other words, it is difficult to define a concrete personal identity.

It seems that none of this is even recognized as a problem. Individuals in this generation are oblivious of the need for relational support that will transmit life experiences. What they require more than anything else is a "technical" kind of support (professional training in general and highly specific skills). Neither the lack of ground, nor the possibility of belonging, emerges as figure nowadays. It is therefore ever more difficult to redress these deficiencies.

Such individuals think that all their needs have been satisfied if they have a fair IQ and are well-informed and skilled in a number of areas. The environment is contacted above all in order to improve these skills and this generation takes for granted their right to receive what they ask for in such cases.

It will seem at first sight that the above statements are overgeneralized and negative. We have, however, preferred to put forward these statements in order to express key issues clearly whilst simultaneously seeking to avoid excessive simplification.

Moving from individual to social experience, the quotations from Maria Teresa Russo and Serge Beaugrand already given suggest that our contemporary society might be described as having *sociopathic* characteristics—the child of the previous social order whose borderline characteristics continue to coexist with those of the new. Of course, we are once again generalizing in order to provide commonly recognizable definitions of experience. Our aim is not to provide a snapshot of the problem, but to seek out the "next"—the intentionality formulated by the problem itself—and to identify the kind of support needed for it to unfold into the field.

In fact, if sufficient and suitable support is available, and if there is a common ground, it is possible for everyone (taking their own personal and generational experience as a starting point), to bring specific skills into the field with which they will be able to modulate variations at the contact-boundary with regularity and precision. For example, we feel confident in suggesting that a member of the third generation would have the advantage

I have this!

of being acutely sensitive in defining him- or herself and others at the contact-boundary—that they would have a marked capacity to detect any confusion of terms and rights and would always be the first to shout out: "The emperor is not wearing any clothes!"

Furthermore, we have described the *risks* of a society with borderline and sociopathic features. When we say risks, we do not mean already existent realities, but potentialities. "The actuality contacted is not an unchanging 'objective' state of affairs that is appropriated, but a potentiality that in contact becomes actual" (Perls et al., 1951/1994, p. 153). As we grow aware of this fact, our sense of impotence should decrease and a sense of responsibility should take its place.

In fact, in describing these different ways of being in or with the world, we feel obliged to foreground the responsibility of all of the generations living together in our contemporary society. This is a key point for two reasons. Firstly because every generation plays a part in co-creating the experiences of the generation that follows it. Secondly, because this very fact brings into question the "generative power" of one generation over another—over their power to prompt and support the following generations. As Russo has put it,

> a lack of 'generativity' is emerging. The power of adults to 'generate,' i.e., to construct a network of relations that is not only affective but also value-based, is diminishing. If adults are lacking in this generative power, there will surely be less conflicts and milder tones of voice. However, this will leave young people to face ethical choices alone, like travelers put out on the street with neither a map nor any luggage. (Russo, 2002, p. 5. Translated from the Italian by A. Spencer)

as the field breaks up into smaller 'chunks'

5.4 Transmitting the World and Weaving Its Fabric: Sustaining Belonging in the Postmodern World

Many authors have presented us with a vision of the contemporary world as the offspring of a series of great and swift transformations and which is now itself going through a dramatic and painful labor as mother or father of the world of the future. They describe the fragmentation of the social fabric and the great difficulty of perceiving the ties that connect us in our common drama. We are unable to attain a well-defined sense of identity, which should arise from and enrich our roots of belonging, the source of our ability to develop ties of intimacy:

deconstruction
abolition is love
'social fabric'

(but) sought, bought rather than in person ??

ground;
★ loss of what is taken for granted (covid, planet)
→ (mild) panic or at least uncertainty → leads to seeking belonging + power (survival)

for who??
eg white etc...

The lapse of community in political societies is not reducible to the neuroses of individuals, who indeed have become 'individuals' because of the lapse of community; nor is it reducible to the bad institutions, for these are maintained by the citizens; it is a disease of the field, and only a kind of group therapy would help. (Perls et al., 1951/1994, pp. 134–135)

Goodman's discussion of the importance of a genuinely communitarian society—of the need for a complete community as the basis from which fragmentation can be overcome (1960/1972)—is as relevant today as ever: "Young people, to grow up, need the world to be made up of situations that have already been closed and need society to be whole once more" (p. 225. Translated from the Italian by A. Spencer).

The great technological, urban, political, and social revolutions of recent years have not brought us any reassuring certainties. The world has progressed, but has left open certain important areas where, notwithstanding all our technical progress, the subject finds him- or herself powerless in the face of events beyond human control. The revolutions, which have been "invented and discovered" in response to particular historical conditions, create an imbalance when they are stillborn or come to be interrupted and inconclusive. This creates a sense of disorientation and an ambiguous value system in the subsequent generations: "A successful revolution establishes a new community. A missed revolution deprives the community that survives of meaning. And a compromised revolution tends to break up the pre-existent community, without providing an adequate substitute" (Goodman, 1960/1972, p. 213. Translated from the Italian by A. Spencer). In the world of today, if our community is to be made whole, the greatest innovation that would make it possible to tie up our situational lose ends would be the skill "to conserve human resources and to develop human capacities."

The following question immediately springs to mind: If we as humans need to fit together in a relational sense, what kind of *specific support* (Spagnuolo Lobb, 1990) can help us to do so? First of all, it would seem necessary to connect generations and experiences, sharing information and resources on the theme. For that reason, one of the aims of this chapter is to stimulate an intergenerational dialogue, in which we as authors would only be giving voice to one part of the field. Secondly, in seeking out answers to the question, we have defined three possible levels—social, therapeutic, and educational—at which we might intervene to sustain networks of belonging.

On a social level, it would be important for us (both as therapists and as

164

or of coexistence in difference?

participants in broader networks of belonging) to construct meeting places and contexts for society, where the social network can, by deconstructing itself and its world, identify emerging social and relational needs and re-situate itself in relation to them, making a new *creative-adjustment.* Every social encounter could become a precious occasion to develop capacities, create new senses of belonging, and thereby enrich the ground. For example, in a context in which awareness of experiences and the assimilation of roles is problematic (see chapter 6), it becomes essential to lend support to these two processes, which are fundamental steps along the way to the construction of networks of belonging: "To recover a strong sense of generative potential, we need first to reestablish an intergenerational dialogue based on communitarian reciprocity: A space for dialogue where values can be shared ... transmitting values in order to create reciprocity" (Russo, 2002, p. 6. Translated from the Italian by A. Spencer). *fabrics ...*

From a psychotherapeutic and educational point of view, we should remember that the fragmentation of the social fabric, reflected in the severing of many ancient ties of belonging, has problematized the construction of a cohesive sense of identity. In this case, identity is no longer reinforced by strong and nourishing relationships; individuals have little desire and ability to instill such relationships in their turn. It is often very difficult for clients and students who are going through such experiences to answer the question *"Who am I?"* This is because they are lacking in the props of belonging that would make them ask *"Whose and for whom am I?"* (Russo, 2002, p. 7).

What we are, in fact, dealing with is an amplification and historicization of an experience which is intrinsic to humanity. The polar dichotomies between autonomy and belonging, individual and society, modernity and tradition, are omnipresent right across human history. These mark the relationships between different generations, the stages of growth, and social roles:

★ *some shame, anxiety, panic is experienced as networks of 'belonging' are reconfigured*

The need to find an equilibrium between what is familiar, known, and secure, and that which is new and risky but at the same time attractive, is one of the basic processes of growth in general—of the growth of individual human beings and of relationships. (Spagnuolo Lobb, 2000, pp. 94–95. Translated from the Italian by A. Spencer)

In modern society, however, our disorientation, when we are asked to situate ourselves in a shared world, is particularly tangible, vivid, and distressing. It is therefore useful to define a paradigm for the transformation

unless 'not feeling safe' (who??)

that this generation—in contrast to its predecessors—has undergone simultaneously on cultural, economic, and social levels. Namely, we have passed from a deterministic and vertical worldview to a model based on a horizontal network, in which knowledge, production, and meanings are constructed (in a manner that might be termed chaotic) through an interaction between equals.

It seems to us that this situation dictates that our primary therapeutic objective should be to permit the problematic nature of the situation to emerge as figure. It will then be possible to support the construction of the basic perceptive and relational figures required to recognize the need for belonging and, subsequently, to enable the subject to carry out the deconstruction work necessary for the construction of new networks of belonging.

In psychotherapy and education, then, we need to reconstruct the fabric of belonging within which the subject can develop his or her capacity to perceive, satisfy the need for, and assimilate, belonging. A necessary prerequisite for this is a reciprocal recognition of the legitimacy of being there for one another in an atmosphere of respect, which does not attempt to cancel out the diversity of roles, responsibilities, and personal experiences. Rather it must draw its vitality from the integration of each individual's limitations and subjectivity. Returning to the words of Beaugrand, we should operate: "in the hope that each individual will discover a rule whereby, rather than being yoked into submission, he or she will discover anew our need for the other, that is to say brotherhood" (1999, p. 141. Translated from the Italian by A. Spencer).

To be able to foster this process, today's psychotherapists and educators need to reflect on what it means to feel legitimized by one's role as co-creator of a therapeutic relationship that focuses on the very value of belonging as a presenting problem. It will thus become evident that legitimacy and belonging are closely interconnected. If belonging means feeling part of a significant field, within which meaningful totality do we recognize ourselves as psychotherapists and educators? To which fabric (existential, social, etc.) do we wish to make reference as sustaining and legitimizing our work to others?

Whose and for whom are we, as psychotherapists and educators?

5.5 Closing Reflections: Whose and for Whom Are We?

In our contemporary context it is becoming evermore important for therapists to find legitimacy in constructing "ties of belonging" within the therapeutic context so as to authorize the patient's need for belonging. We need to be sensitive to the lack of networks of belonging in the patient's ground, and of the way in which ties of belonging are being fractured. We need to become skilled at supporting the individual through our own capacity for intimacy and for creating a sense of belonging (on this topic, see section 3.4 and 3.5 in chapter 3).

The therapist can thus corroborate and lend dignity, not only to the individual patient's need for belonging (and note that patient's disorders are often an expression of the difficulty or impossibility of expressing and responding to this need), but also to that of the whole field of which he or she is a part.

This process should be anchored in the support and potential afforded by the relationship, which will permit the therapist to cope with the experiences of isolation and fragmentation that he or she will inevitably and repeatedly encounter throughout his or her life.

Let us conclude with the telling words of Giorgio Gaber:

> *Belonging is much more than personal salvation*
> *It is the hope of every man who suffers*
> *And just being polite to him won't be enough.*
>
> *It is that vigor you feel when you are part of something*
> *Which overcomes every ounce of selfishness*
> *With that more vital air that is truly contagious.*
>
> *I would be sure that I could change my life*
> *If I could just start saying "we."*[1]

References

Bauman, Z. (2000). *Community: Seeking safety in an insecure world*. Cambridge: Polity.

Bauman, Z., & Tester, K. (2001). *Conversations with Zygmunt Bauman*. Cambridge: Polity.

Beaugrand, S. (1999). A propos d'une production sociale des borderlines [On the social production of borderline cases]. *Cahiers de Gestalt, 6*, 133–142.

Buber, M. (2004). *I and Thou* (R. G. Smith, Trans.) (2nd ed.). London: Continuum.

[1] Belonging Song, 1996, © Warner Chappell Music Italiana Srl Milano. Translated from the Italian by A. Spencer.

(Original work published 1958)

Diamanti, I. (2004, October 24). Le lenti spezzate negli occhiali dei cinquantenni [The broken lenses through which fifty-somethings see the world]. *La Repubblica*, p. 1.

Geertz, C. (1999). *Mondo globale, mondi locali: Cultura e politica alla fine del ventesimo secolo* [Global world, local worlds: Culture and politics at the end of the 20th century] (A. Michler & M. Santoro, Trans.). Bologna: Il Mulino. (Translated from the German. Originally sound recording of *The world in pieces: Culture and politics at the end of the century*. Successively published in *Available light: Anthropological reflections on philosophical topics*, pp. 218–254, by Clifford Geertz, 2001, Princeton, NJ: Princeton University Press)

Giddens, A. (2000). *Runaway world: How globalization is reshaping our lives*. New York: Routledge.

Goodman, P. (1972). *Growing up absurd: Problems of youth in the organized system*. New York: Random House. (Original work published 1960)

Lasch, C. (1978). *The culture of narcissism: American life in an age of diminishing expectations*. New York: Norton.

Perls, F., Hefferline, R., & Goodman, P. (1994). *Gestalt therapy: Excitement and growth in the human personality*. Gouldsboro, ME: The Gestalt Journal Press. (Original work published 1951)

Perls, L. (1968). Two instances of Gestalt therapy. In P. D. Pursglove (Ed.), *Recognitions in Gestalt therapy* (pp. 42–63). New York: Funk & Wagnalls.

Russo, M. T. (2002). L'insegnamento delle humanities e il dialogo tra generazioni [Teaching the humanities and the intergenerational dialogue]. *Babele, 4*, 4–11.

Salonia, G. (1999a). Dialogare nel tempo della frammentazione [Dialogue in the time of fragmentation]. In F. Rametta & M. Naro (Eds.), *Impense adlaboravit. Scritti in onore del Card. Salvatore Pappalardo* (pp. 571–585). Palermo: Pontificia Facoltà Teologica di Sicilia S. Giovanni Evangelista.

Salonia, G. (1999b). In equilibrio tra comunione e libertà [In the balance between communion and liberty]. *Messaggero Cappuccino, 5*, 132–134.

Salonia, G. (2000). La criminalità giovanile tra vecchie e nuove regole. Verso l'integrazione dello straniero nella *polis* [Juvenile delinquency between old and new rules: Towards the integration of the foreigner into the *polis*]. *Quaderni di Gestalt, 30/31*, 100–109.

Salonia, G. (2001). Disagio psichico e risorse relazionali [Psychic disorders and relational resources]. *Quaderni di Gestalt, 32/33*, 13–22.

Spagnuolo Lobb, M. (1990). Il sostegno specifico nelle interruzioni di contatto. *Quaderni di Gestalt, 10/11*, 13–23. (Successively published 1993 as Specific support in the interruption of Contact. *Studies in Gestalt Therapy, 1*, 43–51)

Spagnuolo Lobb, M. (2000). "Papà, mi riconosci?" Accogliere la diversità dei figli oggi ["Daddy, do you recognize me?" Accepting the diversity of children today]. *Quaderni di Gestalt, 30/31*, 94–99.

Spagnuolo Lobb, M. (2001). La teoria del sé in psicoterapia della Gestalt [The theory of the self in Gestalt psychotherapy]. In M. Spagnuolo Lobb (Ed.), *La psi-coterapia della Gestalt. Ermeneutica e clinica* (pp. 86–110). Milan: Angeli.

Spagnuolo Lobb, M., Salonia, G., & Sichera, A. (1996). From the "discomfort of civilization" to creative adjustment: The relationship between individual and community in psychotherapy in the third millennium. *International Journal of Psychotherapy, 1*, 45–53.

6. The Polis as the Ground and Horizon of Therapy

by Michela Gecele and Gianni Francesetti

> *We seek out individual solutions to the problems of the system, individual salvation in the face of common problems.... . It is precisely this withdrawal into overreliance on our individual resources and skills which nourishes the insecurity in the world from which we are trying to flee.*
>
> (Bauman, 2000)[1]

> *No individual can bear such direct contact with all the complexity of the world.*
>
> (Luhmann, 1979)[2]

6.1 Preface

> ✗ *Real psychotherapy is always somewhat subversive of the existing order.*
> (Laura Perls, quoted in Kitzler, 2003)

In our third chapter, we located a specific element of panic attacks in the collapse of the ground during the formation of the contact figure. We also highlighted the manner in which ties of belonging constitute a fundamental element in this ground. We noted how, during stages in the life cycle during which these are significantly deconstructed and remodeled, the ground can lose its support function and, abruptly and temporarily collapsing, open the way for panic. The different manners in which networks of belonging are constructed and the different forms they take (as significant structural elements in the organism–environment field), change in accordance with the social context and with the given historical moment (on this point, cf. chapter 5).

We will now seek to place these observations within a broader social perspective and to analyze the way in which social and cultural changes can

---

[1] Translated from the Italian by A. Spencer.
[2] Translated from the Italian by A. Spencer.

influence the personal and collective ground, the construction and deconstruction of networks of belonging, and the "grounds of ultimate security" which protect us from anxiety.

Our task is a complex one. In carrying it out, we have often found it difficult to formulate ideas that could be shared and communicated, that were coherent and not introjected, but fresh and authentic. It is probable that, in the form and content of the final product, there remain traces of the fragmentation from which these pages were created, however much it has been "chewed" over. We had to deal with fragmentation on many levels: between Real, transmitted and shared "realities," mystifications, myths, and conventions. The panic attack is a phenomenon that ranges across all of these different levels, a lightning flash capable of revealing collective scenarios. Hence, we are trying to establish the road we will follow, the ground we will rest on during our present task. As the psychopathology of every historical period is an expression of the culture of that era (cf. chapter 2), clinical phenomena such as panic attacks should provide us with a key that will help us to "read" more general social phenomena, which, in turn, assist our understanding and help us to find better forms of support for the disorder.

For us Gestalt psychotherapists, assuming a broader, more social perspective does not mean distancing ourselves from the personal. "Social" is just another way of saying "personal."[1] Moreover, psychotherapy cannot estrange itself from politics and society. To do so would be to lose all meaning and to perish. This is not necessarily a question of assuming a "political" stance in accordance with the rules of the political game. Psychotherapy follows other rules. It is rather a question of two worlds that intersect and enrich one other.

"Real psychotherapy is always somewhat subversive of the existing order": But being subversive in a context of fragmentation and chaos, polluted by mystifications that offer answers that cannot be assimilated, requires us to find a meaning born from the power, authenticity, and reality of life itself.

These issues reflect the contemporary concerns of psychotherapy and the role of the profession. However, these issues become yet more pressing when we come to deal with a "field" disorder with relevant social implications, as is the case with panic attacks. This position has already been upheld and explored in the chapter on clinical practice. It constitutes both the starting point and the final destination of all the considerations posited and of the questions raised in this book and particularly of this final chapter in all its complexity.

---

[1] Dan Bloom's lecture, VIII International Congress on Gestalt Therapy and II National Congress FISIG, Naples, Italy, November, 14th–17th, 2002. Oral communication.

6.2 Simplification and Mystification of "Reality" and Experience

In an old joke from the defunct German Democratic Republic, a German worker gets a job in Siberia; aware of how all mail will be read by the censors, he tells his friends: "Let's establish a code: if a letter you get from me is written in ordinary blue ink, it's true; if it's written in red ink, it's false." After a month, his friends get the first letter, written in blue ink: "Everything is wonderful here: the shops are full, food is abundant, apartments are large and properly heated, cinemas show films from the West, there are many beautiful girls ready for an affair—the only thing you can't get is red *ink."* ... *Of course, this is the standard problem of self-reference: since the letter is written in blue, is its entire content therefore not true? The answer is the very fact that the lack of red ink is mentioned signals that it* should *have been written in red ink. The nice point is that this mention of the lack of red ink produces the effect of truth* independently of its own literal truth: *even if red ink really was available, the lie that it is unavailable is the only way to get the true message across in this specific condition of censorship.*

(Zizek, 2002)

Which is the ground that, in disintegrating, plunges us into panic? In this chapter we seek to explore the various pathways opened up by this question. The first line of inquiry, which suggests itself to us, is that the ground that collapses has not been and cannot be assimilated. We might call it "a stage scenery ground," inasmuch as it is false but conventionally defined as true and substantial. The stage scenery ground is made up of assumptions that have been introjected as answers to questions on the meaning of life, on the positions of each one of us in the world, on relationships, work, the family, values, the stages of life, power, and money. These have been introjected in the sense that they have been "swallowed" from outside—that they are not the fruit of the awareness and sharing of needs, limits, and potential. Moreover, such introjections are often built on "mystifications," accepted socially but not originating in the freshness of experience (not even in the experiences of others). These are stereotypical answers. When, individually, we realize that "it isn't the way we believed it was," everything collapses and the resultant terror is accompanied by an overwhelming sense of isolation and distance from the rest of the world. There may also be a sense of guilt and the burden of feeling "different." The pain and disorientation begin to be relieved as soon as an awareness is made to emerge from a social context or a relationship, that the subject's own experience is shared by others and, perhaps, by everybody. Indeed, subjects suffering from panic attacks continue to believe and fear that they are going to go mad and die until they are able, within one or more significant relationships, to make the "real potential ground" "real" in contact.

We are dealing, then, with a profound social deception: That which is defined as *real* is not real and vice versa. Thus, there is no place in a shared "reality" for what subjects really experience. A cartoon by Bucchi uses a work of art dating back to another era and social context to provide a fine illustration of this kind of mystification. The picture shows a reproduction of Edvard Munch's *The Scream* in which the terrifying scream has been replaced by a radiant smile. The caption is "Official Version" (Bucchi, 2004).

When the ground collapses during panic attacks, this fraud is exposed. It then becomes necessary to rebuild new grounds based on the freshness and truth of personal experience.

As far as panic is concerned, an initial mystifying simplification occurs when an exclusively descriptive approach is employed in therapy. The patient is squeezed into a rigid grid of symptoms, which define his or her experience from without. This kind of diagnosis, arrived at without "chewing over" the patient's experiences within the relationship, constitutes a fake ground, to which first the therapist and then the patient have adapted. The anxiety that is born from having little ground is such that the subject scrambles to assume a ground immediately, without worrying about whether it has been assimilated. Patients afflicted by panic attacks are willing to accept this definition because it calms their terror of suffering alone and of not understanding what is happening to them. In this way, their sense of solitude and bewilderment is diminished. Therapists dealing with such cases may also be willing to accept these definitions as they offer a response to the anxiety, which arises from the chaos of that which is indefinite. They therefore attain to a greater sense of orientation. We nonetheless need to pass from this kind of simplification of the symptom to the real com-

the 'belonging' of diagnosis

plexity of the experience, which has already been underlined in the comments on Cristiana's account in chapter 4. We also need to bear in mind the distinction between the phenomenological and the descriptive approach (which is based on the *Diagnostic and Statistical Manual of Mental Disorders–IV*). This latter form of nosography arises from the need for better communication—the need to establish a shared conceptual field. It runs the risk, however, of simplifying individual experiences, and diverse visions of health and sickness to an ever greater extent. It also progressively eliminates all "uncommon" areas from our awareness. This process potentially denies the very experience of the patients. As it goes unseen, its truth is repudiated. "Can I really trust my own experience in this symptom?"—is what Cristiana, in a certain sense, was asking. And in pursuing this question she discovered *"that pins and needles are not necessarily limited to the hands."*

This reduction and simplification of the languages of therapy, and consequently of the patient's experiences, already constitutes a mystification. Neither is it true to say that when we speak about what we have in common, making an effort to construct a common ground, we understand each other any better. On the contrary, experience has shown us that in intercultural or interreligious dialogue, for example, it is only through a profound knowledge and unadulterated experience of belonging to one's own culture that one can begin to approach an encounter with the "Other."

We will discuss the changes to relationships between society, family, and the individual at greater length later on. For the time being, let us just remark that there is often no awareness of these changes to roles and contexts—that they have not been "socially assimilated." We mean to say, returning to the relationship between simplification and mystification, that the complexity of roles, relationships, and life transitions is not socially declared, taught, or shared, and is therefore not considered "real." The subject finds him- or herself going through crucial life changes equipped only with grounds that cannot be assimilated—with what we have called stage scenery grounds. When they begin therapy, individuals suffering panic attacks are unaware of the critical stages of life that they are going through. In the world as defined by the media, it seems that everything in life should be easy and there for the taking. There is a risk that individuals will start trying to play parts described and predefined externally—roles in which fatigue and limitation are illegitimate and voiceless. In this way, individuals risk not finding relational and social space within which to chart and live out their own experiences.

Moving on from this, the following quotation can help us to link this risk to the difficulty of experiencing the needs, limitations, and potentialities inherent in the human condition:

We are afraid to discover not that we are mortal but, rather, that we are immortal. Here, we should link Kierkegaard with Badiou: it is difficult, properly traumatic, for a human animal to accept that his or her life is not just a stupid process of reproduction and pleasure-seeking, but that it is in the service of a Truth. And this is how ideology seems to work today, in our self-proclaimed post-ideological universe: we perform our ideological mandates without assuming them and "taking them seriously": while a father functions as a father, he accompanies his function with a constant flow of ironic/reflexive comments on the stupidity of being a father, and so on. (Zizek, 2002, pp. 69–70)

Experiences, values, and meanings are closely interwoven—indeed, they are intrinsically copresent in and are the expression of a relational field. If awareness is not sufficiently supported in the field, the experience itself and the subject's capacity to "cope with life" will also be reduced.

6.3 The Postmodern Perspective

> *We are living through the end of certainties.*
>
> (Prigogine, 1997)[1]

> *"This is the real trouble!" exclaimed Edward. "It is no longer possible to learn anything which will stay valid for your whole life. Our forefathers were able to stick with the tools that they had acquired during youth. Now, instead, we have to build ourselves all over again every five years, if we do not want to go completely out of fashion."*
>
> (Goethe, 1809/1978)[2]

Amongst the various gauges, always at once necessary and arbitrary, with which we might punctuate and define our world as a figure, we have chosen the temporal scale, which identifies our own time as "late moder-

---

[1] Translated from the Italian by A. Spencer.
[2] Translated from the Italian by A. Spencer.

nity" or "postmodernity" (Chiurazzi, 1999). In the wake of Giovanni Salonia's lucid reading of our contemporary context (Salonia, 1999), we can identify social fragmentation and the complexity of reality as two constituent elements of our time (on this point, see chapter 2).

Faith in a deterministic and definitive form of knowledge has been replaced by an awareness of its irreducible complexity and subjectivity. This has opened the way for fresh explorations of uncertainty and possibilities which accept chaos and unpredictability as constituent elements in knowledge and action (Bocchi & Ceruti, 1985; Fogelman Soulié, 1991; Waldrop, 1992).

The loss of these points of reference has rendered elusive any kind of unifying, essential, clear, and steadfast center—any stable point from which one might look upon the world, understanding it and orienting oneself within it. This leads to the experience of being "off-center," which a number of authors have associated with the postmodern condition (Vattimo, 1984 & 1992).

On another level, the profound historical and political changes that have taken place over the last decades have significantly modified both personal and collective experience. The fall of the Berlin Wall was highly symbolic of the breaking up of the rigid structures of belonging established during the Cold War, which had provided us with a fixed set of coordinates. This moment can be said to have sanctioned the progressive fragmentation and dissolution of political and economic blocs which is still taking place today: "The world is broken up into fragments, in conflict with each other, mutually irreconcilable, struggling for survival" (Geertz, 1999, p. 9. Translated from the Italian by A. Spencer). The loss of these firm points of reference was at first accompanied by the feeling of freedom that possibilities were opening up, which was sometimes euphoric and often markedly individualistic (we need only think of the characteristics of Christopher Lasch's *Culture of Narcissism*).

After this, the loss of every tie of belonging and the difficulty of defining ourselves in a context without consistent points of reference, led to a sense of disorientation and bewilderment (Salonia, 1999, p. 574).

We feel we are lacking in a secure and stable "ubi consistam" from which we can draw on the world in its totality and upon which we can rely. Trust is an indispensable faculty in reducing social complexity, which the individual sets into motion in order to orient him- or herself in the world and to be able to act in it.[1]

---

[1] On trust as an indispensable tool in reducing social complexity which the individual sets

What remains today of the great philosophical and religious systems that
used to be our fundamental reference points? The sociologist Jean François
Lyotard's study, *The Postmodern Condition: A Report on Knowledge*,
originally published in 1979, is a useful guide when dealing with this question. Lyotard describes the "postmodern condition" as "the state of culture
in the wake of the transformations to the 'rules of the game' of science, literature, and arts from the end of the nineteenth century onwards" (1984.
Translated from the Italian by A. Spencer).

These transformations have radically altered the constitution of knowledge:

> Simplifying to the very maximum, we can consider "postmodern" an
> incredulity with regard to metanarratives (Lyotard, 1984). The univer-
> salistic ideal of what Lyotard tellingly refers to as the "grands recits,"
> the great *stories* of modernity, were thrown into crisis and undermined
> by the historical events of the twentieth century: "the metanarratives—
> philosophies of history which form a whole project, stories of the
> emancipation of humanity—of which Christianity, Hegel's philosophy,
> Marxism and economic and political liberalism are the classic exam-
> ples." (Chiurazzi, 1999, p. 55. Translated from the Italian by A.
> Spencer)

Hannah Arendt's illuminating reading of this fall of universal ideals
connects the phenomenon with a crisis of the *polis*:

> For many centuries before us—but now it is no longer so—men went
> into the public sphere because they wished that something of their own
> or something they had in common with others would outlast their ter-
> restrial life... . There is perhaps no more illuminating testimony to the
> loss of the public sphere in the modern age than the near-total disap-
> pearance of any authentic quest for immortality—a loss which has been
> somewhat obscured by the simultaneous abandonment of the meta-
> physical problem of eternity. (1958/1998. Translated from the Italian
> by A. Spencer)

---

in motion in order to orient him- or herself in the world see, for example, Luhmann: "Without
trust, he would not even be able to get up in the morning. He would be assaulted by an inde-
terminate fear and paralyzed by panic... . No individual can bear such direct contact with all the
complexity of the world" (1979. Translated from the Italian by A. Spencer).

This point of view will probably, upon more or less attentive reflection, be shared by all of us readers. As is often the case, however, this passage only deals with one polarity of the experience and of the meanings to be extrapolated from it. Are we really at the end of the great philosophical systems, or are we rather coming face to face with a new way of living and recounting the experience of, for example, God.

Intimate mutual relationships (including our relationship with God) appear problematic at the present time, difficult to reconcile with society and the world. They are poised between two risks. On the one hand, there is the risk of an excess of liberty and the uprooting of thoughts and sentiments from context and relationships. On the other, there is the impossibility of an intimacy that, to survive, should be protected against the invasion of nonprivate space.

Friedrich Nietzsche's dazzling revelation "God is dead" no longer bears testimony to an absolute death. Rather, it reflects the complexity of a relationship and a quest for new questions, which will open up new possibilities and uncertainties and which will seek out an unknown situation on the horizon of the polis.[1]

We have become aware, in the course of these reflections, of a cross-contamination between the various spheres of experience. It is for this reason that we are now touching on religious themes in a text that began with a discussion of the political aspects of our role as therapists today. In the

---

[1] The following quotation from Emmanuel Lévinas should help to shed some light on the kind of religious experience to which we are referring: "The relationship between the Ego and the whole is therefore a relationship with an Other whose face I recognize. I am either innocent or guilty in his or her eyes. Moral conscience is the condition.... . The crisis of religion in contemporary spiritual life derives from an awareness that society has passed beyond love, that a wounded third party listens in on the amorous dialogue and that the society of love itself has wronged him. The lack of universality here stems, not from a lack of generosity, but from the intimate nature of love. Every love—unless love is transformed into judgment and justice—is the love of a couple. The closed society is the couple. The crisis of religion, therefore, derives from the impossibility of isolating oneself with God and forgetting about everyone outside the amorous dialogue" (Riva, 1999, pp. 44–49. Translated from the Italian by A. Spencer).

It is, fortunately, difficult to simplify and reduce (i.e., to introject) these words for "use" within our argument. Some of these suggestions will find a more definite application later on, on various different levels but always in relation to religion as an ethical and relational–social field. Sticking to religious themes, we might ask ourselves if this point of view applies to Christianity alone. What has been the experience of other faiths? How are we to consider the concept of secularism, of being "in search of answers" which, depending on your point of view, can apply to everyone or just to religious or nonreligious individuals? Should this be seen as a commitment or a detachment?

178

same way, as we continue to delve into our experiences, our significance, and our social roles, we will touch on ethics and history.

6.4 Insecurity, Uncertainty, and Fear

> *Anxiety has ceased to be a private issue faced by the individual. Western humanity in general is immersed in anxiety and fear: A determined presentiment of some terrible impending danger has derailed the ontological certainty of every human being. The invasiveness of the anxiety phenomenon, which has undergone a vertiginous growth over the last hundred years, has risen to an unprecedented level of intensity today.*
>
> (Von Gebsattel, quoted in Borgna, 1997)[1]

On a ground already full of uncertainties—such as the great ecological risks that we are currently facing (including the threat of climate change), the uncontrollable potential of science and technology, the intercultural phenomena linked to immigration, the unpredictability of finance and economics on a global level—recent further phenomena have intensified our sense of uncertainty and instability. Namely, terrorism after September 11th and the unprecedented characteristics of the war that we are currently engaged in, have thrust us into a world without clearly defined fronts and boundaries, where our enemies are often elusive and faceless, where dangers are unpredictable, and where no refuge provides absolute security. We have already said that the panic opens out onto experience on many different levels. Let us now try for a moment, setting aside all critical and politically correct deliberations, to consider September 11th as a phenomenon unfolding, not on an individual, but rather on a collective level. Our collective ground collapsed together with the Twin Towers, revealing itself to be mere stage scenery, a papier-mâché façade.

The idea that we can all troop together and fight a traditional style war—that we can "beat" the threats we are faced with and feel secure once more—typifies a notion of security that is essentially superficial, because we can only ever really believe it on a very superficial level. As, for exam-

---

[1] Translated from the Italian by A. Spencer.

179

ple, in a fairy tale told to children, that which is defined as reassuring and necessary is not reassuring and necessary in contemporary society, where the context is not one of adults taking care of children. If the past ground collapses, the ground that provided and defined the individual's sense of "security" (in terms of both certainty and reassurance), it replaced by terror. We all know that fairy tales have much to say to adults, too. There are limitations to the apparently reassuring notion of security, championed at the moment in a battle for the good that will triumph in the end: These principles are being constantly contradicted as the story unfolds. Mankind needs certainties, and when these are not present we construct them. However, today, mass media constantly undermine precisely what they declare to be real. It is as if we were persistently burning our own myths, our own narratives, and our own superstructures. And we are overhasty in doing so, as these should be our foundations.

Insecurity has then become a fundamental characteristic of our present social organization and our individual perception of reality:

> The world in which we are living today ... instead of being increasingly brought under control, seems completely out of control—perpetually elusive... . We find ourselves face to face with risks for which there is no historical precedent... . Many of these risks will strike us regardless of where we live and regardless of our quality of life. (Giddens, 2002. Translated from the Italian by A. Spencer)

Perhaps the real point, as other authors have suggested, is not so much that our uncertainty is greater than that in other historical eras. Possibly the real issue is that we are facing insecurities that are entirely "new." But is insecurity not always a result of novelty, of that which is different from me or us, from what I or we have already integrated?

The discrepancy between experience and that which is made explicit would seem to be particularly telling here. The world is at once defined as safe and unsafe, but, above all, the key message, which is socially propounded and accepted, is that it will only be possible for us to live in a world that is secure.

Perhaps the world is no less stable than it has always been, or perhaps it is more dangerous than ever. The actual novelty is surely that we are currently waking up from the positivistic and narcissistic myth that we can live in a world where security is possible and guaranteed. We are alone in our uncertainty, insecurity, and fear, and, at the same time, we are only prepared to live in a secure world.

180

6.5 The Social Sphere: Between Invasiveness and Inconsistency

> *The commercial mass media are rearranging our neurons, manipulating our emotions, making powerful new connections between deep immaterial needs and material products.*
>
> (Lasn, 1999)[1]

Whose?

The loss of solid ties of belonging is particularly manifest in the fragmentation of our contemporary society. However, as Arendt suggests, this kind of fragmentation is a latent characteristic of mass society:

> The term "public" refers to the world itself, inasmuch as it is common to everyone and distinct from that space which each of us occupies privately ... It is connected with the artificial, with the man-made, as it is connected to the relationships between those who live together in the man-made world. Living together in the world essentially means that a world of things exists and is shared by those who have these things in common, like a table positioned between those who sit around it. The world, like any "in-between" space, at once establishes relationships between and separates individual human beings. The public sphere, inasmuch as it is a common world, at once reunites and impedes us, so to say, from falling on top of each other. What makes mass society so difficult to bear is not, or rather is not principally, the number of people who make it up, but the fact that the world between them has lost its power to reunite them, to establish relationships between them, and to separate them. (Riva, 1999, p. 39. Translated from the Italian by A. Spencer)

The necessary *in-between* space is made real by the shared awareness of moving in a social space that is not defined by individual subjectivity alone. It is the *polis*, the *locus* of the many—the space of dialectic exchange and reciprocal limitation—as opposed to the *oikos*, the *locus* of the few, of the home, of intimacy. The loss of this space is made manifest, in a certain sense, in the internet, where everything can happen in parallel without meaningful encounters taking place.

What is the relationship between the ground, the contact-boundary, and

---

[1] Translated from the Italian by A. Spencer.

the in-between space described by Hannah Arendt? As we underlined in chapter 5, the ground is not only the basis, the preexistent whole against which, bit by bit, the figure is defined. The ground itself, as an in-between space, needs to be created through contact, through the establishment of figures that are then assimilated. But the in-between space is also the contact-boundary itself, the locus where contact takes place, and the self springs into action, where life and growth potential are developed.

The complexity also lies in what we referred to at the beginning of this chapter as "mystification." It is more complex to construct or reconstruct the ground when we assume that it is already there and that it is supporting us, whereas in fact it has not been assimilated and, being a stage scenery ground, collapses.

We are, to some extent, living a life of "as ifs," where introjection is applied above all in the case of the names given to experiences and the contents ascribed to roles and stages of life—where the mass media and social pressures (which differ from those of other historical periods) play an important role in defining and constraining the various areas of experience. The problem is that each of these aspects has been made falsely "public," because we are not here dealing with the meeting place of the polis, but with something purely external, prepackaged, which invades and corrodes the private sphere:

> The presence of others, who see what we see and hear what we hear, reassures us of the existence of the world and of ourselves. While the intimacy of a fully developed private life, the likes of which were unheard of before the advent of the modern era and the concomitant decline of the public dominion, will continue to intensify and enrich the whole scale of subjective emotions and private sentiments, this intensification will increasingly be to the detriment of any certainty in the reality of the world and mankind. (Arendt, 1958/1998. Translated from the Italian by A. Spencer)

The end result of this process, however, is that not even subjective emotions and private sentiments can exist as such if they do not actively contribute to the construction of an "external" reality. The public and private polarities of reality each presuppose the existence of the Other. Just as autonomy and belonging mutually define each other in a continual playoff of figure and ground, the private sphere can only really exist in relation to the social sphere. If the social sphere collapses, otherness can no longer be located in the in-between, at the contact-boundary, in the space and time of novelty and growth. It therefore invades the space of the private. This is a social and relational description of something that we are all living through with regard to the television and other mass media, which bring the external into our homes, into our intimate worlds, without the mediation and the space of a potential encounter with the polis.

Without the locus needed for reciprocal confrontation and recognition (i.e., the polis), it becomes impossible to define, cope with, and communicate experiences. The experience of solitude, like that of death, is unacknowledged and emptied of meaning: "A Card for Every Need," containing ready-made greetings for every occasion and condolences for every kind of bereavement, designed for every possible addressee (brother-in-law, mother-in-law, next door neighbor, etc.), is on sale in many shops in the U.S.A. There is no need to experience and recognize an emotion and the action connected to it, to feel the impulse and to share in it. An externally predefined code comes into effect before and in the place of the experience, substitutes the emotion and the whole process of its definition, its effortful elaboration, and the quest for the right words with which to communicate it.

We perceive our world as a place where communication pervades and is always readily available. We are at the crossroads of streams of messages, which constantly stress that "we are not alone" and that we have the communicative tools to avoid solitude. However, this experience is often far removed from awareness and is not, in a certain sense, real: "Actuality [is] ... a potentiality that in contact becomes actual" (Perls, Hefferline, & Goodman, p. 153). The absence of the polis is only bearable if solitude is anaesthetized and denied. *or at least the mythe (and key trauma;*

Can we then conclude that panic attacks occur, or may occur, when we finally become aware of this solitude? When, paradoxically, our solitude is made real through contact? When we find ourselves in a relationship or context in which we can feel our solitude? It was in this sense that we argued in the clinical section that panic marks the beginning of the solution, a creative-adjustment of the field to an overwhelming reality, which represents the beginnings of a search for the Other. The borders of psychotherapy are thereby extended or, rather, our field of vision opens out to experiences, problems, and possible solutions, which are collective. It may be a myth, it may "always have been like this," but it seems reasonable to us to argue that "once upon a time" people were more aware of the limitations inherent in our humanity. At present, we receive solutions arrived at by others (and there are many of these and they are often invasive) before feeling any need and experiencing our own human limits. Solutions and received prescriptions come to us prematurely and from too many different directions. The consequence is that while a more or less healthy introjection was useful in the past in establishing a stable nucleus around which experiences, roles, and loyalties could be formed, today solutions are unable to come to rest and form a sediment. To experience the limitation posed by solitude, and to then aim for encounters, can stimulate and allow for the construction of new networks of belonging. It gives us a sense of being part of humanity and is therefore therapeutic for ourselves and for others. Having done so, we can go back to taking advantage of the wealth of opportunities, which are effectively presented to us by the internet, globalization, etc. Only after this initial step can we fully take advantage of the creative power of a world which is potentially very much present at the contact-boundary.

The crisis of the polis is a crisis of belonging and, therefore, a crisis of identity. The great cultural, historical, and social changes have profoundly influenced both the various levels of communication and interpersonal relations, both personal and collective health, both social ties and networks of belonging, both identification and differentiation. They have thus exerted a profound influence on individual and social identity.

Ties of belonging can no longer be taken for granted *a priori*, as they were in traditional communities. Neither do they result from an adhesion to, or rebellion against, an ideological or social group. They are, instead, the fruit of a problematic, uncertain, and laborious process, which we no longer embark upon in order to realize a personal ideal or a collective idea with which we identify. Rather, we undertake this task in order to escape from the abyss of solitude and uncertainty—from the chaos that would annihilate us. In a traditional, premodern context, individual identity is not problematic, since it is taken for granted as a manifestation of the community to which the subject belongs. The social ground is consistent and taken for granted. Networks of belonging are not subject to uncertainty, and the individual does not distinguish him- or herself from society as a whole, with which he or she has a confluent relationship (Bauman, 2000).

The dissolution of communitarian ties, which has characterized the modern era, has obliged the subject to resituate him- or herself in relation to reference points that can no longer be taken for granted a priori in relation to his or her existence. The question *"Who am I?"* has grown problematic. The notion of individual identity was born with modernity: "At the very moment in which the community collapses, the notion of identity is invented" (Young, quoted in Bauman, 2000. Translated from the Italian by A. Spencer). The central problem faced by the modern subject is how to construct and maintain a solid and stable identity (Bauman, 1993). "We start thinking about identity when we're not sure of belonging ... 'Identity' is the

184

name we give to our attempts to escape this uncertainty" (Bauman, 2007. Translated from the Italian by A. Spencer).

In fact, it is something of an oversimplification to talk about the experiences that were taken for granted a priori by traditional societies. This is another case of a figure/ground playoff, another playoff between polarities. For us, the figure, that is the object on which our attention is focused, is our own experience as a society, the here and now of our social life. In this sense, "other times and other places" become a single ground, become the grey area against which the figure stands out.[1]

For us, in our present time and place, identity is a strategy whereby the individual can locate him- or herself in a noncommunitarian context. It is constructed through self-recognition within one particular social group as opposed to any other. It is possible only in a context where groups are stable enough to allow a sufficient duration of identification or alienation.

In modernity, the disintegration of the traditional community has been accompanied by the construction of new and "strong" epistemological, social, and personal systems of reference: objective knowledge in science, the invention of new production technologies, the construction of nation states and new social classes, and faith in reason and organization (Salamone, 1998, pp. 62ff.).

As we saw above, we are now living through a period of further disorientation and dislocation. The strong systems of reference, which characterized the modern age, have grown inconsistent. Various metaphors have been used to describe some key characteristics of the mutations undergone by identity in this period: Identity has fragmented into a plurality of selves and its boundaries have grown ephemeral, fluid, indefinite, and protean (Sciolla, 2002; Dunn, 1998). This experience has been accompanied by a sense of disorientation and confusion, which has made the processes of identity construction uncertain and laborious (Salonia, 1999, p. 574; Melucci, 1998).

[1] We feel duty bound to briefly point to the concept of "the invention of tradition" (which refers above all to the African "traditions" invented in response to colonialism). We wish to underline this point here not only to differentiate the ground, but also to ask ourselves if these experiences can be drawn on in our own "here and now." It is also worth noting that, where there are clearer spatial borders, it is easier to structure ties of belonging in terms of "inside" rather than "outside." For most of us, nowadays, the "outside" is indefinite, like the ground, because the majority of places have already been attained or can potentially be reached. There is no neat distinction between known and unknown, explored and unexplored, as there is a widespread sense that everyone knows a fair bit about everywhere. This is the "common knowledge" of those who assume they know but in reality do not. Also on this point, we can observe that we are not only speaking about historical eras. It is as much a question of perspectives and possibilities: The accessibility of the world today varies according to the place and context into which the individual is born.

6.6 Forms of Disorder

> *I think that children understand with their bodies that the present moment will never be repeated. Their sensibilities tell them that the present will fly away at the same speed as their bones lengthen, creaking with growth. They gaze wide-eyed into this devastating reality.*
>
> (Yoshimoto, 1997)[1]

> *At the fragmentation stage, the subject's level of confusion increases dramatically ... The potentially devastating question that arises is this: "What is real and what is not?"*
>
> (Salonia, 2000)[2]

The disturbances that accompany the difficulty of self-definition can take forms so subtle and unpronounced that they are never directly observed clinically. Nonetheless, they reduce the individual's capacity to take initiatives, plan, act in solidarity, and open out to a common social dimension (Crespi, 2002). "It becomes very difficult to realize oneself when one is overcome with thousands of possible networks of belonging and an infinite number of possibilities that are often unattainable—when one is faced with the relativization of every norm" (Salonia, 1999, p. 574. Translated from the Italian by A. Spencer). A number of observers have indeed noted an increasingly widespread ill-being, which is indefinite, vague, sometimes depressive, sometimes anxious, and difficult to pin down in terms of clear psychopathological categories or precise sociopathological manifestations.[3]

---

[1] Translated from the Italian by A. Spencer.

[2] Translated from the Italian by A. Spencer.

[3] This general ill-being can also manifest itself in more evident clinical disorders. Hence, the increase in identity disorder, personality disorders, and acute symptoms in general (Melucci, 1996; Ehrenberg, 2000; Pavan, 2002).

The rise in the number of individuals suffering from panic attacks is another such example (Gerdes, 1995). Panic attacks are most common in contexts characterized by interpersonal ties and social networks which are fragile, uncertain, and fragmentary (Pavan, 2002), but which simultaneously afford the individual the possibility of attaining to the kind of awareness panic represents, the "laceration" to which we referred earlier.

or identity with (fundamentalist) *
eg incel ... complete introjection ←
... which was proud of GT/IMG!

Sociopathological behaviors can, in part, be understood as an outward expression of the individual's difficulty in constructing his or her personal identity—a process that always occurs through the recognition of the Other in a continuous and significant relationship. Violence today is often accompanied by an experience of existential emptiness, a nonperception of limits and a blindness towards the needs, pain, and even existence of the Other-as-subject (Beaugrand, 1999; Salonia, 2000). This "relational immaturity" manifests itself in violence at the very moments when the control and the norms of society become uncertain and undefined, with the result that violence can be avoided only through a capacity to recognize the Other's dignity, otherness, and personality. Where personal vulnerability encounters a collective experience of disorientation, psychopathic or sociopathic behavior can easily result. This is due to the lack of sufficient relational support (from the family or community) to contain the personal disturbance and to orientate the individual through ties of belonging. *don't agree*

To give another example, substance abuse has also been profoundly altered by our contemporary context. It no longer represents an attempt to differentiate oneself by rebelling against a social norm but rather stems from an inability to live through meaningful experiences. This leads to an internal vacuum (Beaugrand, 1999) and a relational desert, which often fails to inspire the sorrow that would afford meaning to experience. Rather, meaningful experience is passed through with an anaesthetized indifference in which substance abuse at least offers an opportunity to "feel" something.

Returning to the quotation from Slavoj Zizek's *Welcome to the Desert of the Real* (section 2), this widespread ill-being could be defined as a "social disorder of the personality function" in the narcissistic society. Let us consider roles and ties of loyalty with this point in mind. Our roles continue to limit us without being a living and fully assimilated resource.[1] We are

---

[1] To illustrate this point further, we cite the continuation of Zizek's *Welcome to the Desert of the Real*: "The recent Dreamworks animated blockbuster Shrek (Andrew Adamson and Vicky Jenson, 2001) expresses this predominant functioning of ideology perfectly: the standard fairytale storyline (the hero and his endearingly confused comic helper go to defeat the dragon and save the princess from its clutches) is clothed in jokingly Brechtian 'extraneations' (when the large crowd observes the wedding in the church, it is given instructions on how to react, as in the faked spontaneity of a TV show: 'Laugh!', 'Respectful silence!'), politically correct twists (after the kiss between the two lovers, it is not the ugly ogre who turns into a beautiful prince, but is the beautiful princess who turns into a plump ordinary girl), ironic stabs at female vanity (while the sleeping princess awaits her savior's kiss, she quickly arranges her hair so that she appears more beautiful), unexpected reversals of bad into good characters (the evil dragon turns out to be a caring female who later helps the heroes), up to anachronistic references to modern mores and popular culture. Instead of prais-

187

it's not absence of belonging
but of belonging to 'cult'
eg fundamentalism that
preys on disillusionment?

* ie too much
belonging! ie
introjection!

here describing a disorder at various levels of the contact sequence whereby
we contact and assimilate the new. We have often denied, and still continue
to deny, the complexity of the experience of being a father, for example. It
therefore then becomes easy to be ironic, often intelligently about the role
of the father itself. Once again, none of this is inevitable. It is rather a risk
we can face up to more competently if we continue to confront viewpoints
with experiences. Another aspect of this social disorder is eloquently expressed in the following statement by James Hillman (1995): "Even though
we want ideas, we have yet to learn how to manage them well. We burn
them out too rapidly. We free ourselves of them by immediately putting
them into practice" (Translated from the Italian by A. Spencer).

The contexts we are describing, our contexts, are characterized by the
presence of a secure ground (albeit a stage scenery ground) and not by an
emergency. It may be, however, that the laceration can open up when the
individual enters into his or her "private" world of experience, without having been defined, conditioned, and anaesthetized from without. That which
is private and intimate is in reality universal. It is the human experience of
humanity's limitations, of our place in the cosmos, and in such cases a relational ground is lacking where this experience can be expressed, shared,
processed, and assimilated. The experience of limitation and solitude is
universal and inherent in the human condition. What is specific to the current situation is that the necessary social support in listening to, identifying
with, coping with, and communicating this experience is lacking.

Complexity, fragmentation, and insecurity have thereby become constituent elements of our organism–environment field. Some of those "im-
mense areas of relatively permanent confluence," which "are indispensable
as the underlying unaware background of the aware backgrounds of experience" (Perls et al., 1951/1994, p. 232), have become problematic. Our insecurity stems from the fact that those elements of the ground, which were
taken for granted through confluence, have now become a problematic figure. To continue the quotation:

ing these displacements and reinscriptions too readily as potentially 'subversive' and elevat-
ing *Shrek* into yet another 'site of resistance,' we should focus on the obvious fact that,
through all these displacements, *the same old story is being told.* In short, the true function
of these displacements and subversions is precisely to make the traditional story relevant to
our 'postmodern' age—and thus to prevent us from replacing it with a new narrative. No
wonder the finale of the film consists of an ironic version of 'I'm a Believer,' the old Mon-
kees' hit from the 1960s: this is how we are believers today—we make fun of our beliefs,
while continuing to practice them, that is, to rely on them as the underlying structure of our
daily practices" (2002, p. 70).

We are in confluence with everything we are fundamentally, unprob-
lematically, or irremediably dependent on ... A child is in confluence
with his family, an adult with his community, a man with the universe.
If one is forced to become aware of these grounds of ultimate security
the "bottom drops out" and the anxiety that one feels is metaphysical.
(p. 232)

6.7 Panic: An Emerging Figure of the Social Field

> The individual, to construct and define
> himself, always needs to be face to face with
> another. Social fragmentation can therefore
> thrust the subject into a state of bewilderment.
>
> (Salonia, 1999)[1]

How can these knotty problems of our contemporary world emerge in
the therapeutic relationship and in the suffering of individuals afflicted by
panic attacks? In what way can panic attacks be viewed as a feature emerging from our contemporary organism–environment field?

The anxiety we feel when the "bottom drops out" strikes at the very
moments when our confluence with our networks of belonging is problematized or interrupted, leaving us acutely aware of the fragility of our
certainties, of those grounds we take for granted. The following description
by one 32-year-old patient, who was just beginning to find some meaning
for her ill-being, is typical:

Until a while ago, I thought I was okay apart from the panic attacks.
Now I've realized that I have always lived with an undercurrent of fear
that will never let me be, that I have always lived in a state of uncertainty. My parents are divorced and live in two different places. I'm an
only child and if they get sick I'll be the only person to look after them.
I live alone and I've never experienced an intimate family life, whatever that means. I have a temping job that gives me no security and
means that I have to reinvent myself professionally every three months.
I have a boyfriend whom I've been with for six years. He still lives
with his parents and we don't feel up to making any plans beyond what
we're going to do the next weekend. I feel that my days and my weeks

[1] Translated from the Italian by A. Spencer.

are broken up into little bits—that I myself am broken up into little bits. And I can't hold them all together. The balance of my whole life is hanging by a thread. Everything's precarious and I'm starting to realize that, after all, it's not so strange I'm suffering from panic attacks.

In the contemporary world ties of belonging are transitory, fluid, iridescent, and fragile. There is an ever increasing likelihood of becoming aware of their unbearable and terrifying "lightness."

When this happens we experience a profound sense of isolation, a petrifying solitude that propels us into terror and opens up the precipice of the absence of the Other. We perceive an overwhelming and terrifying solitude:

> I suddenly feel as if I'm in the dark, a tiny being in a foreign place. I am overcome with a terror that manifests itself as an unbearable physical anxiety because everything is completely indifferent to me, completely alien, neither good nor bad. There are no real "people," just "things." So I feel as if I hardly exist myself.

The "false ground of knowledge for life" has collapsed, together with that of the individual's assumed autonomy, which had made it impossible to accept or to go looking for support. This patient's panic attacks gradually subsided as she attained more and more awareness of her roots ("My personal history has been broken up by the continuous changes undergone by my family") and managed to build up more stable and significant ties of affective belonging.

Solitude is, indeed, a key theme when dealing with patients suffering from panic attacks. What with the fragmentation of networks of belonging and the crisis of the polis, feeling alone becomes not just painful, but unbearable and terrifying (on this point, see chapter 3).

Individual solitude is often generated and amplified by social fragmentation. The uncertainty of networks of belonging contributes to a general climate of precariousness and insecurity, which can have a significant effect on subjects suffering from panic attacks. They often experience an intense fear of losing everything: personal affects, the people who are dear to them, social position, economic security, health, and life itself. This fragility becomes unbearable when the capacity to give meaning to all that is precarious is lacking. As one patient affirms: "I cannot bear to think that my wife will die one day. When this thought comes into my mind, everything collapses. I can avoid panic only by considering suicide." Another adds:

Panic has made me realize that everything is useless: I could lose everything. Everything I do is useless, as it is clear to me that it will all be over sooner or later. In fact I reckon that my panic attacks are my most lucid moments, when I really see things in all their cruelty.

These observations might be connected to our difficulty in accepting our limitations, which various authors have put forward as a defining characteristic of our time.[1]

From a certain point of view for the authors and readers of this text (belonging to a definite sociocultural horizon) "there are no limits" in space or time. Most places can be reached easily, directly, and through communication. Human and artificial memory, at least as far as the past is concerned, is well-nigh infinite. The stages of the life cycle and the various ages are no longer clearly circumscribed (Romano, 2004). Limitations and boundaries are not given to us. Rather, we invent, create, and construct them together. We are now not so much faced with overcoming individual and social difficulty of choosing whether to accept or rebel against them (a dominant concern in previous decades), as with redefining them as borders and as phases of passage. This is an effort worth making since, if we refine our awareness of borders and transitions, of the in-between spaces (in time, space, and life experience) which lead us to the new, we will be "justified" in feeling the weariness and excitement of the process and, subsequently, to assimilate the transformation we have undergone. To further illustrate what we are saying, let us briefly return to Cristiana's description of the changes and novelties which had characterized her life in the year leading up to the onset of her symptoms (cf. chapter 4):

> House-hunting and marriage-planning. Choice of house and furniture. Completion of academic degree (January–February, 2000). Another death in the family—a cousin (April 2000). Final preparations for marriage (Spring, 2000) and marriage itself (June, 2000). Living in temporary accommodation while waiting for house to become available (June–October, 2000).

poor you!

---

[1] "We have passed from a world based on humanity as the children of God to a world for which the most important value lies in overcoming every limit. Religious discourse ... reduces man to a finite, limited dimension ... With the advent of scientific discourse ... the limitation function has passed from being a founding principle to being public enemy number one" (Beaugrand, 1999, pp. 133–142. Translated from the Italian by A. Spencer).

It is essential to realize that unease is legitimate, that weariness and disorientation are normal in the moments of life when such changes are taking place.

The difficulty of defining limits is one of the constituent characteristics of the so-called "narcissistic society," for which success and conquest, well-being and effectiveness, progress and certainty, possession and strength, are the figure. Recent historical and social developments have introduced into the figure elements that had previously been relegated to the background: limitation, and with this fallibility, impotence, precariousness, fragility, loss, and pain.

This is the very point where panic can strike. The brittle defenses, which prevented limitation from becoming a figure, have been irremediably shattered with the result that we have been brutally reawakened to the precariousness of every success and the fragility of every certainty. Fragmentation and complexity have turned insecurity and precariousness into a figure, without our ability to draw support from the assimilation and sharing of our limitations.

From a social perspective, we can consider panic disorder in our context as a field phenomenon, which expresses (i.e., makes a figure of) the perception of terror that a narcissistic society feels in the face of precariousness and fragmentation when it lacks the support of the polis. This collapse has struck us individually, in a state of isolation because the myth of self-sufficiency and the fragmentation of society have deprived us of the experience (and sometimes even of the memory) of the support, which can emerge as a result of giving voice to and sharing in our own fragility.

Panic can thus be seen as the failure of the narcissistic society. It could, however, also be a step towards its cure, since this terror has led our society to perceive its own weakness and to invoke the Other, in the unique, fragile hope of finding a ground that will allow us to transform terror into pain, precariousness into a precious transience, and weakness into a shared resource.[1]

The collapse of certainties and securities has caught us unawares in a context of narcissism and fragmentation, where limitations have been removed and replaced with efficiency and where the kinds of encounter that should generate sharing and solidarity have been rendered impossible by the myth of self-sufficiency.

Panic, in this situation, is a fall without a safety net.

[1] On the need to found social ties upon the solidarity in and sharing of the common experience of limitation, of pain, and of the finite, see Crespi (2002) who explores Axel Honneth's theory of "collective existentialism."

6.8 Specific Support in the Private Sphere and in the Polis

> *The aim of the historical analysis being carried out here is to trace the alienation of the modern world—its twofold fleeing from the earth to the universe and from the world to the ego—back to its origins. This should bring us to an understanding of the nature of society, exploring how it developed and manifested itself up to the moment when it was overcome by a new and, as yet, unknown era.*
>
> (Arendt, 1958/1998)[1]

A clinically and socially relevant issue thus arises: Namely, how are we to support the construction of networks of belonging which can sustain the individual in coping with solitude, limitations, and the precariousness of a context characterized by fragmentation and complexity? "We are left facing a brutal question mark: With what ties can we hold together such diverse and strongly differentiated subjectivities?" (Salonia, 1999, p. 575. Translated from the Italian by A. Spencer). If we translate and personalize this question, the sense of impotence that it initially generates should be, at least to some extent, diminished: "What support can we therapists provide in the process of building bridges between such diverse and strongly differenti- *or?* ated subjectivities?" In this way, we are moving inexorably from the intimate level of therapy to a social and political plane. Indeed, it is one of the basic assumptions of this book as a whole that a need is emerging in the field of psychotherapy and society for a broadening of the skills and activities of those practicing our profession. It is, however, necessary to clarify what we mean by "support." We are referring above all to the process of sustaining awareness and the processes of assimilation through the relationship and the contact sequence.

In saying this, we are drawing together a number of points made in the preceding paragraphs, as we believe that any separation of "diagnosis" from "cure," albeit necessary for the purposes of exposition, is inevitably artificial. The fact that we can now complete our passage between psychotherapy and politics or, better, that we can continue to occupy this boundary area should be taken as evidence that we feel justified and sure of ourselves

---

[1] Translated from the Italian by A. Spencer.

in doing so—that we are neither oversure of ourselves nor troubled with overwhelming feelings of inadequacy.

Hence, we ourselves exemplify what we are writing about, inasmuch as we are exposing ourselves to certain risks by writing on social rather than psychological themes, claiming neither that we are specifically qualified to do so nor that such issues do not concern us. We are responding to a task that requires the expertise of many different professions. We are not trying to express an absolute truth, simply to contribute to its construction. It would not be constructive either to stay silent on the matter, offering no contribution, or to merely assume that we are necessarily "in the right." We feel that it is important to dare, to push ourselves beyond ourselves, towards the Other, towards the new. Naturally, whatever we say will be a simplification, given that we are describing(human)relationships,(humanity)in our time, and considering the historical–evolutionary dimension with which we are dealing. We are trying to open out a window onto the flux of which we ourselves are part. We have drawn the courage to do so from the support afforded to us by our ties of belonging to the community of psychotherapists in general and our affiliation to the Gestalt movement in particular, which implies a shared awareness of the competences and limitations of every one of us. We are also sustained by our sense of a shared direction—that of constructing new networks of belonging (we might, then, indulge a bit in playing with words and, borrowing the terms of the previous chapter, ask: Does this book presuppose a tie of belonging or is it aimed at creating one?).

Coming, now, to our reformulated version of Salonia's question: The support we need as therapists is partly that which we start out with and partly that which we are trying to develop as we read and write these pages, sharing them with others, and consequently broadening the field of research and dialogue. The tools required are those necessary for life in a globalized world—the tools that will enable us to broaden our awareness so as to locate our own being in such a vast context. Living locally in a globalized world tends to intensify our sense of limitation and impotence. Staying in relationships, even with those who are far away, establishing ties and connections with those who are different from us, who lie on the other side of a boundary, always keeping one window open to the world (to borrow an expression that is currently as relevant as it has been abused), can further equip us. In a world where a dialectical space (an in-between locus, a polis) is lacking, everything is very direct, speedy, immediately, and easily reversible. There is no mediation. This can lead to fear, loneliness, and a sense of impotence or, alternatively, to an impression of omnipotence. We may need support in dealing with a sensation of being too small for emotions and possibilities that seem bigger than they are. There is a certain circularity between political and clinical tasks. The therapist, too, is a citizen of the polis and his or her two worlds have or should share a common history of loyalty. It is fundamental to recognize the new spaces of the polis: Politics may be a cure and the cure may be political when we take politics to mean, not just the administration of public things, but the nature of participation in social relationships.

This weighing up of the roles of politics and psychotherapy has carried us "head-on" into the boundary territory with which we are dealing. We now feel able to reflect more fully on certain social dynamics. The reflections that follow are, obviously, just points of view and, as such, are relative. Yet we do not wish to be excessively relativistic. It is important to stress relativity, so as not to promote ideas that may become "unhinged" from their context, so as to avoid one's own belonging from degenerating into fundamentalism. However, to exaggerate relativity would lead, in a certain sense, to the kind of contact interruption that typifies narcissistic societies: The falling into a dialogue with oneself, individually seeking out ones own limitations with no faith in the possibility that one might be corrected or contradicted by others. Trust (as already noted in the quotation in footnote 6) is a central issue for borderline and narcissistic societies, and we are here at the very boundary between clinical and social themes. Our greatest task is to form the ground of trust in both the therapeutic field and in a broader network of egalitarian relationships:

> The reality of the public sphere is founded upon the simultaneous presence of the innumerable perspectives and aspects in which the common world emerges. It is therefore impossible to find either a common measure or a common denominator. Indeed, although the common world represents the common meeting ground, those who are present there occupy diverse positions, and the position of one can no more coincide with that of another than two objects can occupy the same space. Being seen and heard by others derives its importance from the fact that each one of us sees and hears from a different position. This is the significance of public life, in contrast to which even the richest and most satisfying of family lives can only offer the prolongation or multiplication of one's own individual position, with its various aspects and perspectives. The subjectivity of the private sphere can be prolonged and multiplied in a family to such an extent that its weight may even be felt in the public sphere. However, this private "world" can never reveal the full sum of the aspects revealed by a single object to a multitude of

spectators. Reality can only appear sure and certain when things are seen by many from a variety of points of view without their identity changing, so that those who stand around any given thing see the same thing despite doing so in totally diverse ways ... If the identity of the object can no longer be defined, common human nature, and, to an even lesser degree, the unnatural conformism of mass society, will be unable to impede the destruction of the common world, which is usually preceded by the destruction of the multiplicity of perspectives from which it presents itself to plural humanity. (Arendt, 1958/1998. Translated from the Italian by A. Spencer)

This passage operates on two levels: Describing diversity of points of view and at the same time giving our readers a firsthand experience of them. Indeed, Hannah Arendt's perspective on the relationship between the polis, the individual, and the private sphere is quite different from ours. We are dealing with different time cycles. Whereas Arendt demonstrates her theories by moving from the Greek polis towards modernity, the temporal model put forward by Giovanni Salonia (to which repeated reference is made throughout this book) offers a reading based on the modernity–postmodernity transition, which has taken place during psychotherapy's first centenary. These two visions thus differ in rhythm, structure, and framing. However, there is no contradiction between them, inasmuch as they both assume a greater value through being shared, discussed, and criticized, insofar as they offer sustenance to experience and to the construction of meaning. Let us try to relate them to each other. According to Arendt, the polis is opposed to the private space of the home, wherein material requirements and needs are dealt with. The "outside" is the space for free, co-constructed thought: of exchange, confrontation, vitality, and action. More recently (but is it really an "elsewhere" in time, space and experience?) politics became increasingly dedicated to the service of the material, progressively depriving the home and the family of this role.

The distinguishing feature of the domestic sphere was that human beings lived there together in response to their needs and necessities. They were propelled there by life itself which requires the company of others for the survival of the individual and of the species ... The dominion of the *polis*, on the other hand, was the sphere of liberty, and, if there was any relationship between these two spheres, the control of needs in the life of the domestic sphere was obviously a prerequisite for the freedom of the *polis*. Under no circumstances could politics be viewed as nothing more than a means for protecting society. (Arendt, 1958/1998. Translated from the Italian by A. Spencer)

Salonia, instead, discusses the changes that our relationships with authority and with limitations have undergone over the last century. We have passed from being a "vertical" society, founded on the recognition of authority, through a phase of rebellion, to the individualism and subjectivity of the narcissistic society (to the "death of the fathers") and then, finally, to the fragmentation of the borderline society. In opposing external rules the individual has become increasingly isolated and powerless (first through belonging to clearly defined groups, then alone, opposing themselves to these very ties of belonging).

> The question that beset Freud—how to educate individuals in the reality principle—is a problem that typifies his contextual background in a symbiotic society. In today's narcissistic society, a far more radical question arises: Namely, who makes the rules? To what extent are we obliged to respect reality? No reality is seen as preestablished and beyond modification. Where is it written that reality cannot be modified? Who says so? In the narcissistic society, the greatest sin is that of "not being oneself," of "betraying oneself." The face of the Other, who is perceived as a purveyor of the rules and pretexts of belonging, as an obstacle to one's own self-fulfillment, is gradually eroded. (Salonia, 2000, p. 104. Translated from the Italian by A. Spencer)

Thought in the modern world has increasingly withdrawn into itself, abandoning common spaces and actions, becoming at once impotent and omnipotent. Again, we need to pause for a moment to consider a number of questions. Are we here exploring the real history of humanity, or just a metaphor? Can this really reflect the various forms of experience undergone by every unique individual in every diverse community? Is this a myth, which is going to provide us with direction and support?

Both Arendt's and Salonia's perspectives shed light on the manner in which the modern subject has come unstuck from his or her context, from significant relationships and actions. To attempt to take all the weight of human destiny onto one's shoulders would be a grandiose undertaking, doomed to failure:

> "When destiny, in whatever form, calls us individually by name, beneath our anxiety and fear there is always a kind of attraction. This is

197

because mankind does not just desire to live. We also want to understand and accept our destiny at the most profound possible level, even if it means exposing ourselves to danger and destruction" (Marai, 2001). For a Gestalt therapist, reading this quotation is similar to that which somebody religious might experience upon reading words describing human experience with sensitivity and acumen, but from a secular point of view. There is all the weariness and the burden of daring, of challenging destiny and the Gods (hubris). There is also an awareness of human limitations and an acceptance that annihilation will be the consequence of daring too much is the starting point. There is no hope and no faith, as the experience being described here is one of solitude in which no one shares and for which no support is available. Hope lies in relationships. In the absence of relationships, only the human fear of choices remains.[1] If there is not a sufficient level of support, the individual may be afraid of self-destruction, of falling to pieces. There is thus a risk of desensitivization or of proceeding to a tragic dimension of solitude. (Gecele, in press. Translated from the Italian by A. Spencer)

The political strategy required to cure the fragmentation of our present time would sustain the capacity of the oikos and polis to exist side-by-side, as complex as they are.

[1] "The etymology of the term decision (*caedo, caedere*) refers to 'beating' or 'hitting.' This first Latin meaning certainly does not refer to a rational process. It suggests an ugly kind of power 'beat, hit, strike.' The second meaning connects *caedo, caedere* with sexual relations, such as those we can see when birds mate. A third significance is 'kill, slaughter, assassinate, destroy, immolate.' A fourth is 'break, shatter, smash.' *Caedo*, in its turn, can be traced back to the sanscrit *khidati*, 'squash, flatten,' *kheda*, 'hammer.' ... We need not wonder, then, that our decisions are so tortured, so 'agonizing,' since decisions bring us close to death" (Hillman, 1995, quoted in Gecele, in press. Translated from the Italian by A. Spencer).

6.9 The Other Faces of Fragmentation

> *From the beginning, then, Empire sets in motion an ethico-political dynamic that lies at the heart of its juridical concept. This juridical concept involves two fundamental tendencies: first, the notion of a right that is affirmed in the construction of a new order that envelope the entire space of what is considers civilization, a boundless, universal space; and second, a notion of rights that encompasses all time within its ethical foundation. Empire exhausts historical time, suspends history, and summons the past and future within its own ethical order. In other words, Empire presents its order as permanent, eternal and necessary*
>
> (Hardt & Negri, 2000)

In an attempt to identify one of the possible polarities of contemporary fragmentation, it is worth briefly examining the concept of *Empire* as defined by Michael Hardt and Antonio Negri in their work of that title (2000). What is empire for us and how does our notion of it compare to that of the authors of the text? First of all, let us consider how it relates to the contemporary fragmentation to which we have been referring. Does it contradict or complement the concept that we have been putting forward? We feel confident in affirming that empire can be seen as the opposite polarity of fragmentation. From our point of view it is, perhaps, a space of possibility. However, it is also a space devoid of temporal and spatial boundaries—the sensations and experiences which it produces are those of confluence. Time stands still. It is interesting to compare our perspective with that of Hardt and Negri. This suspension of time—its being rendered absolute—perhaps explains our own caution in delving too far into comparisons between our own time and "the rest of history," notwithstanding the usefulness and necessity of focusing in on a clear figure (the "here and now" of our society) set against a ground, so as to better understand its details and its form.

If belonging is confused with confluence (with a consequent invasion of private space and collapse of the polis), it can easily end up being discarded altogether, especially by those with borderline or narcissistic experiences. We might perhaps argue that the fragmentation born of the narcissistic society's "flight from belonging" can find temporary relief in the confluence of the empire. However, there will then be another countermovement, an often violent rejection of ties of belonging. There is a repeated circularity of movement, a continuous playoff between these two polarities.

In an undifferentiated and fluid context, such as that of empire, ties of belonging are neither clear nor stable. Instead, they are iridescent and various. Within the apparently immobile sphere of empire exist occasional novel openings for individual and group creativity and productivity. In this situation, representation loses its meaning, since it narrows us down to a single tie of belonging. There is a shift from the vertical to the transversal. In such contexts, it is necessary to identify new forms of support and to take care—in therapy as in politics—that they are fluid, open and flexible, favoring appropriate forms of belonging. This kind of creativity will sometimes involve calling the assumed ground into question to an almost excessive extent. There is a risk of losing our sense of direction and descending into the disorientation and confusion that can lead to panic attacks. The support offered by the therapist is that of a fellow citizen with a special skill, someone who is struggling through the same difficulties as his or her patient in attempting to establish networks of belonging.

The means to get beyond the crisis is the ontological displacement of the subject. The most important change therefore takes place inside humanity, since with the end of modernity also ends the hope of finding something in which we can identify ourselves outside the community, outside humanity, outside cooperation, and outside the critical and contradictory relationships that each person finds in the non-place, that is, in the world and the multitude. (Hardt & Negri, 2000, pp. 385–386)

In both the fiction and nonfiction of our time, we often come across themes closely related to the phenomena we are describing.

Let us return to our particular subject matter. We suggest that the specific support required consists of defining boundaries, helping the subject to distinguish his or her body, home, and cosmos. This must be accomplished in such a way as to avoid the loss of creativity amid the chaotic sea of fragmentation, where the difficulty lies not only in having meaningful encounters with others, but also in staying separate from them. Intimacy may become too easy where there is no separation or structure. We need distinct forms of language for the home and the cosmos, but what we need most of all is a language in itself. At the most fundamental level, the support needed should consist of restoring names and substance to things and experiences through sharing, thereby redefining boundaries. Consequently, the meaning is restored to those moments when we come "face to face with the Other."[1] It is for this reason that we are focusing on the support that might be provided through the recovery of the polis, inasmuch as this is a construct of humanity which—as a space for meeting with others and constructing reality—goes beyond the simplest production–reproduction model. Considering the polis as a mythic locus, a possible or metaphorical reality, we can perhaps claim that those who were involved in its public life were blessed with both a ground of security (that their survival was guaranteed), and a ground of meaning and values, which was constructed together.

All of this is to say that, whilst the private can be the locus of the family as a production–reproduction unit, it can also contain an ensemble of individuals who never encounter each other or a union that is regulated from outside and that is therefore not really private (e.g., on an extreme level, the family as target of advertisements, the home invaded by "external" objects, which have been introjected without being assimilated, the direct and unmediated assault of the private sphere with information from the public domain). It is often the case that all of these situations coexist simultaneously. For this reason a truly intimate encounter needs to involve an opening outwards (not in the fear of losing ones own subjectivity, but rather with the end of rediscovering it) to the novelty, growth, and action which we associate with communication.

> We have learnt a little too late that the root of action lies not in thought but in willingness to assume responsibility ... If one wishes to do only those things with which no one possibly could argue, there would no longer be any action, or rather it would be unnecessary as others would already have taken up the possibility. In contrast, every real action is such that no one else but only you can perform it. (Rasmussen, 1972/2005. Translated from the Italian by A. Spencer)

---

[1] "The increase in crimes against the personality—like the rise in personality disorders—can be deciphered as a violent/desperate/destructive but nonetheless 'meaningful' cry for an enormous absence in a world of subjectivity and fragmentation: The face of the Other. There has been a telling invocation for the 'return of the Other' a noteworthy suggestion of the openings which, in our present time, there can be for creativity and for our task of being human. Only by lending an ear to the subjectivities of others, neither refusing nor disqualifying their points of view ... can we open the way for new relationships. In our period of fragmentation and subjectivity, the formation of relationships has come to represent the greatest challenge" (Salonia, 2000, pp. 105–106. Translated from the Italian by A. Spencer).

As Hanif Kureishi put it in an interview about his book *Intimacy*: "Twenty years ago it was political to try to make a revolution and change society, while now politics comes down to two bodies in a basement making love who can recreate the whole world." Confronted with statements like this, we can only recall the old lesson of Critical Theory: when we try to preserve the authentic intimate sphere of privacy against the onslaught of instrumental/objectivized "alienated" public exchange, it is privacy itself which becomes a totally objectivized "commodified" sphere. Withdrawal into privacy today means adopting formulas of private authenticity propagated by the recent culture industry—from taking lessons in spiritual enlightenment, and following the latest cultural and other fashions, to engaging in jogging and body-building ... Against this kind of privacy, we should emphasize that, today, the only way of breaking out of the constraints of "alienated" commodification is to invent a new collectivity. Today, more than ever, the lesson of Marguerite Duras's novels is relevant: the way—the only way—to have an intense and fulfilling personal (sexual) relationship is not for the couple to look into each other's eyes, forgetting the world around them, but, while holding hands, to look together outside, at a third point (the Cause for which both are fighting, in which both are engaged) ... The ultimate result of global subjectivization is not that "objective reality" disappears, but that our subjectivity itself disappears, turns into a trifling whim, while social reality continues its course. (Zizek, 2002, pp. 85–86)

It is therefore unrealistic to talk about private space as something distinct from the public space of the polis. Where there is no private space, there is no polis, and vice versa. It is true that one possible source of protection from fragmentation is sometimes sought in the rigidity of ties of belonging. Nevertheless, these no longer consist so much in the use of social introjections preexistent in a firmly established environment, as in the adhesion to rules and convictions which guarantee one's belonging to a group but which cannot be discussed, leave no room for novelty, and verge on fanaticism. Fanaticism is not simply a passive and dogmatic adhesion to external rules. Rather, it can be seen as a reaction to an urgent need to construct a rigid context, so as to avoid chaos and to escape from an unbearable sense of disorientation. In a certain sense, then, we might ask ourselves if fundamentalism could be seen as responding to a need to resist the invasion of the private space (e.g., by the media).

Healthy belonging should involve a capacity to differentiate, as well as to share. There is a risk that belonging without differentiation will result in fundamentalism: white Spremay

> In fragmentary societies, small groups offer protection from fragmenta-tion. However, if these are not versed in the "other" language and in contact with the "other" sphere of the *polis*, they may become nests of fundamentalism, an alternative *polis*, running the risk of falling into patterns of behavior and language which are ever more symbiotic and self-referential. There follows a progressive and "staunch" transforma-tion of every "outsider" from guest (*hospis*) into enemy (*hostis*). (Salo-nia, 1999, p. 577. Translated from the Italian by A. Spencer)

The risk of fundamentalism[1] is particularly present in our current period, and we need to face up to it with new strategies of belonging:

> The battleground emerging in the twenty-first century will see funda-mentalism deployed against cosmopolitan tolerance. In an increasingly globalized world, where information and images are commonly trans-mitted everywhere, we find ourselves in contact with others who think and live differently from us on a daily basis. The cosmopolitans wel-come and revel in this cultural complexity; the fundamentalists find it disturbing and threatening, and, in areas characterized by a strong sense of ethnic, religious, or nationalist identity, they take refuge in a re-newed and radicalized form of tradition—and, often, in forms of vio-lence. (Giddens, 2002. Translated from the Italian by A. Spencer)

We are here referring to fanaticism and cosmopolitanism not as posi-tions defining identifiable social groups, but rather as an attitude, which can be assumed on a personal and individual level, which is not necessarily as-sociated with religious, social, and cultural ties of belonging.

The recent increase in insecurity has brought about two apparently con-tradictory changes to our behavior with regard to our sense of belonging. Research carried out in the U.S.A. a year after the attack on the Twin Tow-

---

[1] As we can gather from the following quotation, there is also a risk of responding to fundamentalism with behavior which is, in itself, fundamentalist: "The apparently modest relativization of one's own position is the mode of appearance of its very opposite, of privi-leging one's own position of enunciation. Compare the struggle and pain of the 'fundamen-talist' with the serene peace of the liberal democrat who, from his safe subjective position, ironically dismisses every full-fledged engagement, every 'dogmatic' taking sides" (Zizek, 2002, p. 78).

ers demonstrated that individuals tend to have set up more rigid and precise boundaries with regard to whom they include in and exclude from their groups, and that Americans have become less open to intercultural integration and are increasingly in favor of restrictions to the civil rights of foreigners (American Psychological Association monitor, September, 2002). At the same time, the heartbreak and pain of the September 11th, which can still be felt at Ground Zero, has dramatically undermined the American and Western sense of being part of a special, untouchable, and invulnerable world. There has been a concomitant increase in a shared sense of uncertainty and vulnerability with which other areas of the world were already familiar. This "sharing" may contribute to an increased sensitivity to the suffering of the Other, an increased degree of neighborliness and understanding, and a greater willingness to offer help to strangers. These are not so much (or are not only) characteristics of neatly defined and contrasting positions adopted by specific social or political groups, as they are a sign that diverse needs and experiences are emerging between social groups or single individuals who are seeking out new definitions of belonging (of including, excluding, or welcoming others, and of protecting themselves). It is very tempting to define oneself prematurely in order to escape from the prevalent uncertainty. However, such a reaction would impede the necessary maturation of new creative-adjustments, taking into account the complexity of the issues we are faced with and the diverse and often contrasting needs we are dealing with, at the risk of simply reproducing series after series of sterile antinomies.

Something other than belonging

— abolition ??

6.10 Which Values Can Support Us Along the Way?

> *Where is such a "memory" nowadays?*
> *Might the loss of this "moral memory"—a*
> *horrible expression!—not account for the*
> *crumbling away of all our duties, of love, of*
> *marriage, of friendship, of faith? Nothing is*
> *left. Nothing is rooted. Everything is short-*
> *lived, breathing only for a short while. Yet*
> *values such as justice, truth, beauty, and all*
> *the greatest goods in general require time,*
> *stability, and memory. Otherwise they de-*
> *generate. Those who are unwilling to carry*
> *forward the responsibility of the past and to*
> *shape the future are suffering from "amne-*
> *sia."*
>
> (Bonhoeffer, quoted in Rasmussen, 1972/2005)[1]

> *Beauty means holding something in your*
> *hands, then letting it go. You cannot cling on*
> *to the sea, to the smile of friends as they*
> *travel far away from you.*
>
> (Yoshimoto, 1997)[2]

Such an apparently natural process as that of "allowing new creative-adjustments to mature," requires a great deal of support (both self-support and support from the environment). At the moment in which this direction has been defined, we believe that, as therapists, we have all the necessary skills to play a significant role in this process. Yet, it is also important to ask ourselves which criteria we should observe. Should we observe the extrinsic criteria of ethical correctness or criteria intrinsic to the process of contacting, meeting, and growing? This question is not only relevant here. It is also highly pertinent to our previous consideration of fundamentalism. Our answer will probably differ according to whether we respond as therapists or as citizens. We would nonetheless maintain that, in our contemporary context, there are many points of overlap between these two levels.

---

[1] Translated from the Italian by A. Spencer.
[2] Translated from the Italian by A. Spencer.

Gestalt therapy attends to the forming of the figure, rather than the figure formed ... Content is thus of secondary import. Rather, what *is* crucial is the elasticity of how content is found and made. So long as this fluidity is maintained, discovery is supported and encouraged. This is Gestalt therapy's evaluation. Values can be wisdom's best fruits. Ethics as a mode for evaluating the formed figure is indispensable. It is part of the social compact and assures civil safety. But ethics is not psychotherapy. A just society may be the foundation for optimum fulfillment; it may also be one of the conditions for increased fluidity in contact and one of its consequences. But this, like growth itself ... , is a by-product of psychotherapy. Ethics is both a concern for just ends and a way to ensure its means. But ethical weather patterns are fickle; the climate for approved and condemned behaviors is always changing. The quest for a "preferred" or even a "just" figure impairs the free play of figure formation. Rather, the ethics of Gestalt therapy is intrinsic to the contact process: it is the self-justifying light of the emerging figure. (Bloom, 2003, p. 73)

In the social field that we have dealt with so far in this chapter, there is an emergent need to redefine or, rather, to sustain the quest for a network of social ties that would facilitate processes of identification and differentiation, enabling us to develop sufficiently solid and flexible networks of belonging capable of supporting us even in our moments of direst need.

In such a situation, in which the very connecting fabric of social life is being progressively unwoven, human conversation cannot be exclusively devoted to informative, rhetorical, and persuasive ends (which are all that is required of it in social contexts where networks of belonging are firmly established or in vertical groups). It will, instead, be required to serve other functions related to the very meaning and possibility of living together. (Salonia, 1999, p. 575. Translated from the Italian by A. Spencer)

It is therefore of the utmost importance to actively promote and support the development of communicative skills, especially in our own period, in which the term communication is frequently abused and even "profaned." All the evidence we need of the importance of our communicative and relational skills can be found in the field itself.

Communication is the basis on which networks of belonging are built up and consolidated, together with the locus of the polis. At the same time, it is also the tool with which we can redefine the limits and confines of a truly private locus, namely the oikos. In this light, Jürgen Habermas' definition of communication as the ethical action par excellence proves to be particularly pregnant with meaning for our contemporary context.

Now is not the moment to assert personal independence from social norms. Belonging and autonomy are no longer diametrically opposed polarities. We no longer need to emancipate ourselves from the ties of tradition and social conformity, as was the case in the 1950s and 1960s. Then it was indeed necessary to break away from our consolidated ties of belonging in order to forge new affiliations (upheld by the very requirements of opposition) that provided the ground for our actions (e.g., belonging to the students', labor, feminist, hippie movements, etc.). Whilst in that period of rebellion it made sense to see autonomy and belonging as opposites, to do so today is only to leave the subject in narcissistic isolation and devoid of support.

To be autonomous, we need no longer struggle against the established "powers that be." Autonomy is not opposed to belonging but, rather, belonging is the problematic, not to be taken for granted ground in which autonomy should, to the greatest possible extent, be rooted. In our complex, fragmentary, and uncertain postmodern society, belonging is the fluid ground (or liquid, as Bauman would put it) on which we must try to establish an autonomy that can never be definitive. Indeed, to be revolutionary at the present time is not to oppose, but rather to believe in something. It is for this reason that, as therapists today, we are particularly concerned with ethics and values. In the past, by contrast, therapy consisted rather in sustaining individual autonomy and emphasizing his or her personal skills. "Real psychotherapy is always somewhat subversive of the existing order" (Laura Perls, quoted by Kitzler, 2003, p. 105), inasmuch as it supports the polarities emerging in the field. Can we go so far as to say that a missed encounter is, today, a missed ethical encounter?

The challenge posed by complexity consists in paving the way for personal encounters, and therefore to a social coexistence consisting neither in chaos (whereby the personal and social worlds dissolve into a sea of non-communicative monads, potentially descending into psychopathology and sociopathology), nor in fanaticism (which avoids the terror of chaos by denying dialogue and refusing to differentiate or recognize the Other), nor in narcissism (which avoids the terror of being tied down through solitude and exasperated self-differentiation).

As we have seen, these notions are extremely pertinent to our work with patients suffering from panic attacks (see section 5 of chapter 3). In the past, dependency was a symptom that suggested that the patient was seeking autonomy through self-sufficiency. Today, in contrast, it suggests that the individual is seeking to construct a tie of belonging, which will help the subject to cope with limitations, solitude, and precariousness. As Salonia has stressed, "symptom" is a word that is for ever in search of a sentence and, as the context changes, so does the sentence that gives meaning to the word.

In dealing with panic attacks, then, we as therapists come into contact with both the specific facts of the patient's life and the more general issue of uncertain and fragmentary networks of belonging. Inasmuch as we ourselves are also an expression of the context in which we live, we share this latter experience with our patients. Issues of fragmentation and uncertainty are a universal and general concern at this time, a constituent factor in every individual's subjectivity. The creative-adjustments with which different individuals react to these phenomena may vary considerably—depending on the levels of support with which they are able to provide themselves or which they can draw from their context.

As we saw in the clinical cases described in chapter 3, personal history can be a factor leading to panic disorder. But we should not forget that every personal history is, in part, also a manifestation of the context from which it springs, just as every figure is the expression of a ground. Panic attacks, like every life phenomenon, are unique and personal idiographic points of meeting between the motivations behind personal history and the history of these motivations in a broader sense: between the most intimate relationships and the social and cultural atmosphere in which they were forged.

The capacity to continue to "be" in the midst of all the complexity, uncertainty, and fluidity of ones own networks of belonging, while at the same time being receptive to new ties of belonging (even if they consist in nothing more than sharing in a common destiny of uncertainty and rootlessness), is a central factor in any "creative and adjusted" meeting that may take place between organism and environment in the postmodern world. It is important to regard this capacity, not just as part of the personal heritage of the individual, but rather as a resource of the collective, which, through a network of relationships, provides ground and meaning for each individual's quest for identity.

Nevertheless, our present situation leads us to conclude that, rather than finding a safe road to follow, we need to pursue myriad winding pathways that lead to no certain outcome. Along the way we will seek, not so much the end of our journey, but rather a means to proceed through the moments *for me, embracing this loss of (what was) taking for granted; so much a / abolition of power relations structures of oppression*

of panic which occasionally afflict us and the many meetings with others' hands at work and other eyes looking out at the world—with other agents who will, sometimes, support us in our efforts to support others.

which will mean panic, shame, uncertainty, humility, humiliation, and giving something up that I hold dear....

References

American Psychiatric Association. (1994). *Diagnostic and statistical manual of mental disorders* (4th ed.). Washington, DC: American Psychiatric Association.

Arendt, H. (1998). *The human condition* (2nd ed.). Chicago: University of Chicago Press. (Original work published 1958)

Bauman, Z. (2000). *Community: Seeking safety in an insecure world.* Cambridge: Polity.

Bauman, Z. (1993). *Postmodern ethics.* Oxford: Blackwell.

Bauman, Z. (2007). *Liquid times: Living in an age of uncertainty.* Cambridge: Polity.

Beaugrand, S. (1999). A propos d'une production sociale des borderlines [On the social production of borderline cases]. *Cahiers de Gestalt, 6,* 133–142.

Bloom, D. J. (2003). "Tiger! Tiger! Burning bright"—Aesthetic values as clinical values in Gestalt therapy. In M. Spagnuolo Lobb & N. Amendt-Lyon (Eds.), *Creative license: The art of Gestalt therapy* (pp. 63–78). Vienna & New York: Springer.

Bocchi, G., & Ceruti, M. (Eds.). (1985). *La sfida della complessità* [The challenge of complexity]. Milan: Feltrinelli.

Borgna, E. (1997). *Le figure dell'ansia* [The figures of anxiety]. Milan: Feltrinelli.

Bucchi, M. (2004, April 23). La finestra sul cortile [Rear window]. *La Repubblica,* p. 21.

Chiurazzi, G. (1999). *Il postmoderno* [The postmodern]. Turin: Paravia.

Crespi, F. (2002). *Le identità distruttive e il problema della solidarietà* [Destructive identities and the problem of solidarity]. International Seminar in Memory of Alberto Melucci: Identità e movimenti sociali in una società planetaria. Milan, 11–12 October 2002.

Dunn, R. G. (1998). *Identity crises: A social critique of postmodernity.* Minneapolis: University of Minnesota Press.

Ehrenberg, A. (2000). *La fatigue d'être soi: Dépression et société* [The fatigue of being oneself: Depression and society]. Paris: O. Jacob.

Fogelman Soulié, F. (Ed.). (1991). *Les théories de la complexité* [Theories of complexity]. Paris: Seuil.

Geertz, C. (1999). *Mondo globale, mondi locali: Cultura e politica alla fine del ventesimo secolo* [Global world, local worlds: Culture and politics at the end of the 20th century] (A. Michler & M. Santoro, Trans.). Bologna: Il Mulino. (Translated from the German. Originally sound recording of *The world in pieces: Culture and politics at the end of the century.* Successively published in *Available light: Anthropological reflections on philosophical topics*, pp. 218–254, by Clifford Geertz, 2001, Princeton, NJ: Princeton University Press)

Gerdes, T., Yates, W.R., & Clancy, G. (1995). Increasing identification and referral of panic disorder over the past decade. *Psychosomatics, 36*(5), 480–486.

Giddens, A. (2000). *Runaway world: How globalization is reshaping our lives.* New York: Routledge.

Goethe, J. (1978). *Elective affinities* (R. J. Hollingdale, Trans.). London: Penguin. (Original work published 1809)

Hardt, M., & Negri, A. (2000). *Empire.* Cambridge, MA: Harvard University Press.

Hillman, J. (1995). *Kinds of power: A guide to its intelligent uses.* New York & London: Currency Doubleday.

Kitzler, R. (2003). Creativity as Gestalt therapy. In M. Spagnuolo Lobb & N. Amendt-Lyon (Eds.), *Creative license: The art of Gestalt therapy* (pp. 101–111). Vienna & New York: Springer.

Lasch, C. (1978). *The culture of narcissism: American life in an age of diminishing expectations.* New York: Norton.

Lasn, K. (1999). *Culture jam: The uncooling of America.* New York: Eagle Brook.

Luhmann, N. (1979). *Trust and power: Two works by Niklas Luhmann* (H. Davis, J. Raffan, & K. Rooney, Trans.). Chichester & New York: Wiley. (Original works published 1973 and 1975)

Lyotard, J. F. (1984). *The postmodern condition: A report on knowledge* (G. Bennington & B. Massumi, Trans.). Minneapolis: University of Minnesota Press.

Marai, S. (2001). *Embers* (C. B. Janeway, Trans.). New York: Knopf.

Melucci, A. (Ed.). (1998). *Fine della modernità?* [The end of modernity?]. Milan: Guerini e Ass.

Pavan, L. (2002). *L'identità fra continuità e cambiamento. Psicopatologia dell'attacco di panico e delle psicosi acute* [Identity between continuity and change: The psychopathology of panic attacks and acute psychoses]. Milan: Angeli.

Perls, F., Hefferline, R., & Goodman, P. (1994). *Gestalt therapy: Excitement and growth in the human personality.* Gouldsboro, ME: The Gestalt Journal Press. (Original work published 1951)

Prigogine, I. (1997). *The end of certainty: Time, chaos, and the new laws of nature.* New York: Free Press.

Pursglove, P. D. (Ed.). (1968). *Recognitions in Gestalt therapy.* New York: Funk & Wagnalls.

Rasmussen, L. L. (2005). *Dietrich Bonhoeffer: Reality and resistance.* London: Westminster John Knox. (Original work published 1972)

Riva, F. (1999). *Il pensiero dell'altro* [The thought of the Other]. Rome: Edizioni Lavoro.

Romano, R. G. (2004). *Ciclo di vita e dinamiche educative nella società postmo-*

derna [The life cycle and educational dynamics in postmodern society]. Milan: Angeli.

Salamone, N. (1998). Perchè postmodernità? [Why Postmodernity?]. In A. Melucci (Ed.), *Fine della modernità?* (pp. 47–82). Milan: Guerini e Ass.

Salonia, G. (1999). Dialogare nel tempo della frammentazione [Dialogue in the time of fragmentation]. In F. Rametta & M. Naro (Eds.), *Impense adlaboravit. Scritti in onore del Card. Salvatore Pappalardo* (pp. 571–585). Palermo: Pontificia Facoltà Teologica di Sicilia S. Giovanni Evangelista

Salonia, G. (2000). La criminalità giovanile tra vecchie e nuove regole. Verso l'integrazione dello straniero nella *polis* [Juvenile delinquency between old and new rules: Towards the integration of the foreigner into the *polis*]. *Quaderni di Gestalt, 30/31,* 100–109.

Sciolla, L. (2002). *Identità minime. La difficile "libertà di essere"* [Minimal identities: The difficult "freedom of being"]. International Seminar in Memory of Alberto Melucci: Identità e movimenti sociali in una società planetaria, Milan, 11–12 October 2002.

Spagnuolo Lobb, M., & Amendt-Lyon, N. (Eds.). (2003). *Creative license: The art of Gestalt therapy.* Vienna & New York: Springer.

Vattimo, G. (1984). *Al di là del soggetto* [Beyond the subject]. Milan: Feltrinelli.

Vattimo, G. (1992). *The transparent society* (D. Webb, Trans.). Cambridge: Polity.

Waldrop, M. M. (1992). *Complexity: The emerging science at the edge of order and chaos.* New York: Simon & Schuster.

Yoshimoto, B. (1997). *Amrita* (R. F. Wasden, Trans.). London: Faber and Faber.

Zizek, S. (2002). *Welcome to the desert of the real.* London: Verso.

Glossary

by Elisabetta Conte

Creative-Adjustment. According to Gestalt therapy theory, human nature can be understood through consideration of the process whereby the organism establishes contact with the surrounding environment. This process is called creative-adjustment. The term refers to an active interaction that takes place at the very boundary of contact, through which creativity, as an expression of individual uniqueness, is combined with the reciprocal adaptation required by society. The assimilation of the new, of that which is other than oneself, is expressive of the influence of environment and society upon the individual organism. It suggests the polarities involved in adaptation and reciprocity. The positive agency of individual assertiveness—inasmuch as it enables each subject to make contact with, manipulate, and change his or her surrounding environment—is indicative of the ostensible polarities involved in uniqueness and creativity, as is the way in which every new experience is assimilated into the experiential baggage of the individual. Creative-adjustment integrates the apparently opposed urges towards uniqueness and belonging (cf. Perls, Hefferline, & Goodman, 1951; Perls, 1942/1969; Spagnuolo Lobb, Salonia, & Sichera, 1996; Wheeler, 1991).

Organism–Environment Field. This central concept in Gestalt therapy theory has its origins in K. Lewin's *field theory*, which maintains that human behavior cannot be described or explained in isolation, without reference to the environment in which it takes place. Organism and environment are in a reciprocal relationship. Experience is unitary and cannot be traced to any single aspect within that relationship. It rather consists in the shared truth of the *field* in question which is constantly being created and recreated through the reciprocal interaction of its components. The concept of field is indissolubly linked to that of the contact-boundary, which lies at the very heart of Gestalt therapy theory. We are therefore not so much concerned with representing the field as a kind of topological mental–behavioral map, as Lewin saw it, as with redefining it as a common middle ground between organism and environment. The holistic Gestalt therapy concept of the organism–environment field thus allows for a broad and inclusive phenomenological vision (cf. Cavaleri & Lombardo, 2001; Cavaleri, 2003; Spagnuolo Lobb, 2001a).

Contact Sequence. This term refers to the temporal dimension of a contact episode, whereby, at any given time or place, an organism and an environment initiate, maintain, and bring to a conclusion a contact experience. It refers to a dynamic process of continual change, defining the relationship between the moment in which a contact episode unfolds, and the changing experiences that determine the organism–environment interaction taking place. The sequence of contact, or rather of contact-withdrawal, is a unitary process consisting of four distinct stages: **fore-contact** (the first, preliminary stage), **contact** (the concrete realization of contact), **final contact** (the absolute and spontaneous fulfillment of contact), and **post-contact** (withdrawal from contact and assimilation of the new experience gained).

Each stage of the sequence involves both *figure* and *ground*. In each of these successive figure/ground situations, the energy that sustains the organism and spurs on the activity of the self belongs to both organism and environment. In the fore-contact stage, a stimulus or interest arises from the ground, giving rise to the *figure/ground process*. During contact, the initial interest or stimulus, which has now become ground, provides a set of possibilities on the basis of which choices are made through deliberate self-orientation and manipulation of reality. At the final contact stage, both organism and environment become ground, as the culmination of contact emerges as figure. During the post-contact stage, as the subject withdraws contact and assimilates the experience that he or she has just undergone, there is a fluid interaction between organism and environment which cannot be described in terms of figure/ground (cf. Cavaleri, 2003; Perls et al., 1951; Salonia, 1989; Spagnuolo Lobb, 2001a).

Contact-boundary. In accordance with its unitary, holistic vision, Gestalt therapy defines the contact-boundary as the liminal space, the "third dimension," wherein the organism comes into contact with its surrounding environment. The contact-boundary does not, then, belong to any single individual. It rather constitutes the "in-between" space in which the various confining parts meet in all their diversity and undergo transformation. Interaction, experience, and growth take place in this ever changing middle ground. It is a place of living relationships, of desire, rejection, perception, communication, emotion, and all that is vital to the interaction of organism and environment. The boundary is not, ultimately, a place of separation or division. Far from representing the border, which separates organism from environment, it serves the double purpose of delimiting and protecting the individual at the same time as placing him or her in relation to the surrounding environment (cf. Cavaleri, 2003; Perls et al., 1951).

Confluence. Confluence is a condition of nondifferentiation between organism and environment. It is characterized by the lack of any perception of the boundary, delimiting the self and a lack of contact and awareness. Confluence can be described as a type of contact with what is not figure at a given moment. It is the natural consequence of a contact episode. Confluence is encountered at the fore-contact stage (see contact sequence) as a sudden blocking of excitement. In such cases, the need or stimulus arising from the environment is not felt, as the boundary lines between organism and environment are not sufficient for a figure to emerge. This prevents the subject from recognizing novelty and excitement. The individual tends to react by grasping at the familiar and habitual—at that which, inasmuch as it is already known to him or her, can bring with it no new interest or satisfaction (cf. Cavaleri, 2003; Perls et al., 1951; Salonia, 1989).

Awareness. Gestalt therapy theory holds awareness to be the most vital human faculty, since human beings are defined as active and aware subjects. Awareness is defined in specific terms as a continuum of experience consisting in contact, sensory perception, excitement, and the formation of Gestalt. Awareness is a quality of contact, that "presence" at the contact-boundary, which makes fluid and spontaneous contact possible. It is the faculty that enables organisms to fully experience contact with the environment with all their senses. It is not, then, verbal or memorial in quality, nor can it be viewed as a reflection upon a problem. Neither can it be traced back to the individual alone, since it is clearly related to the field, too. Awareness is a unitary process. The subject becomes immediately and spontaneously aware of the field and is thus able to construct figure/ground relationships. It is a structured and creative process that constitutes, in itself, a solution to problems (cf. Cavaleri, 2003; Poster & Polster, 1974; Perls et al., 1951; Salonia, 1986; Spagnuolo Lobb, 2004).

Contact. This is the basic conceptual paradigm of Gestalt therapy theory for understanding the psychological life of mankind. The organism–environment relationship is seen as the constitutional cornerstone of human identity. Every interaction between an individual and the animate or inanimate components of his or her environment involves contact. Contact phenomenology constitutes the "here-and-now" of organism–environment relations, the space in which those relations are made visually manifest. Through contact, the organism encounters environmental novelties that provide excitement and facilitate growth. Contact is characterized by the awareness of a novelty which can be assimilated (or rejected) and of the behavior that should be assumed under the circumstances in question. Contact is not just a facet of human life: It represents the founding principle of life itself (cf. Cavaleri, 2003; Poster & Polster, 1974; Perls et al., 1951; Salonia, 1986; Spagnuolo Lobb, 2004).

Figure/Ground Dynamic. This concept derives from theoretical constructs originally formulated by proponents of Gestalt psychology. It originates in studies on human perception, which demonstrated that human beings organize what they perceive into individual figures that stand out against a background. On the basis of this principle, Gestalt therapy conceives of the process of contact as the gradual formation of a figure against the background, or context, of the organism—environment field. Psychological experience thus consists of the elements of the surrounding field arranging themselves around a need that becomes the figure, organizing the field and the relationships within it.

The figure incorporates and unites the need and energy of the organism with the possibilities offered by the environment. The ground, inasmuch as it is composed of unmade, incipient, and assimilated contacts, is itself not lacking in structure and contributes to the definition of the figure (cf. Cavaleri & Lombardo, 2001; Cavaleri, 2003; Salonia, 1989).

Egotism. Egotism is the form of contact interruption most common in the final contact stage (see contact sequence). It consists in an excessive control on the part of the self in its ego function at the culmination of contact, at the very moment when the organism should be at his or her most abandoned in exchanging with the environment. The fear of assimilating that which is other than oneself prevents the relaxation of volition. The organism, afraid to face the "confusion" and "oblivion" of the new, falls into excessive introspection, caution, and thought, curbing his or her natural spontaneity (cf. Cavaleri, 2003; Perls et al., 1951).

Intentionality. This concept derives from the phenomenological school of philosophy that defines the essence of humanity in the "transcendence of self"—in the ability of the individual to knowingly, intentionally, and deliberately enter into contact with the surrounding world. The individual is viewed as active and aware, capable of directing and orienting his or her behavior on the basis of "meanings" that he himself or she herself has elaborated. If we want to understand any individual, then, understanding the forms through which his or her intention is expressed must be a key priority, as it is in this way that he or she relates to the world. Healthy intentionality makes the ego functions of self spontaneous and active, enabling the individual to intensify or limit contact, either assimilating the various possibilities or rejecting them. The direction in which an organism moves is defined both *through* and *in* healthy contact between organism and environment (cf. Cavaleri, 2003; Salonia, 1989; Salonia, 1993).

Contact Interruptions. Contact interruption takes place when the healthy excitement, which sustains and mobilizes the self through the various stages of contact, proves to be lacking in self- or relational support and is stymied, transformed into anxiety or anguish which the individual seeks to evade by breaking off contact. The self loses its bearings, its sense of direction, and its ability to react appropriately. The cause of interruption is neither behavioral nor linked to intrapsychic defense mechanisms. Interruption is rather an expression of a failed intentionality of contact. The ways in which contact interruption is manifested are related to the stages of the contact sequence at which the contact excitement is blocked.

A number of recent theoretical reviews have suggested that contact interruption should be redefined, arguing that neither contact in itself nor intention are interrupted, but rather the healthy spontaneity of the organism (cf. Cavaleri, 2003; Salonia, 1989; Salonia, 1993; Spagnuolo Lobb, 2001a; Spagnuolo Lobb, 2001b).

Introjection. Introjection is the type of contact interruption (see contact sequence) that takes place in the first substage of contact (orientation). At this stage, a need or interest emerges in the organism–environment field. This is accompanied by excitement and a growing impulse to contact the environment. However, the organism is unable to identify with this need and experiences a sense of emptiness, which he or she seeks to fill out by identifying in a uncritical manner with preconceptions about the experience (introjections). The organism is thus unable to either identify with his or her own original need or interest, which is perceived as immature and reprehensible, or to distance that to which it does not correspond. The individual abandons his or her personal critical and discriminatory faculties. This frustration of the aware identification with an emerging need limits the immediate vitality with which the subject responds to the excitement, impeding the orientation of the organism within the environment (cf. Cavaleri, 2003; Perls et al., 1951; Salonia, 1989).

Projection. Projection is the type of contact interruption (see contact sequence) that takes place in the second substage of contact (manipulation). At this stage, a need having emerged and the individual's excitement having been aroused, the organism directs itself towards the environment. However, the organism feels unable to sustain its own excitement. The emotion triggered is not anchored in the active sense of self. It thus remains detached, since the subject does not recognize it as his or her own and instead projects it out onto the environment, attributing his or her own feelings to others. The organism actively manipulates the surrounding environment, but is unable to reach the next level of contact, as action is essentially aimed at reducing levels of tension (cf. Cavaleri, 2003; Perls et al., 1951; Salonia, 1989).

Retroflection. Retroflection is the type of contact interruption (see contact sequence) that takes place in the third substage of contact (action). At this stage, the organism is ready to act and to achieve full contact. However, action is blocked because the individual becomes afraid that contact will be destructive or result in conflict, and draws the energy that had been directed outwards back into him or herself. The environment of the retroflective individual consists primarily within him- or herself, since the energies that had been mobilized have all been channeled back into the individual and the individual's body. This phenomenon can result in fear of forming attachments, of losing control, and of placing too much trust in the surrounding environment (cf. Cavaleri, 2003; Kepner, 1997; Perls et al., 1951; Salonia, 1989).

Self. This term is used to describe the complex system of contacts necessary for adaptation in a difficult field. It is neither a fixed structure within the organism nor an isolated psychic incident. It is rather a process, a function, the expression of an interaction within the field. Self can be said to exist every time interaction takes place. Self belongs to both the organism and the environment, and transcends any dualism that might be perceived between the two. It in fact operates in the marginal space in which contact between the organism and the environment takes place and represents the unitary expression of both. Self embodies the creative-adjustment of the organism–environment field and it unfolds across the various stages of contact. Contact is the final aim of self.

Functions of Self. These are some of the various experiential structures of self, categories of experience, which function integrally. The use of non-phenomenological psychological terms in a phenomenological context has made it very difficult to understand the theory of self and its functions. Gestalt therapy defines the id, ego, and personality functions as constituting the organism's capacity to relate to its environment. The **ego function** is the volitional, decision-making agency of self. It is the active and intentional faculty that makes decisions based on identification with some aspects of the field and other decisions based on a rejection of other aspects. In a holistic vision of self, the ego function operates within a continuous process of interchange with the other functions. In particular, the ego function is the creative faculty of self, which acts upon information derived from the id and personality functions. The **id function** is the background of experience from which various possibilities and needs emerge from within. It is indicative of the organism's capacity to make contact with its environment in that it determines that which the organism will need. It refers to physical needs, unresolved past situations, and the initial sentiments that connect an organism to its environment. The **personality function** refers to that which self has become by assimilating past contacts into the organism. It thus represents the way in which each individual defines him- or herself on the basis of personal history. The personality function refers to the different kinds of behavior that the individual adopts in the course of interpersonal relationships and, in particular, the taking on of responsibilities, the lessons learned from personal experience, and the social roles of the individual. It also implies changes connected to individual growth, such as becoming an adult, a partner, or a parent (cf. Cavaleri, 2003; Muller, 1989; Perls et al., 1951; Spagnuolo Lobb, 2001a; Spagnuolo Lobb, 2001b).

Specific Support. This term refers to the individual therapeutic interventions that are tailor-made for each patient and for each particular interruption of the contact sequence as the therapeutic relationship develops. Specific support helps the organism to renew its spontaneity, providing the necessary support for the self as it encounters the environment, and enabling it to overcome any impediments to contact. Specific support, then, responds to each patient's particular needs, helping him or her to overcome obstacles emerging at any specific relational moment. It functions above all through the deconstruction and subsequent assimilation of the dysfunctional process. Specific support enables the individual to develop new and creative solutions based on his or her own experience in the field. Each specific support intervention looks to the "next," sustaining the intentionality towards which the organism is moving (cf. Spagnuolo Lobb, 1993).

References

Cavaleri, P. (2003). *La profondità della superficie* [The depth of surfaces]. Milan: Angeli.

Cavaleri, P., & Lombardo, G. (2001). *La comunicazione come competenza strategica* [Communication as a strategic skill]. Caltanissetta-Rome: Sciascia Editore.

Kepner, J. I. (1993). *Body process: Working with the body in psychotherapy.* Cleveland: Gestalt Institute of Cleveland Book Series.

Muller, B. (1989). Diagnosi di strutture narcisistiche di vissuto e di comportamento [Diagnosing narcissistic experiences and behaviors]. *Quaderni di Gestalt, 8/9,* 25–44.

Perls, F. (1969). *Ego, hunger, and aggression: The beginning of Gestalt therapy.* New York: Random House. (Original work published 1942)

Perls, F. Hefferline, R., & Goodman, P. (1951). *Gestalt therapy: Excitement and growth in the human personality.* New York: Julian Press.

Polster, E., & Polster, M. (1974). *Gestalt therapy integrated: Contours of theory and practice.* New York: Vintage Books.

Salonia, G. (1986). La consapevolezza nella teoria e nella pratica della psicoterapia della Gestalt [Awareness in the theory and practice of Gestalt psychotherapy]. *Quaderni di Gestalt, 3,* 125–146.

Salonia, G. (1989). Tempi e modi di contatto [Times and modalities of contact]. *Quaderni di Gestalt, 8/9,* 155–164.

Salonia, G. (1993). Time and relation: Relational deliberateness as hermeneutic horizon in Gestalt therapy. *Studies in Gestalt Therapy, 1,* 7–19.

Spagnuolo Lobb, M. (1993). Specific support in the interruption of contact. *Studies in Gestalt Therapy, 1,* 43–51.

Spagnuolo Lobb, M. (2001a). From the epistemology of self to clinical specificity in Gestalt psychotherapy. In J. M. Robine, *Contact and relationship in a field perspective* (pp. 49–65). Bordeaux: L'Exprimerie.

Spagnuolo Lobb, M. (2001b). La teoria del sé in psicoterapia della Gestalt [The theory of the self in Gestalt psychotherapy]. In M. Spagnuolo Lobb (Ed.), *Psicoterapia della Gestalt. Ermeneutica e Clinica* (pp. 86–110). Milan: Angeli.

Spagnuolo Lobb, M. (2004). L'awareness dans la pratique post-moderne de la Gestalt-thérapie [Awareness in the postmodern practice of Gestalt therapy], *Gestalt*, Société Française de Gestalt (Ed.), *XV*(27), 41–58.

Spagnuolo Lobb, M., Salonia, G., & Sichera, A. (1996). From the "discomfort of civilization" to creative adjustment: The relationship between individual and community in psychotherapy in the third millennium. *International Journal of Psychotherapy, 1,* 45–53.

Wheeler, G. (1991). *Gestalt reconsidered.* Cleveland: The Gestalt Institute of Cleveland Press.

Authors

Dan Bloom, J. D., L.C.S.W., is a psychotherapist in New York City. He studied with Laura Perls, Isadore From, Richard Kitzler, and Patrick Kelley. He is a full member of the New York Institute for Gestalt Therapy and its past President, and is also a full member of the European Association for Gestalt Therapy. He is President-elect of the Association for the Advancement of Gestalt Therapy, an international community. He teaches and lectures internationally. His writings have appeared in various professional journals in many different languages. He is editor-in-chief of *Studies in Gestalt Therapy. Dialogical Bridges* (www.studies-in-gestalt.org).

Eugenio Borgna, psychiatrist with a phenomenological orientation, is Clinical Director Emeritus at the Ospedale Maggiore of Novara and Professor at the Nervous and Mental Ailments Clinic of the University of Milan. He is the author of numerous articles, chapters, and books on psychopathology, exploring its phenomenological and epistemological grounding, its painful clinical complexity, and its poetic and artistic expressions.

Elisabetta Conte, psychologist, Gestalt psychotherapist, teaches on the Gestalt Psychotherapy Training Programs of the Istituto di Gestalt H.C.C. Together with Maria Mione, she is the joint coordinator of the Institute's branch in Venice. She has published many papers in the field of psychotherapy. She is part of the editorial board of the journal *Quaderni di Gestalt*.

Cristiana Filippi holds a degree in Communication Studies, specializing in cultural anthropology. She is also a qualified Gestalt counselor. She works on research, education, and rehabilitation projects connected to psychological and psychiatric disorders.

Gianni Francesetti, psychiatrist, Gestalt psychotherapist, teaches on the Gestalt Psychotherapy Training Programs of the Istituto di Gestalt H.C.C. He is in charge of the Master's course in Gestalt Counseling at the Turin branch of the Institute. He is an Associate Member of the New York Institute for Gestalt Therapy. He is the SIPG (Italian Gestalt Psychotherapy Association) representative to the EAGT (European Association for Gestalt Therapy), a member of the EAGT Training Standards Committee, and a member of the executive board of FIAP (Italian Federation of Psychotherapy Associations). He is on the editorial board of *Quaderni di Gestalt* and of *Studies in Gestalt Therapy. Dialogical bridges.* He has authored articles, chapters, and books in the field of psychiatry and psychotherapy.

Michela Gecele, psychiatrist, Gestalt psychotherapist, teaches on the Gestalt Psychotherapy Training Programs of the Istituto di Gestalt H.C.C. She is in charge of the Master's course in Gestalt Counseling at the Catania branch of the Institute. She is an Associate Member of the New York Institute for Gestalt Therapy and a member of the Human Rights and Social Responsibility Committee of the EAGT (European Association for Gestalt Therapy). She has been working for thirteen years in a public mental health service, and for three years she has coordinated a psychological and psychiatric prevention and support service for immigrants. She has authored articles, chapters, and books in the field of psychiatry, psychotherapy, and transcultural matters. She is on the editorial board of the journal *Quaderni di Gestalt.*

Maria Mione, psychologist, Gestalt psychotherapist, teaches on the Gestalt Psychotherapy Training Programs of the Istituto di Gestalt H.C.C. Together with Elisabetta Conte, she is the joint coordinator of the Institute's branch in Venice. She has published many papers in the field of psychotherapy. She is on the editorial board of the journal *Quaderni di Gestalt.*

Giovanni Salonia, psychologist, Gestalt psychotherapist, teaches Social Psychology at the Lumsa University in Palermo and Learning Processes and Franciscanism at the Pontifico Ateneo Antoniano in Rome. He is Director of the Istituto di Gestalt H.C.C. and of the first and second level Master's program in Phenomenological-Relational Psychopathology that is run in collaboration with the Università Cattolica del Sacro Cuore in Rome. He is internationally renowned as a teacher and is a visiting professor at several universities in Italy and abroad. He is a full member of the New

York Institute for Gestalt Therapy and a past President of the FISIG (Italian Federation of Gestalt Psychotherapy Schools). He has authored many articles, chapters, and books, some of which, including *Kairòs* and *Sulla felicità e dintorni* (On Happiness and Thereabouts), have been translated into other languages.

Margherita Spagnuolo Lobb, psychologist, Gestalt psychotherapist, is Director of the Istituto di Gestalt H.C.C., an internationally renowned teacher and visiting professor at various institutes and universities in Italy and abroad. She is a full member of the New York Institute for Gestalt Therapy and past President of the FIAP (Italian Federation of Psychotherapy Associations) and of the EAGT (European Association for Gestalt Therapy). She is President of the SIPG (Italian Gestalt Therapy Association). She is also the editor of the journal *Quaderni di Gestalt* and co-editor of *Studies in Gestalt Therapy. Dialogical Bridges*. She has authored many articles, chapters, and books, some of which have been translated into other languages. She is the editor, together with Nancy Amendt-Lyon, of *Creative License: The Art of Gestalt Therapy* and the editor of *Psicoterapia della Gestalt. Ermeneutica e clinica* (Gestalt Psychotherapy: Hermeneutics and Clinical Practice).

Printed in Great Britain
by Amazon